William Henry (Uncle Billy) Gibbons

William Henry (Uncle Billy) Gibbons

The Life of a Central Texas Ranching Legend

Donald B. Wigley

E-BookTime, LLC
Montgomery, Alabama

William Henry (Uncle Billy) Gibbons
The Life of a Central Texas Ranching Legend

Copyright © 2022 by Donald B. Wigley

All rights reserved. No part of this book may be reproduced or transmitted in any form or by any means, electronic or mechanical, including photocopying, recording, or by any information storage and retrieval system, without permission in writing from the copyright owner.

Library of Congress Control Number: 2022902020

ISBN: 978-1-60862-831-5

First Edition
Published February 2022
E-BookTime, LLC
6598 Pumpkin Road
Montgomery, AL 36108
www.e-booktime.com

Dedicated To

*My Beloved Mother-In-Law
Billie Louise McGregor Adams
Granddaughter of W. H. (Uncle Billy) Gibbons*

*A wonderful lady who had
a significant impact
on my life
and the life of my family*

Contents

Introduction xi

Chapter One – *The Beginnings* 1
    Origin of the Name 1
    Alternative Spelling of the Name 3

Chapter Two – *Irish Immigration to America* 5
    The Gibbons Family of Athlone, Ireland 8
    Immigration of the Gibbons Family 10

Chapter Three – *The Family Line of Charles Paul Gibbons* ... 13
    George William Gibbons 17
    Winifred Chapel Gibbons 19
    Mary Emily Gibbons 21
    Mattie Elliott Gibbons 23
    Charles Paul Gibbons, Jr. 24
    William Henry Gibbons 26
    Lydia Brown Gibbons 27
    Timeline for Charles Paul Gibbons 30

Chapter Four – *The Family Line of Michael Giblin* 31
    Timeline for Michael Giblin 33

Chapter Five – *The Family Line of Winifred Gibbons* 35
    Timeline for Winifred Gibbons Chapple Fennell 39

Chapter Six – *The Family Line of Marie Theresa Gibbons* ... 41
    Timeline for Marie Theresa Gibbons Elliott 47

Chapter Seven – *The Family Line of John J. Gibbons* 49
    Timeline for John J. Gibbons 51

Chapter Eight – *The Family Line of Adelia Beatrice Gibbons* ... 53
    Martin Brooks 58
    Marie Theresa Brooks Elliott 59
    Michael Edward Brooks 62
    John J. Brooks 63
    Winifred C. Brooks 64

Contents

    Orson Brooks 68
    George Edward Brooks 69
    William H. Brooks 70
    Charles Ward Brooks 72
    Luella Delia Brooks 73
    Raymond J. Brooks 75
    Milton Brooks 76
    Timeline for Adelia Beatrice Gibbons Brooks 77

Chapter Nine – *The Family Line of William Henry Gibbons* 79
    Immigration to the US 79
    Gone to Texas 81
    The Move to Brady Creek 84
    Wedding Bells 86
    Family and Fortune 88
    James Edward Gibbons 93
    John William Gibbons 95
    Mary Adelia Gibbons 97
    John Clarke McGregor 104
    Taylor Gibbons McGregor 107
    Mary Forrestine McGregor 110
    Fanora Mae McGregor 113
    Billie Louise McGregor 115
    The Legacy of William Henry (Uncle Billy) Gibbons 121
    Timeline for William Henry Gibbons 124

Chapter Ten – *The Ancestry of Mary Virginia Taylor Gibbons* 125
    Davenport Family 127
    John Taylor 131
    William T. Taylor 133
    James Taylor the Elder 135
    The Norman Family 136
    Bludworth Family 139
    Conclusion of the Taylor Ancestry 140

Contents

Chapter Eleven – *The Ancestry of Forrest Edwin McGregor* 141
    Immigration 141
    Bartlett McGregor 143
    William (The Preacher) McGregor 145
    Timeline for William (The Preacher) Mcgregor 151
    John McGregor 152
    The Descendents of Bartlett McGregor the Immigrant 160
    Bartlett McGregor, Jr. 168
    Joel Henderson McGregor 175
    James Clarke McGregor 183

Chapter Twelve – *The Ancestry of Martha Elizabeth Graham* 189

Chapter Thirteen – *Swiss and German Connections* 199

Chapter Fourteen – *Conclusion* 205

Appendix A – *Transcription of Letter from Maria Theresa
    Gibbons Elliott to William Henry Gibbons 1888* 207

Appendix B – *Drownings in Roundtree Cave, San Saba County,
    Texas by J. Tom Meador* 213

Appendix C – *A Short Biography of Orson H. Elliott* 217

Appendix D – *W. H. Gibbons Family Bible* 221

Appendix E – *Deed Transfer W. H. Gibbons to O. H. Eliott* 225

Appendix F – *Hannon Family Register* 227

Appendix G – *Formal Requests from Billy Gibbons for Dates
    with Mollie Taylor* 229

Bibliography 231

Index 237

Introduction

One of my first experiences as an 11-year-old Boy Scout in 1958 was to attend summer camp at Camp Billy Gibbons, located in San Saba County, Texas. The Boy Scout camp was near the small town of Richland Springs, about 30 miles south of my home in Brownwood, Texas, which was located near the geographical center of Texas. The name of the man for whom the camp was named meant nothing to me at that time, other than that it was a really cool place to camp, swim, explore, and fish – at least according to some of the older Scouts in my troop. This turned out to be true. Camp Billy Gibbons was located in a very remote but beautiful area, situated along the junction of Brady Creek and the San Saba River.

It was a memorable week of learning and outdoor fun. Little did I realize that 11 years later I would marry one of the Great Granddaughters of Billy Gibbons, an Irish immigrant during the last Potato Famine. It was then that I began to learn about the man himself – a self-made man who was not only a hugely successful pioneer livestock rancher, but a banker, owner of real estate across the state, and more importantly, a generous man who was a benefactor of schools, churches, the Boy Scouts, and people in need throughout the area he now called home.

He was truly a legend in his own time.

Also included are affiliated family lines of McGregor, Taylor, Graham, and Ulmer.

Chapter One

The Beginnings

Origin of the Name

According to *SurnameDB.Com*, "This interesting surname is of early medieval English origin, and is a patronymic form of Gibbon, which is a diminutive of Gibb, a pet form of the given name 'Gilbert'. Gilbert derives from 'Gislebert', a Norman personal 'name' composed of the Germanic elements 'gisil', hostage, noble youth, and 'berht', bright, famous. This given name enjoyed considerable popularity in England during the Middle Ages, partly as a result of the fame of St. Gilbert of Sempringham (1085 - 1189), the founder of the only native English monastic order. Richard Gibun is listed in the 1202 Pipe Rolls of Sussex. In some instances the surname may be patronymic from the Germanic personal name 'Gebwine', from 'geba', gift, and 'wine', friend. Ralph Gibiun is noted in the 1176 Pipe Rolls of Oxfordshire. The full patronymic form of the name emerges in the 1379 Poll Tax Returns of Yorkshire, with the entry of one Roger Gibonson. On April 30, 1557, Richard, son of Hugh Gibbons, was christened at St. Michael Bassishaw, London. On April 14, 1635, James Gibbons, aged 21 yrs., embarked from London on the ship 'Increase', bound for New England.

"The first recorded spelling of the family name is shown to be that of John Gibbons, Jesuit, and Doctor of Philosophy at the German College, Rome, which was dated 1544, in the 'Ecclesiastical Records of Rome', during the reign of King Henry VIII, known as 'Bluff King Hal', 1509 - 1547. Surnames became necessary when governments introduced personal taxation. In England this was known as Poll Tax. Throughout the centuries, surnames in every country have continued to 'develop' often leading to astonishing variants of the original spelling."

In 2014, based upon a database of over 4 billion people (55.5% of the world's population) created by the website *Forebears.IO*, about 82,000 people worldwide bore the surname Gibbons. About 50% of those live in the United States, and of those, 8% reside in California and about the same percentage in New York. The surname exists in 115 countries, and the top five countries, in addition to the US are England (23%), Canada (6.5%), Australia (6.3%), and Ireland (4.4%). These five countries account for 90% of the surname Gibbons in the world.

William Henry (Uncle Billy) Gibbons

Alternative Spelling of the Name

An interesting notice was published in the *San Francisco Chronicle* in 1900 with regard to the obituary of Winifred Gibbons Fennell, the oldest daughter of Michael and Mary Glennon Gibbons. When she died on November 9, 1899, a standard obituary was published the next day listing all of her relatives. An alternative obituary was not published in the *San Francisco Chronicle* until August 4, 1900, about 8 months after her death. This obituary, located through the GenealogyBank.Com web-site, is as follows: "FENNELL - In this city, November 28, 1899, Winifred, beloved wife of William Fennell, and oldest daughter of the late Michael Giblin of the Parish of Taugh, County Roscommon, and sister of the following: The Hon. Michael Giblin of Roscommon, Patrick Giblin, alias Charles Paul Gibbons, of San Francisco; William Giblin, alias William P. Gibbons of San Saba County, State of Texas; Mrs. Maria Teresa Elliott, nee Maria Giblin; Mrs. Delia Brooks, nee Bridget Giblin, a native of Taugh, age 60 years (Athlone, County Roscommon papers, please copy). Requiescat in pace."

Discounting the error for the middle initial of William Henry Gibbons, this does reveal some interesting data for the Gibbons family. But who was the Honorable Michael Giblin, who was still in Roscommon, and did not immigrate? Were there actually seven Gibbons, or Giblin, children? It seems likely that there were. If he were one of the oldest children, it is probable that he remained in Ireland to support his parents and to inherit the successful business interests of his father.

According to *Thom's Directory of Ireland*, there was a Michael Giblin who was serving as a Roscommon Town Commissioner in 1873. If serving as a Town Commissioner makes you "The Honorable", then this could possibly be the Michael Giblin who did not immigrate with his siblings, but there is no definitive proof that this is the case. It also could be his father, also named Michael Giblin, who was still alive at this time.

A search of International Genealogical Index microfiche from County Roscommon revealed several records which provide supporting documentation for this name. Athlone actually straddles the border between County Westmeath and County Roscommon, separated by the River Shannon, with Westmeath on the east bank and Roscommon on the west.

The Beginnings

On February 22, 1836, a Patricium Giblin was christened at Kiltoom, County Roscommon, Ireland. He was the son of Michaelis Giblin and Mariae Glennon. He became Charles Paul Gibbons in the United States. His birth year is sometime in 1836, dependent upon how long his parents waited before the christening.

On October 1, 1842, a Marie Giblin was christened on this date, along with the names of her parents: Michaeles Giblin and Maris Glennon. This may reflect a Latinized spelling of the names by the Catholic Church in Ireland at that time, but it does establish a year of birth for Marie Theresa Gibbons Elliott of 1842 or earlier, much earlier than she would later admit to in US census records.

On August 8, 1851, a Gulielmum Giblin was christened in Loughglynn and Lisacull Parish, County Roscommon, Ireland. Gulielmum is the Latin form for William, and his father was listed as Michaelis Giblin.

On August 25, 1872, Brigida Giblin was married to Thomas Brooks in County Roscommon, Cam and Kiltoom Parish. This parish is adjacent to both St. Mary's Parish in County Westmeath, and also Taughmaconnell Parish in County Roscommon. This not only validates the given name change for Delia Gibbons, but also provides a verifiable marriage date for Thomas Brooks and Delia.

Despite the documented proof that the surname Giblin was associated with the family of Michael and Mary Gibbons in Ireland, because the surname Gibbons and, in some cases, different given names, were used by all of the children once they arrived in the United States, the remainder of this document will address them by the anglicized version of their names.

Chapter Two

Irish Immigration to America

Due to conditions in Ireland in the middle of the nineteenth century, it was not a difficult decision for all of the Gibbons children to seek a better life and more opportunities for success in the New World.

The catalyst for immigration was the Irish Potato Famine, which began in 1845. This event caused a huge spike in emigration to America as people lost all hope in their ability to survive in Ireland due to successive potato crop failures in the late 1840s, and the failure of the British government to provide timely and adequate relief measures. The increase to 85,000 immigrants who fled from Irish ports in 1847 involved all classes and regions of the country and was exacerbated by the suspension of the government public works programs in the spring and the closing of the government run soup kitchens in the fall.

According to *Irish Immigration to America, 1630 – 1921* by Dr. Catherine B. Shannon, famine refugees continued to flow into America in very high numbers between 1848 and 1853, reaching over 200,000 in 1851. Current estimates indicate that at least 1.5 million emigrants left Ireland between 1846 and 1855, with the majority traveling to America. About 120,000 passengers traveled from Ireland to Boston from 1841 to 1851, and it is probable that a considerable number of the 22,000 who arrived from English and Scottish ports such as Liverpool and Glasgow were also Irish. While all these immigrants did not stay in Boston, they profoundly altered the ethnic demography of Boston and the surrounding area. By 1855, 25%-27% of the population consisted of Irish born people and represented 85% of the resident foreign born.

Irish immigrant numbers to the United States fell to around 50,000 per year in the early 1860s with the return of better times, but rose again to almost 100,000 per year from 1864 to 1868 when recession and a minor potato failure reappeared.

According to the HistoryPlace.Com website, famine immigrants were the first big wave of poor refugees ever to arrive in the U.S., and Americans were simply overwhelmed. Upon arrival in America, the Irish found the going to be quite tough. With no one to help them, they immediately settled into the lowest rung of society and waged a daily battle for survival.

The roughest welcome of all was in Boston, Massachusetts, an Anglo-Saxon city with a population of about 115,000. In 1847, the first big year of Famine emigration, the city was swamped with 37,000 Irish Catholics arriving by sea and land. The newly arrived Irishmen settled with their families into enclaves that became exclusively Irish near the Boston waterfront, then in the North End section and in East Boston. Irishmen took any unskilled jobs they could find such as cleaning yards and stables, unloading ships, and pushing carts.

And once again, they fell victim to unscrupulous landlords. This time it was Boston landlords who sub-divided former Yankee dwellings into cheap housing, charging Irish families up to $1.50 a week to live in a single nine-by-eleven foot room with no water, sanitation, ventilation or daylight.

There were only a limited number of unskilled jobs available. Intense rivalry quickly developed between the Irish and working class Bostonians over these jobs. In Ireland, a working man might earn eight cents a day. In America, he could earn up to a dollar a day. Bostonians feared being undercut by hungry Irish willing to work for less than the going rate. Their resentment, combined with growing anti-Irish and anti-Catholic sentiment among all classes in Boston led to 'No Irish Need Apply' signs being posted in shop windows, factory gates and workshop doors throughout the city.

New York, three times the size of Boston, was better able to absorb its incoming Irish. Throughout the Famine years, 75 percent of the Irish coming to America landed in New York. In 1847, about 52,000 Irish arrived in the city which had a total population of 372,000.

In New York, the Irish did not face the degree of prejudice found in Boston. Instead, they were confronted by shifty characters and con artists. Confused Irish, fresh off the farm and suffering from culture shock, were taken advantage of the moment they set foot on shore.

The penniless Irish who remained in Manhattan stayed crowded together close to the docks where they sought work as unskilled dock workers. They found cheap housing wherever they could, with many families living in musty cellars. Abandoned houses near the waterfront that once belonged to wealthy merchants were converted into crowded tenements. Shoddy wooden tenements also sprang up overnight in yards and back alleys to be rented out room by room at high prices. Similar to Boston, New York experienced a high rate of infant mortality and a dramatic rise in crime as men and boys cooped-up in squalid shanties let off steam by drinking and getting in fights.

U.S. immigration records indicate that by 1850, the Irish made up 43 percent of the foreign-born population. Up to ninety percent of the Irish arriving in America remained in cities. New York now had more Irish-born citizens than Dublin. Unlike other nationalities that came to America seeking wide open spaces, the Irish chose to huddle in the cities partly because they were the poorest of all the immigrants arriving, and partly out of a desire to recreate the close-knit communities they had cherished back in Ireland.

For some, like the Gibbons family, the key to the better life they were seeking was to escape the squalid conditions they had encountered in the large cities of the east, and make their way into the vast reaches of the country, where the prejudices against the new immigrants were minimal.

The Gibbons Family of Athlone, Ireland

The family line of William Henry Gibbons was firmly rooted in Ireland. According to parish records, he was born on October 4, 1846 in Athlone, County Roscommon, Ireland to Michael Edward Gibbons and Mary Glennon Gibbons. Michael Gibbons was born in Athlone around 1820, and died in December of 1896. He was a merchant and was reportedly comfortably wealthy. The parents of Michael were William Gibbons, born around 1798, and Molly McLaughlin, born around 1800. It has been reported on FamilySearch.Org that Molly McLaughlin was the daughter of John McLaughlin and Maria Guilfoyle, but no references were provided to justify the relationship. Mary Glennon was the daughter of William Glennon and Mary Brooks, born about 1821, and died April 19, 1874.

A Michael Gibbons of Westmeath was listed in *Griffith's Valuation, 1847 – 1864*, the first full-scale valuation of property in Ireland. The date of the valuation was 1854. His landlord was Francis Adams, and he had a house on 3/4 of an English acre, making his annual valuation calculate to 7 shillings. This may be the Michael Gibbons, father of the immigrant Gibbons children, but no definitive proof can be determined from the data. There were seven Michael Gibbons in County Roscommon.

Michael and Mary Gibbons had seven children, four boys and three girls, based upon the obituary of Winifred Gibbons Fennell. The Gibbons children, all born in County Westmeath or Roscommon, Ireland were:

> Charles Paul Gibbons, born March, 1836
> Michael Gibbons, born about 1839
> Winifred T., born 1841
> Marie (often called Maria) Theresa Gibbons, born August 27, 1842
> William Henry Gibbons, born October 4, 1846
> John J. Gibbons, born about 1847
> Adelia (Delia) Beatrice Gibbons, born about 1857, or earlier

The children were all educated in the Roman Catholic faith and tradition at St. Mary's Convent in Athlone. This schooling also provided a solid education which prepared them for better starting positions in their new lives once they immigrated to America. Billy Gibbons maintained his faith throughout his life, even though there were no Catholic churches in close proximately to his ultimate home in San Saba County, Texas. He was also supportive of other Christian faiths – ultimately, his children became members of Methodist, Disciples of Christ, and Southern Baptist churches in Richland Springs.

All of the Gibbons children who left Ireland immigrated to America with the encouragement and support of their parents. Some immigrated together, and remained closely linked geographically for the rest of their lives; others immigrated on their own and literally scattered throughout the world. Despite geographical separation, all of the children and their families remained in close contact throughout their lives. Eventually, five of the children who immigrated ended up in the San Francisco area. Despite very strong encouragement from his sister Marie, Billy Gibbons resisted the lure of his family and remained tied to his land in Central Texas.

Beginning with the eldest of the immigrant children, Charles Paul Gibbons, the following chapters will document the lives of each of the children of Michael Edward and Mary Glennon Gibbons, their descendents, and some of their affiliated families.

Immigration of the Gibbons Family

The immigration of the Gibbons children spanned both of the peak Irish migration periods which came about due to the potato famines. Because of the relative prosperity of Michael Gibbons, and the education provided through the Catholic Church, his children fared much better than many of the other immigrants, who left home with almost nothing. Michael was able to provide for both transportation and startup money to help his children get established in America. For example, it is reported that Billy Gibbons was provided a ticket in steerage for $35, plus $500 to help him get established once he arrived. They were expected to succeed with this stipend, and almost without exception, they became very successful in their new lives.

In addition, the Gibbons families did not linger long in the big cities on the east coast, mainly Boston and New York, like so many of the Irish. There, the Irish faced discrimination and many other difficulties, while the Gibbons sons and daughters went to pioneering areas where their roots did not have a stigma. The initial stipend provided by their father gave them a distinct advantage over many of their Irish peers, who came basically with nothing.

Based upon his obituary in 1922, Charles Paul Gibbons was the eldest of the Gibbons children, born in about 1836, according to the parish records, or in 1840, according to what he told the census takers. The 1900 census of San Francisco County, California, states that he was the first to immigrate, arriving in New York in 1848, which seems unlikely since he would have been only eight to twelve years old. More than likely, he immigrated in 1858 or 1859, along with the eldest daughter, Winifred T. Gibbons, born in 1841, and one of their sisters, Marie Theresa Gibbons, born in 1842. They landed in the New York City area and established residency there. According to the "Taughmaconnell Parish Baptismal Records", Marie was born in 1842, and the 1900 Census states she immigrated in 1859. There is a strong probability that John J. Gibbons also came with this group, although he was only about 11 years old at the time.

After establishing residency in the New York City area, Charles and Winifred became Naturalized Citizens in Brooklyn on almost the same day. Charles was naturalized on May 4, 1860, in the Common Pleas Court of New York County. His address was listed as 60 Bergen Street in Brooklyn, New York. His sister Winifred, who had married Thomas Chapple (sometimes spelled Chappel) prior to leaving Ireland, was a witness to the proceedings. Charles, in turn, was the witness to the naturalization of Winifred five days later, on May 9, 1860, in City Court of Brooklyn, New York. Winifred and family were living on 3rd Avenue, New York City, at the time. Marie was not naturalized by 1900, according to the census.

The four siblings, Charles, Winifred, Marie, and John, left the East Coast immediately after naturalization of Charles and Winifred, and soon were established in San Francisco. The first documented evidence of their presence in San Francisco was the purchase of property on Mission Street in 1860, as reported in the *San Francisco Chronicle* on October 27, 1940, when the property was sold by the heirs of Charles P. Gibbons for a 7000 percent profit. In addition, in his obituary published in the August 30, 1922 issue of the *Chronicle* it was reported that he arrived in the city in 1860, moving from New York.

The San Francisco City Directory published December, 1865, lists all four of the men in the family: Thomas Chapple was a jeweler in the Mission District, which eventually became the area of San Francisco where all five of the California families made their permanent residences. On the same city directory, Charles P. Gibbons, John J. Gibbons, and Orson Elliott, new husband of Marie Theresa Gibbons, were all listed as living in the same building: West side of Leavenworth between Washington and Jackson. Charles was listed as a jeweler, John as a canvasser, and Orson was a bookseller.

Charles and Winifred remained in San Francisco the rest of their lives, but Marie and John J. both sought better opportunities far and wide, only ultimately to return to San Francisco to live out their days close by their families. Adelia Gibbons Brooks, called Delia by her family, was born about 1857, and was therefore much younger. She and her husband Thomas Brooks joined them in the Mission District after their immigration in 1888.

The notable exception of the children who immigrated was William Henry Gibbons. Allured by the financial success of some of his siblings in San Francisco, Billy Gibbons immigrated to the United States in 1867, but sought his fortune in a totally different way: on the backs of sheep and cattle in a remote, but beautiful area of Central Texas.

According to the 1900 San Saba County, Texas census, William Henry Gibbons immigrated in 1860, traveling first to New York, and then on to Boston. However, he would have been only 14 at the time. Many reports state a date of immigration of 1867, which is much more likely. In addition, it was said that the success of his brothers in the real estate market of California inspired him to immigrate. In 1860, his oldest brother Charles had just relocated from the New York area, and had yet to establish himself. Billy Gibbons did not become a naturalized citizen until 1871.

Delia did not immigrate until 1888, according to the 1900 California Census. Based upon a letter written to Billy Gibbons from his sister Marie (see Appendix A), she had married Thomas A. Brooks in Ireland and evidently remained with her son Michael Edward Brooks, who was born in Ireland in 1884. Shortly after Michael was born, Thomas immigrated to America to seek better employment opportunities. According to the 1900 census, he returned to Ireland in 1888 and brought his family back to America with him.

The 1910 Census has some interesting dates for the immigration of the couple: Delia in 1872 and Thomas in 1884. The 1884 immigration date for Thomas would have matched the scenario above, but Delia would have been 11 in 1872 (if her stated birth date of 1861 is accurate, which is unlikely). This possible scenario for an early immigration of Delia will be discussed later in more detail in Chapter Eight.

The following chapters will document the experiences in the New World of each of the children of Michael Edward and Mary Gibbons, telling their histories as well as the stories of their descendents. The lives of the siblings of William Henry Gibbons will be addressed first, followed by a more detailed documentation of the life and descendents of W. H. "Billy" Gibbons, including details of families affiliated with him through marriage.

Chapter Three

The Family Line of Charles Paul Gibbons

Charles Paul Gibbons was the oldest of the Gibbons children, and was born in March of 1836 in or near Athlone, in County Westmeath. It was reported in August, 1900 in the San Francisco Chronicle that his birth name was actually Patrick Giblin, from the Baptismal Records of Taughmaconnell Parish, County Roscommon. However, he lived his life in the United States as Charles P. Gibbons, and that is how he will be addressed in the remainder of this volume.

Charles immigrated in the late 1850s, landed in New York City, and resided in the area until after he became a Naturalized citizen of the United States on May 4, 1860. As stated earlier, he left almost immediately to travel to the west coast, arriving in San Francisco later that year. By the time of the 1870 census, he had permanently established his residence in the San Francisco area, living with his sister Winifred and brother-in-law Thomas Chapple in the Mission District, at the corner of Fair Oaks and 26th.

Charles continued to live with Winifred and Thomas until his marriage about 1875 to Lydia Brown Macy, daughter of Daniel Folger Macy and Mary Brown Macy. Lydia was born on May 22, 1849 in Nantucket, Massachusetts. Her family had relocated to San Francisco by 1866, when Daniel registered to vote.

Charles and Lydia began their rather large family almost immediately. The 1900 census indicates they had eight children, seven of whom were still alive as of 1900. Their living children were all born in San Francisco:

The Family Line of Charles Paul Gibbons

George William Gibbons	b. July 10, 1875
Winifred Chapel Gibbons	b. February 11, 1877
Mary Emily Gibbons	b. March 17, 1879
Mattie Elliott Gibbons	b. May 25, 1884
Charles Paul Gibbons, Jr.	b. April 7, 1887
William Henry Gibbons	b. February 20, 1889
Lydia Brown Gibbons	b. February 15, 1892

The following sections of this chapter will provide more detail in the life of his children and their descendents.

The Charles P. Gibbons Family
Left to Right: Charles Jr., Lydia, Baby Lydia, George W., Charles Sr., and William

The San Francisco City Directory is a very important reference in tracking not only the residences of individuals, but also their professional life. Charles had his initial listing in the San Francisco City Directory as a jeweler in 1865, then was listed in various professions, such as a real estate broker, stock broker, and in mining for a number of years before he began concentrating professionally as a fire Insurance broker. Beginning in 1886, he worked as a solicitor for several insurance companies, and two of his sons, Charles P. Gibbons, Jr., and William Henry, followed him in the profession.

The following is a listing of the references for Charles in San Francisco City Directories, along with his residences as he flourished in a long and storied career in both real estate and insurance:

1865 - Charles P. Gibbons, jeweler, Leavenworth bet Washington and Jackson
1866 - Charles P. Gibbons, jeweler, Leavenworth bet Washington and Jackson
1875 - Charles P. Gibbons, real estate agent, r W s Guerrero bet 25th and 26th
1876 - Charles P. Gibbons, dwl 2608 Mission, no occupation listed
1877 - Charles P. Gibbons, stock broker, 2608 Mission
1878 - Charles P. Gibbons, broker, 2608 Mission
1879 - Charles P. Gibbons, speculator, 2608 Mission
1880 - Charles P. Gibbons, mining, 2608 Mission
1881 - Charles P. Gibbons, stockdealer, 2608 Mission
1882 - C. P. Gibbons, Speculator, residence 2608 Mission
1883 - Charles P. Gibbons, Real Estate, r. 2608 Mission
1884 - Charles P. Gibbons, Real Estate, r. 2608 Mission
1885 - Charles P. Gibbons, Real Estate, residence 2608 Mission
1886 - Charles P. Gibbons, Solicitor and Surveyor, H. M. Newhall r 2608 Mission
1887 - Charles P. Gibbons, Insurance Solicitor, H. M. Newhall r 2608 Mission
1888 - Charles P. Gibbons, Insurance Solicitor, H. M. Newhall r 2608 Mission
1889 - Charles P. Gibbons, Insurance Solicitor, H. M. Newhall r 844 Capp
1890 - Charles P. Gibbons, Insurance Solicitor, H. M. Newhall r 844 Capp
1891 - Charles P. Gibbons, Insurance Solicitor, H. M. Newhall r 844 Capp
1892 - Charles P. Gibbons, Insurance Solicitor, H. M. Newhall r 844 Capp
1893 - Charles P. Gibbons, Insurance Solicitor, H. M. Newhall r 844 Capp
1894 - Charles P. Gibbons, Insurance Solicitor, H. M. Newhall r 844 Capp
1895 - Charles P. Gibbons, Insurance Solicitor, H. M. Newhall r 844 Capp
1896 - Charles P. Gibbons, Solicitor, Atlas Assurance Company, r 844 Capp
1900 - Charles P. Gibbons, Solicitor, Atlas Assurance Company, r 844 Capp
1901 - Charles P. Gibbons, Solicitor, Atlas Assurance Company, r 844 Capp
1902 - Charles P. Gibbons, Solicitor, Atlas Assurance Company, r 844 Capp

1903 - Charles P. Gibbons, Solicitor, Atlas Assurance Company, r 844 Capp
1904 - Charles P. Gibbons, Solicitor, Atlas Assurance Company, r 844 Capp
1905 - Charles P. Gibbons, Solicitor, Atlas Assurance Company, r 844 Capp
1907 - Charles P. Gibbons, insurance, r. 844 Capp
1908 - Charles P. Gibbons, insurance, r. 844 Capp
1909 - Charles P. Gibbons, fire, life and accident ins., r 844 Capp
1910 - Charles P. Gibbons, insurance, r. 844 Capp
1911 - Charles P. Gibbons, insurance, r. 844 Capp
1912 - Charles P. Gibbons, insurance, r. 844 Capp

Charles partially retired in 1907, then fully retired about 1913. He and Lydia continued to be listed in the San Francisco City Directory, but only as residents. Charles P. Gibbons, Jr., continued to run the insurance business under the name Charles P. Gibbons and Son.

Lydia Macy Gibbons died on April 10, 1918, followed four years later by Charles P. Gibbons, Sr., when he died on August 28, 1922, at the age of 86. Both are buried in the Greenlawn Memorial Park in San Mateo, California. His professional career was recognized in his Obituary published in the *San Francisco Chronicle* on August 29, 1922:

PIONEER INSURANCE MAN OF SF DIES
After an illness of several weeks, Charles P. Gibbons, 82, a pioneer insurance man, died Monday night at his home, 884 Capp Street. Funeral services will be held this afternoon from undertaking parlors at Divisadero and Post Streets. Gibbons came to California from New York in 1860 and made extensive real estate investments in San Francisco. He later engaged in the insurance business, from which he retired in the latter part of 1907. He was a prominent Odd Fellow and is survived by six children, George W. Gibbons, Mrs. A. W. Turpin, Mrs. Mae E. Green, Mrs. Charles W. Harry, Charles P. Gibbons, Jr., W. H. Gibbons, and Mrs. Gus Schaefer of Honolulu.

George William Gibbons

George W. Gibbons was the eldest child born to Charles P. and Lydia Gibbons, arriving on July 10, 1875. According to the San Francisco City Directory, it appears that he initially joined his father in the insurance business at age 16, working as an adjuster for the same company in 1891 while still living at home.

He was evidently not a good fit in the insurance business because he then disappears from the Directory until 1899, where he was listed with no occupation and living at 2616 Mission. The previous year, he was listed on the "Great Registers of California" while living at the same address, with an occupation of painter. In 1902, he was listed as a bartender, living on 3rd street.

He left San Francisco after 1902, and disappeared from records for a period of time. On September 12, 1918, he registered for the draft in Gilroy, Santa Clara County, where he listed his address as the Central Hotel, and his occupation as Ranch Laborer. Two years later, on the 1920 Census of Gustine, Merced County, California, he was listed as a Widower working as a Construction Painter. He stated an age of 44, and that his father was born in Ireland and his mother in Massachusetts. The only other record found of his late wife was a statement on the 1930 San Francisco County Census that he was first married at age 23, or in about 1898.

The next major documented event in the life of George W. Gibbons was the issuance of a marriage license on July 11, 1923, to George and Mrs. Wilhelmina Kohrn Egan, a widow of German descent. His address on the license was the Seneca Hotel, and her address was 14 Walter Street. The wedding took place on July 18, 1923, in San Francisco.

After their marriage, George and Wilhelmina, or Minnie as she was commonly called, continued to reside at her house at 14 Walter Street. George had steady employment as a Salesman in real estate until the 1930 Census, where his occupation was once again listed as a painter, this time in his own shop. They were still living at 14 Walter St. The mar-riage seems to have been a happy one, and lasted the rest of their lives. There were no children as a result of the union.

In 1939, George and Minnie no longer appeared on the San Francisco City Directory, indicating they had retired and relocated or taken a long vacation. They were listed on the 1940 Census for Chico, Butte County, California, living at the Richardson Springs Hotel, and listing their status as retired. The Richardson Springs Hotel was a popular vacation and retirement spot for San Franciscans attracted by the warm springs there.

In the San Francisco City Directory for 1941, they were back at 14 Walter Street, where they lived until George's death on March 29, 1944, in San Francisco. Wilhelmina died 10 years later, on February 27, 1954, also in San Francisco. They are buried side by side in the Greenlawn Memorial Park in San Mateo, where many of their Gibbons relatives are buried.

Winifred Chapel Gibbons

Winifred Chapel Gibbons was the second child and oldest daughter of Charles Paul and Lydia Gibbons. She was born February 11, 1877, in San Francisco, and was named after Charles' sister, Winifred Gibbons Chapple.

Winifred married Andrew Walker Turpin November 1, 1898, in San Francisco. They operated various boarding houses and hotels in San Francisco, including the Turpin House and the Turpin Hotel over the next 20 years, until Andrew's death on June 26, 1923.

Andrew and Winifred had one child, Ruth E. Turpin, born July 17, 1905. After Andrew's death, Winifred and Ruth lived in Honolulu with her sister Lydia Gibbons Schaefer for a period of time, long enough to be counted there on the 1930 census. They returned to San Francisco for the 1940 census.

Ruth Turpin waited until her mid thirties to get married, but after the 1940 Census, she finally married, and she picked an interesting character to wed. She married Charles Herbert Veil, a pilot in World War I. According to information from FindAGrave.Com, Charles Veil was born in Big Run, Pennsylvania, and grew up in East Palestine, Ohio. On April 12, 1917, Veil enlisted in France's Service Aeronautique and underwent aviation, aerobatic, and gunnery training at Avord, Pau, and the G.D.E. He earned his brevet on the Caudron on October 20, 1917, and he graduated from the training pipeline on December 16, 1917. He was assigned to Escadrille SPA 150 and served with that unit at the Front through October 9, 1918. On that date, Veil was commissioned as a First Lieutenant in the United States Army Air Service, but he continued to fly with his French comrades in SPA 150 until the Armistice ended the war on November 11, 1918. He was awarded France's Croix de Guerre with three Palms as well as the Medaille Militaire for his combat service and his destruction of three enemy aircraft.

While still in Paris, Veil pulled off a memorable stunt. He successfully flew a fighter through the Arc de Triumphe by rolling the aircraft on its side and kicking in some upside rudder just before passing through the arc. Veil was honorably discharged on September 8, 1919, in Garden City, New York.

He even wrote a book about his flying experiences, called *Adventure's a Wench*. Ironically, he was killed in an auto crash, according the September 9, 1949, edition of the *San Francisco Chronicle*. He was a passenger with two friends when a speed racer drove through an intersection and broadsided his car.

A few years after this tragedy, Ruth's mother, Winifred Chapel Gibbons Turpin also died. The date was June 30, 1952, in San Mateo, California, but it is unknown where she is buried. Ruth Turpin Veil passed away in 1982, in Honolulu, Hawaii, according to the Social Security Death Index.

Mary Emily Gibbons

The third child born to Charles Paul and Lydia Gibbons was another daughter, Mary Emily Gibbons, born March 17, 1879, in San Francisco. Mary Emily, who was called Mae, was married, according to the *San Francisco Chronicle*, October 18, 1896, Edition, to Wallace L. Thompson, the son of Judge and Mrs. A. W. Thompson. The service and reception took place at the residence of the bride's parents, 844 Capp Street, the Rev. Thomas Chalmers Easton of the Twenty-third Street Presbyterian officiating.

It is uncertain what happened to husband number one, but Mae was evidently a very lovely young lady, per the newspaper, and in about 1905, she married J. Charles Green, the most prominent outdoor advertising executive in the San Francisco area. His company, the J. Charles Green Company, owned almost all of the billboard advertising in San Jose, and at one time, he was also the owner of the Auditorium Rink.

What appeared to be an ideal marriage soon took a surprising turn. J. Charles had been married previously to Belle, who became his first wife in 1892. Belle suffered fits of violent temper, and in 1904, he placed her in a sanatorium in Alameda County. Then, while on business in Utah, he had obtained a divorce from Belle Green, which was granted under the normal proceedings of that state. After about a year, he married Mae Gibbons.

In 1909, Belle Green was adjudged to be an incompetent person, and her mother was granted letters of guardianship. As soon as this was done, the mother filed a divorce suit against J. Charles Green, alleging that the initial divorce granted in Utah was illegal, and that he had committed bigamy when he married Mae. This suit asked for a divorce and a division of all his property, plus an allowance of $500 a month, plus attorney's fees. Even though J. Charles had offered to pay a monthly stipend to support the cost of the sanatorium, this was not sufficient for the mother. The suit dragged on for three years, until the mother agreed to a settlement of $150 per month.

With that issue finally behind them, another tragedy struck. Two years later, on September 21, 1914, J. Charles was late coming down for breakfast. When Mae Green went upstairs to check on him, she found him dead in bed due to heart failure.

About six years later, Mae remarried, this time without all the drama. Her third husband was Frederick Joseph Giblin, which was ironic since her family's name was Giblin prior to immigrating. Mae and Frederick were married sometime after 1920. Although they had no children, it was a marriage which lasted until their deaths: Mae in 1943, and Frederick a year later. Mae was buried in the Greenlawn Memorial Park in San Mateo, and Frederick in the Holy Cross Catholic Cemetery nearby. Both cemeteries were the final resting places for many of the Gibbons siblings and their descendents.

Mattie Elliott Gibbons

Mattie Elliott Gibbons was born May 25, 1884, in San Francisco. She was the fourth surviving child of Charles P. and Lydia Gibbons, but Mattie was probably preceded by another sibling who did not survive infancy. In the 1910 California Census, it was stated that Lydia had borne 8 children, 7 of whom were still alive. It is likely that the eighth child was born in the five year gap between Mae and Mattie.

Mattie married William J. Harry, an advertiser, on September 15, 1904, in San Francisco, and they had one son, Willard Charles Harry, born August 10, 1907.

William Harry passed away on Christmas Day 1960, and Mattie on January 25, 1966. William was cremated, and Mattie was buried in Cypress Lawn Memorial Park in San Mateo.

Charles Paul Gibbons, Jr.

The second son born to Charles and Lydia was his namesake, Charles Paul Gibbons, Jr. He was born on April 7, 1887, in San Francisco. Charles, Jr., was not only a namesake, he followed his father into the insurance industry, and spent his entire career working for Charles P. Gibbons and Son, Insurance.

According to the *San Francisco Chronicle*, dated October 26, 1911, Miss Mildred (Milve) Ruth Loveland, the pretty and charming daughter of Mr. and Mrs. Walter G. Loveland, became the bride of Charles P. Gibbons. Their son Charles P. Gibbons, III, was born on December 29, 1912. He initially was called Charles P. III, but often the newspapers dropped the Jr. from his father's name, and Charles III became Charles, Jr.

Charles III deviated from the traditional Gibbons residences in San Francisco, and moved to Los Angeles around 1949, where he lived until his death in 1974.

Charles, Jr., and Milve also had a daughter, Jane Loveland Gibbons, born June 19, 1921. Jane and her betrothed, William Schimpferman, made headlines in the *San Francisco Chronicle* when they announced that, although they were to have been married on February 14, 1940, they had found their dream apartment on Telegraph Hill in San Francisco on November 7, 1939, and they decided to move up the wedding to November 9, 1939. They had a successful marriage which produced two children, Linda and Bruce.

However, all articles in the *Chronicle* did not contain such good news for Charles, Jr. On September 13, 1928 he woke up to these headlines:

REALTY MAN ACCUSED BY WIFE OF DRINKING
Charles P. Gibbons, real estate and insurance man with offices at 315 Montgomery, was made a defendent in a divorce suit filed yesterday by his wife, Milva R. Gibbons.

Needless to say, the divorce went through rather quickly after that headline. However, Charles did not remain single for long. On February 7, 1930, Charles married Marguerite Lord, and both became very active in San Francisco Society, receiving many mentions of their activities in the *Chronicle*. Although they had no children, they remained married until his death on December 27, 1941.

His obituary in the *San Francisco Chronicle* reads as follows:

OBITUARY
CHARLES P. GIBBONS
Funeral Services for Charles P. Gibbons, member of a pioneer San Francisco family and for 30 years an insurance broker here, will be held today (Monday) at 11 a.m. Mr. Gibbons died Saturday at the University of California Hospital after a short illness. He was 54. The present insurance firm of Charles P. Gibbons and Son, with offices at 354 Pine Street, was founded by Mr. Gibbons' father in 1865. Survivors include his wife, Marguerite Gibbons, a son, Charles P. Gibbons III, and a daughter Mrs. Jane Schimpferman.

William Henry Gibbons

William Henry Gibbons was the third and final son of Charles P. and Lydia Gibbons. He was born in San Francisco on February 20, 1889, and was named after his uncle, William Henry (Billy) Gibbons. Like his brother Charles Jr., William followed in his father's footsteps, and became well known in the insurance business.

William received many accolades during his career, and was recognized several times in the industry periodical, "The Adjuster". In the 1922 Volume, it was written:

"Gibbons Joint Assistant General Agent.
The appointment of W. H. Gibbons to the important office of joint assistant general agent of the big general agency of Edward Brown & Sons, where he will have charge under Mr. Arthur M. Brown of the underwriting in connection with his former duties as manager of the loss department, pleases everybody. For thirty-five years Mr. Gibbons has been a faithful servant of this office beginning when the firm was known as Brown, Craig & Co. (when it was established) in 1885. He has filled practically every desk in the office and served a term in the field, covering both Pacific Coast and Mountain territory. In 1906 the office of agencies was created for him and for some time past he has had charge of the claims department. He has taken an active part in all movements undertaken for the improvement of Coast underwriting conditions and is a past president of the Fire Underwriters' Association of the Pacific."

W. H. Gibbons married Anna Mary Rehage in San Francisco on June 23, 1917. They began their married life in San Francisco, but by the time of the 1930 Census, they had relocated to nearby San Mateo, California. They remained in San Mateo the rest of their lives.

W. H. and Anna had one daughter, Lydia, who was born October 15, 1918, in San Francisco, and named after his mother. Lydia lived with them until age 32, when she married Edwin Harold Din in San Mateo. William Henry Gibbons died May 3, 1951, and is buried in Greenlawn Memorial Park in San Mateo.

Lydia Brown Gibbons

The final child of Charles Paul and Lydia Macy Gibbons was Lydia Brown Gibbons, born February 15, 1892, in San Francisco. Like so many of the Gibbons descendents, Lydia Brown Gibbons led a unique, interesting life, including a trip to Hawaii as a teenager. A notice appeared in the Honolulu newspaper, the *Pacific Commercial Advertiser,* on January 10th, 1909, that "J. Charles and Mae Green, along with Miss Lydia Brown Gibbons (sister of Mae Green), Herbert Green (son of J. Charles Green), and Mrs. Kate Harker, formed a jolly party, and set the record for a trip from Hilo to the Volcano House in his seven seater touring car, of one hour and twenty-seven minutes. After a brief rest, they went to the volcano on horseback."

Evidently, Lydia met an important person on this trip, because a notice appeared four months later in the *Pacific Commercial Advertiser*, dated April 16, 1909, that Charles P. Gibbons arrived in Honolulu on the S.S. *Manchuria* from San Francisco on April 15, 1909, along with his daughter, Miss Lydia B. Gibbons, age 17. Two weeks later came the notice from the *Pacific Commercial Advertiser* Society Page, May 2, 1909: An engagement luncheon was given last Tuesday by Mrs. F. A. Schaefer in honor of Miss Lydia Gibbons, the fiancée of Mr. Gustave Schaefer.

Four months later, on August 21, 1909, this notice appeared in the *Oakland Tribune*:

GIBBONS-SCHAEFER WEDDING
Mr. and Mrs. Charles Paul Gibbons have issued invitations to the marriage of their daughter, Lydia, to Gustav Edmund Schaefer. The ceremony will take place on Friday evening, August 27, at half past eight o'clock at the First Presbyterian Church. A reception will follow at the Fairmont Hotel. The groom is the son of one of the wealthiest men in Honolulu, where he and his wife in the future will reside.

The August 28th edition of the *Chronicle* had huge headlines, along with the story:

LYDIA GIBBONS BRIDE OF GUSTAVE SCHAEFFER (The paper got so excited they misspelled his name – it should be Gustav E. Schaefer)

"The wedding of Miss Lydia Gibbons, daughter of Mr. and Mrs. Charles Gibbons and Gustave Schaffer, which took place last evening at the First Presbyterian Church, was a brilliant affair, which was of more than local interest, owing to the effect that the groom is one of the more prominent men of the Hawaiian Islands, and the bride, who is one of the popular girls in the younger social set, has a wide acquaintance outside of her home city...After a honeymoon trip spent in the southern part of the state, Mr. Schaeffer and his bride will sail for Honolulu, where they will make their home."

Gustav and Lydia arrived back in Honolulu in September where she assumed her new role as a supportive wife in an idyllic environment. Lydia and Gustav had two daughters, Lydia Macy born December 10, 1910, and Barbara Corrine, born January 31, 1914. Both girls married native born Hawaii men, and lived in the islands the rest of their lives.

A short biography of Gustav Schaefer, written in 1917, was published on GenealogyTrails.com website:

SCHAEFER, GUSTAV EDMUND, secretary F. A. Schaefer & Co., Ltd., Honolulu; born January 19, 1888, in Honolulu; son of Frederick August and Elizabeth (Robertson) Schaefer; married August 27, 1909, Lydia Brown Gibbons, in San Francisco; two daughters, Lydia Macy and Barbara Corrine; received early education in private and grammar schools of Honolulu, one and one-half years at Lawrenceville, N. J., and six months business course at Throop Institute, Pasadena, Cal. Entered employ of F. A. Schaefer & Co. 1907 of which firm is now secretary. Captain of Infantry, Officers Reserve Corps, U. S. Army, former Captain 1st Infantry, National Guard of Hawaii. Member Pacific, Oahu Country, Myrtle Boat, and Aero Clubs.

Charles and Lydia sailed to Hawaii in May of 1914 to meet their new granddaughters, and then Lydia Schaefer brought her two daughters on their first visit to the mainland to meet the rest of the Gibbons family in June of 1917. The Gibbons family connection remained strong. Winifred Gibbons Turpin and her daughter were living with the Schaefers on the 1930 census, following the death of A. W. Turpin in 1923. Winifred and Ruth returned to live in San Francisco by the time of the 1940 Census.

After a marriage that lasted almost 50 years, Gustav died on April 4, 1957. Lydia passed away 14 years later, on February 10, 1971. Both are buried in the O'ahu Cemetery, Honolulu, Hawaii.

The Family Line of Charles Paul Gibbons

Timeline for Charles Paul Gibbons

1836   Charles Paul Gibbons brother of W. H. Gibbons born in Ireland
1859   Immigrated to America
1860   Became Naturalized Citizen in Brooklyn, NY
1860   Arrived in San Francisco, purchased real estate in Mission District
1865   Working as a jeweler in SF
1870   Listed on SF Census, living with Thomas and Winifred Chapple
1874   Married Lydia Brown Macy
1875   Son George William Gibbons born in SF
1875   Began work in Real Estate and as a stock broker
1877   Daughter Winifred Chapel Gibbons born in SF
1879   Daughter Mary Emily (Mae) Gibbons born in SF
1884   Daughter Mattie Elliott Gibbons born in SF
1886   Began career in insurance
1887   Son Charles Paul Gibbons, Jr. born in SF
1889   Son William Henry Gibbons born in SF
1892   Daughter Lydia Brown Gibbons born in SF
1913   Retires completely
1918   Death of Lydia Brown Macy Gibbons
1922   Death of Charles Paul Gibbons, Sr.

Chapter Four

The Family Line of Michael Giblin

Michael Giblin was the only one of the children of Michael and Mary Giblin who chose not to immigrate to America. In doing so, he also chose to retain the family name of Giblin rather than Americanizing it.

According to SurnameDB.Com, the name, which has been recorded with a wide variety of spellings including Gibben, Gibbin, Giblett, Giblin, Gibling, Gibbon and Gubbin, is a medieval English surname, but of Anglo-Saxon and Olde German pre-7th century origins. As stated earlier, the variations all originated from a shortened form of the given name Gilbert. Changing the name from Giblin to Gibbons was probably done because Gibbons was considered to be more Americanized.

It is interesting that today, there are more Giblins in the United States (4136), Great Britain (1850), and Australia (1080), than there are in Ireland (648). The Gibbons surname, particularly in the United States, is about ten times more prevalent than Giblin.

In the years 1847-1864, the most common county where Giblins were found in *Griffiths Valuation* was Roscommon, where 63 families with the Giblin surname lived. There was one Giblin family in County Westmeath during that same period.

According to the *Ireland Civil Registration Index, 1845 - 1958*, there is a listing for a Michael Giblin, born in Athlone in 1839, who remained in Ireland during all of the Potato Famine immigrations. He died in Athlone in 1922 at age 83. He meets all the date criteria for the seventh child of Michael and Mary Glennon Giblin, but once again, this is not definitive proof of his ancestry.

As listed in the parish records of County Roscommon, Ireland, Michael married Bridget Galvin in the Taughmaconnell Parish of the Roman Catholic Diocese of Clonfert, County Roscommon, on January 8, 1875. A Priest by the name of John Walsh performed the ceremony.

Michael Giblin was listed on the 1901 and the 1911 census of Roscommon County, along with his wife Bridget. There were two lodgers listed on the 1901 census, and a lodger and a servant on the 1911 census. The 1911 census indicates Bridget never had children, and had been married to Michael for 37 years.

Brideswell is in the Electoral Division of Ballynamona, in Civil Parish of Cam, in the Barony of Athlone, in the County of Roscommon. Thomas Brooks and Delia Gibbons were married in Cam Parish in 1872, validating that the location was consistent with the location of some of the other Gibbons children.

The house where Michael and Bridget lived was described in the 1901 census as stone or brick, with a thatch or wooden roof. There were two to four rooms in the house, and the dwelling was described as second class out of four possible classes.

Michael was listed as age 60 and Bridget as age 45 in the 1901 census. By 1911, Michael had picked up a few extra years, and was now listed as 73. However, Bridget has somehow aged 23 years, and was now listed as 68. Both were born in County Roscommon. Michael's age in 1911 is consistent with the reported birth date of 1839, as shown in the Civil Registration Index at the time of his death.

Because Michael and Bridget were childless, his death marked the end of his family line.

Timeline for Michael Giblin

1839   Michael Gibbons born in Athlone, County Roscommon, Ireland
1873   Served as Roscommon Town Commissioner
1875   Married to Bridget Galvin in Taughmaconnell Parish, Roscommon
1901   Listed on 1901 Census, County Roscommon
1911   Listed on 1911 Census, County Roscommon
1922   Died in County Roscommon

Chapter Five

The Family Line of Winifred Gibbons

Winifred T. Gibbons was the second child and oldest daughter of Michael and Mary Gibbons. She was born in 1841 in Athlone, County Westmeath, Ireland. Winifred was married to Thomas Chapple before she immigrated to America, although the exact date of the marriage is unknown. Thomas was born in England in 1831, according to the 1870 San Francisco County Census.

Winifred and Thomas immigrated to America in 1859, probably accompanied by Charles P. Gibbons, Marie Theresa Gibbons, and John J. Gibbons. Winifred and Charles both became naturalized citizens in 1860, and then headed west to San Francisco, along with their siblings. The Chapples established residence near Fair Oaks and 26th Street in the Mission District, and never left the area. Charles was living with them in 1870, then moved to his own residence when he and Lydia Brown Macy were married in about 1875.

Thomas Chapple Jeweler was listed on the 1866 San Francisco Directory, living on the north side of San Jose Railroad near Guerrero; Guerrero is very close to Fair Oaks and 26th. Thomas Chapple Real Estate was listed on the 1867-1868 San Francisco Directory, dwelling on Fair Oaks near Navy. Thomas was listed on the 1870 census with Winifred and Charles, but died in 1871. Winifred Chapple was listed in the San Francisco City Directories starting in 1874 through 1879 as a widow living on the corner of Fair Oaks and 26th.

Winifred Gibbons Chapple remarried around 1886, this time to another Irishman, William Fennell, who was born in Ireland around 1840. He

The Family Line of Winifred Gibbons

was naturalized in San Francisco in 1867. William was a harnessmaker, and moved into Winifred's house after their marriage and continued with his business. The marriage seemed to be quite stable – until Winifred became deathly ill and events took a grim turn.

Winifred died on November 28, 1899. Her obituary appeared in the next day's issue of the *San Francisco Chronicle*, stating:

FENNELL - In this city, November 28, Winifred Fennell, beloved wife of William Fennell, and sister of Charles P. Gibbons, Mrs. O. H. Elliott, Mrs. Thomas Brooks, William Gibbons, and the late John J. Gibbons, a native of Ireland, age 58 years. Notice of funeral hereafter.

The funeral was conducted and Winifred was buried at Holy Cross Catholic Cemetery in Colma, San Mateo County.

An issue existed with the location of her will, and the headlines began. The first story hit the papers on Thursday, December 7, 1899: on page 7 in the *San Francisco Call* it was reported that William Fennell's property was going to be searched that day by Mrs. Marie T. Elliott and Deputy Sheriff Charles Fancher for the will of Mrs. Winifred Fennell. Mrs. Elliott had signed an affidavit stating that three days before she died, Mrs. Fennell had shown her a will which bequeathed the estate, valued at $15,000 to Mrs. Delia Brooks, Miss Winifred Brooks, Mr. William Fennell, Mrs. Elliott, and Mrs. Elliott's daughter. Mrs. Elliott alleges that the day after Mrs. Fennell died, Mr. Fennell forbade her from entering her late sister's residence stating that he knew there was a will and if he found it, he would break it. Mrs. Elliott said that unless restrained by the Court, Mr. Fennell would destroy the will so the Court ordered the search of the property.

On Thursday, February 22, 1900 on page 12 of the *San Francisco Chronicle* it is reported that Judge Coffey took testimony from Winifred's sisters about her will being destroyed by her surviving husband so that he could have the estate. A search was ordered and made at her house at 441 Fair Oaks Street several days after her death. This search was conducted in an unusual manner by digging up the ground where they thought she had buried the documents. Maria Elliott of 842 Capp Street said she was with her sister Winifred one time when she unearthed the will. It was buried with sole tradership papers and her marriage certificate to Mr. Chapple, her first husband. She had buried them at the roots of a Panama lily in her garden. Maria said Winifred then moved the documents to a hole she dug under the house near the front entrance. Later it was reported that Winifred moved them to the store house hiding them among newspapers. Mrs. Elliott said that Mrs. Fennell hid her bank book and will and other papers from her husband William to prevent him from getting it. Her estate was her separate property and worth $10,000.

According to Orson H. Elliott, Fennell thought Mrs. Elliott had the will, but Orson told Fennell that it was in the house. Mr. Fennell refused to allow them into the house after the funeral. Previous to her death Delia Brooks and Maria Elliott asked Winifred about the location of her will, she replied on her death bed, "you know." They had seen her wrap it in oilcloth and place it in a chest made of pine wood that was brought from Ireland. They locked the chest and Delia took it away. The chest was found broken open when the searchers arrived. The searchers then dug under the Panama lily, under the house and other spots where the ground had been disturbed. The storehouse was also searched without success. The will appointed Mrs. Elliott executrix and bequests were made to her and Mrs. Brooks as well as to their daughters. The will was made in 1890, but Mr. Fennell says it was not made before the time of his wife's death in 1899.

On Saturday, March 10, 1900 on page 12 of the *San Francisco Call* it was reported that the will had been found in a tin box in a woodshed in the rear of the decedent's home. Maria T. Elliott and Delia B. Brooks were named Executrices of the Will. The article stated that the will said the same thing Maria and Delia said it would say prior to its finding. It gives to one sister, Mrs. Delia Brooks, the lot and the cottage of the deceased on Fair Oaks Street, near Twenty-sixth, with her furniture, wearing apparel and jewelry, and to Mrs. Maria Teresa Elliott, another sister, the adjoining lot. The third lot was to be sold and the $1000 given to the second husband of the deceased, William Fennell. The remainder of the estate is to be divided between Mrs. Fennell's brothers and sisters. It was filed for probate, and the sad story was hopefully put to rest.

However, it was reported on Wednesday, April 11, 1900, in the *San Francisco Chronicle*, it was reported Judge Coffey authorized Mrs. Maria T. Elliott to administer Winifred Fennell's estate. Bond was fixed at $10,000. Winifred's husband, William Fennell sued the public administrator for the money and personal property of which the administrator took possession because his interest was diminished by the finding of the will.

On Friday, April 5, 1901 on page 8 of the *San Francisco Call*, it is reported the Estate of Winifred Fennell through Executrix Maria Teresa Elliott transferred to William Fennell a lot on E line of Fair Oaks Street, 135 N. of Twenty-sixth. N 25 by E 125. $1450. Mr. Fennell was no longer living in Winifred's house on Fair Oaks – the 1901 San Francisco City Directory shows him now living downtown, at 417 Kearney.

Maria Elliott was a very strong and determined person, and she was determined that Delia would receive the house, furniture, and other items bequeathed to her in the will, exactly as Winifred had intended. This was more important to her than her own inheritance because Delia had lived without a lot of comfort in her life. All five of the other siblings had become very successful in the United States, but Delia's husband Thomas had always struggled for work and to make ends meet. The fact that they now had their own house and furnishings which they had always dreamed of having finally put a happy ending to the story.

Just for the record, the properties belonging to Thomas and Winifred Chapple on the 400 Block of Fair Oaks, specifically 433, 441, and 443 Fair Oaks, are valued in 2021 at an average of $2 million each. 443 Fair Oaks is described on Redfin.Com as "Miraculously intact, a triumphant testimony to the craftsmanship & intrinsic modernity of Victorian architectural ideas."

Timeline for Winifred Gibbons Chapple Fennell

1841 Winifred Gibbons born in Athlone, Ireland
1859 Immigrated to America
1860 Became a Naturalized citizen in Brooklyn, New York
1860 Relocated to San Francisco; listed on 1860 Census
1865 Thomas is listed in the SF City Directories as a jeweler living near 26th street
1870 Listed on San Francisco County Census
1871 Death of Thomas Chapple
1874 Winifred Chapple, widow, living at Fair Oaks and 26th Street
1880 Listed on San Francisco County Census
1886 Married William Fennell
1899 Death of Winifred Chapple Fennell
1900 Search for will hidden from William Fennell by Winifred Gibbons
1900 Will found and probated

Chapter Six

The Family Line of Marie Theresa Gibbons

Based upon the Parish Baptismal Records for Taughmaconnell Parish in County Roscommon, Ireland, Marie Theresa Gibbons was born to Michael and Mary Glennon Gibbons on August 27, 1842, in Diocese Clonfert. In later life, she often went by Maria Theresa, but in the Parish Records as well as correspondence to her siblings, she was Marie. Also in later life, she consistently stated a birth date of 1848, but the parish records show her true date of birth to be six years earlier.

According to the 1900 San Francisco County Census, she immigrated to America in 1859 at age 17, and more than likely was accompanied by her brother, Charles Paul Gibbons, her sister Winifred T. Gibbons Chapple and Winifred's husband Thomas, and possibly her brother John J. Gibbons. The 1900 census does not indicate that she was naturalized as of the date of the census, but Charles and Winifred were naturalized in New York in 1860.

All four of the siblings appear to have immediately left for San Francisco. Marie was definitely there by September 5, 1864, when she married Orson H. Elliott in San Francisco. Orson was born January 28, 1842, in Illinois, a member of a Mormon family which journeyed to Utah when the Mormons were no longer welcome in their base of Nauvoo, Illinois. They traveled to Utah with the Robert Wimmer Company, leaving in July, 1852 with 258 individuals and 71 wagons. They arrived in the Salt Lake valley on 15 September 1852.

Orson was baptized into the Church of Jesus Christ of Latter-day Saints on 6 November 1853 at the age of eleven. In 1860 he was listed in the Cumberland Township, Sierra County, California Census at the age of 18. A more detailed account of Orson Elliott's early life is presented in Appendix C.

In 1865, Orson and Marie were listed in the San Francisco City Directory in a dwelling on the west side of Leavenworth Street, between Washington and Jackson Streets. Also living there were Charles P. Gibbons and John J. Gibbons.

Orson Hyde Elliott **Marie Theresa Elliott**

Also in 1865, it was reported in the *Gold Hills Daily News*, Gold Hills, Nevada, with a dateline of San Francisco that Orson H. Elliott, whose feet were frozen during a trip on the Pacific from Victoria to this port, because the officers of the vessel refused to furnish him with bed or bedding, and compelled him to sleep on deck without covering, recovered a judgement this morning, for $10,000 against the California Steam Navigation Company.

By the time of the 1870 Census, the Elliotts had relocated to Box Elder County, Utah, just to the west of Salt Lake City. Orson was listed with an occupation of bookseller, and Marie was keeping house. Orson remained involved in book publishing or selling for much of the rest of his life. In the book *Corrinne Utah*, Orson was serving in another occupation, as Justice of the Peace, when in January, 1873, he arrested 5 men and sent them to trial in probate court at Brigham City.

Next comes the big surprise. The General Land Office of Texas has an excellent website which lists some of the earliest land acquisitions and transfers. On that site we find this entry:

Texas Land Title Abstracts
District: Bexar
County: San Saba
Grantee: W. H. Gibbons
Patentee: O. H. Elliott
Patent Date: 30 Apr 1881
Patent #: 214
Patent Volume: 12
Acres: 80
Class: Bexar Preemption
File: 2509

These 80 acres of land were surveyed on request from W. H. Gibbons on June 16th, 1877, in order to transfer the land to M. T. Elliott and O. H. Elliott, his sister and brother-in-law. The grant states that O. H. Elliott had actually settled on the land and cultivated it as a homestead, beginning June 16, 1877. At the same time, O. H. Elliott purchased an ajoining 80 acres from W. H. Bainbridge, the business partner of W. H. Gibbons under a similar arrangement. Orson Elliott had just made the move from being a West Coast bookseller to becoming a San Saba County, Texas, farmer. The 160 acre tract was located just to the north of what is now the Colorado River Bend State Park, in east central San Saba County.

This land was acquired under a Preemption Grant. The Preemption land grant program allowed settlers to claim land on the vacant public domain and provided a process through which settlers could title the land once they met the established criteria. The first preemption act was passed by the Republic of Texas in 1845, and allowed for the settlement of up to 320 acres of vacant public land. An 1854 act reduced the preemption amount to 160 acres and the first preemption program was canceled in 1856. Preemption grants of 160 acres were reinstated in 1866 and continued until 1898.

Orson was listed, with Marie, on the 1880 San Saba County Census, still actively working as a farmer:

Osburn Elliotte	Male	37	1843	Illinois	Married	Farmer
Mariah Elliotte	Female	32	1848	Ireland	Married	Keeping House
James Forstad	Male	28	1852	Norway	Single	Servant Laborer

Mr. Forstad was probably the only Norwegian servant in the county at that time, and maybe even the only one in the entire state of Texas.

However, it was soon evident that farming was not going to be a permanent occupation for the Elliotts. The actual land transfer took place in 1881, after all the prerequisites had been taken care of. Even before the land transfer was complete, they were already looking at opportunities elsewhere. Orson submitted a Passport Application March 13, 1876, in Galveston, Texas. On the application, he was described as 34 years old male, 5' 10" in his stocking feet, high round forehead, blue eyes, large pointed nose, a large mouth, short chin, dark brown hair, and light complexion with a sharp face. At that time, a single passport was sufficient for the entire family to travel.

Another passport application was submitted on Jan 4, 1883, at age 41 with the same physical description. The word 'Wife' was handwritten in parentheses, indicating Marie was traveling with him. Shortly after that, the Elliotts disposed of their San Saba County land and made an even bigger move, this time to South America to sell books in Chile.

In a letter written to Billy Gibbons by Marie Elliott in 1888, she described some of their experiences in South America (See Appendix A for a complete transcription of the letter, and a scan of the letter itself). The Elliots went first to Chile to sell books there, but were not very successful, primarily due to a Cholera epidemic. The epidemic forced them to take a harrowing 65-mile trip over the Andes into Argentina where they reestablished their book selling business in Buenos Aires.

They were made a wholesale offer to sell their business, which they were planning to accept and to return to California in May or June of 1888. According to the letter, the Elliotts planned first to go to New

York, then to Texas for a visit with Billy Gibbons and his family. Their final destination was to be Los Angeles. The next record found for them was back in San Francisco, where Orson was listed on the Great Registers of California as having registered to vote on October 27, 1890. They were back living at 842 Capp, next door to Marie's brother, Charles. They continued to live at that address for the next 12 years.

Orson and Marie were listed on the 1900 San Francisco County census, with an added surprise. In addition to Orson and Marie, a 19-year-old daughter Marie T. Elliott was listed, with a birth date of May, 1881, in California. In 1881, the Elliotts were still in Texas, not California. A search of the California Death Index found Marie T. Elliott listed with a death date of February 19, 1955 in Napa, California. Her birth date was listed as May 9, 1877, in another country, presumably Ireland. Her mother's name was listed as Brooks, and the father's name was blank.

FindAGrave.Com reflects that she was buried in Colma, San Mateo County, California, in the Holy Cross Catholic Cemetery, with a death date matching the death record. So, who was this mysterious Marie T. Elliott?

The 1930 Census of Daly City, San Mateo County, California gives us a more definitive answer. The census record for Spencer F. Pepper and his wife, Luella D. Pepper, lists a large extended family living in their household:

1930 Census Daly City, San Mateo County, CA

Name	Sex	Age	Year	Birthplace	Relation
Spencer F Pepper	Male	33	1897	California	Head
Luella D Pepper	Female	25	1905	California	Wife
Marie T Elliott	Female	41	1889	California	Sister
Bert J Lasswell	Male	19	1911	California	Nephew
Ida May Lasswell	Female	14	1916	California	Niece
Edna L Lasswell	Female	11	1919	California	Niece
Alma J Kuebler	Female	46	1884	Minnesota	Servant

The pieces have now fallen into place: Luella D. Pepper is the daughter of Adelia Gibbons Brooks, and Marie T. Elliott is listed as her sister. The three Lasswells listed are the children of Winifred Brooks Lasswell, another daughter of Adelia Brooks. This establishes Marie T. Elliott conclusively as a daughter of Adelia as well. More detail on Marie T.

Brooks Elliott as the birth child of Adelia B. Gibbons Brooks will be covered in Chapter Eight.

Marie T. Brooks Elliott was considered by Orson and Marie to be their adopted daughter, but it is unknown if this was a legal adoption or not. She was sometimes referred to as a foster child. The relationship between Marie Brooks Elliott and her adoptive parents was soon ended with the death of Marie Gibbons Elliott. More details about Marie Theresa Brooks Elliott will be covered in Chapter Eight.

The obituary from the *San Francisco Call Bulletin* dated January 11, 1902, states: "ELLIOTT - In this city, Jan 8, 1902, Maria Teresa, beloved wife of Orson H. Elliott, a native of Ireland, age 53 years, 4 months and 12 days. Friends and acquaintances are respectfully invited to attend the funeral tomorrow (Sunday) from her late residence, 842 Capp Street, at 12 o'clock, thence to St. Peter's Church, Alabama Street, between Twenty-fourth and Twenty-fifth, at 1 o'clock, where services will be held. Interment at Holy Cross Cemetery, by carriage."

Orson Hyde Elliott died on September 5, 1909, in San Diego, California, and is buried next to Marie Teresa in the Holy Cross Cemetery, Colma, California.

Timeline for Marie Theresa Gibbons Elliott

1842   Marie Theresa Gibbons born in Roscommon County, Ireland
1859   Immigrated to Brooklyn, New York
1860   Traveled with siblings to San Francisco
1864   Married Orson Hyde Elliott in San Francisco
1865   Living with her husband, brothers Charles P. Gibbons and John J. Gibbons
1870   Listed on Census of Box Elder County, Utah
1877   Settled and cultivated 160 acres of land in San Saba County, Texas
1880   Listed on Census of San Saba County, Texas
1881   Patent for land in San Saba County granted
1883   Traveled to South America to sell books
1888   Returned from South America
1890   Living in San Francisco
1900   Listed on 1900 Census in San Francisco, along with daughter Marie
1902   Death of Marie Theresa Gibbons Elliott
1909   Death of Orson Hyde Elliott

Chapter Seven

The Family Line of John J. Gibbons

As stated earlier, John J. Gibbons, the sixth child of Michael and Mary Gibbons, was born about 1847 in Ireland, and immigrated to America in 1859 with his brother Charles Paul and his sisters Winifred T. Gibbons Chapple and Marie Theresa Gibbons. He moved west to San Francisco with these siblings, and is listed in the San Francisco Directory for 1865-1866 as a book canvasser (peddler), living with his brother Charles P. Gibbons, and his sister Marie and her new husband Orson Elliott.

There were several references to John in the letter written by Marie Theresa Elliott to Billy Gibbons from Buenos Aires in 1888 (See Appendix A). In this letter, she stated that John was planning to bring his family "out to San Francisco" in May, 1888. It is possible that he had left his family in Ireland while he established himself in America, and was planning for them to join him at a later date. Evidently, John's wife lived close geographically to Delia, because the letter states that she would bring Delia and her family with her. Marie was anxious for Delia to leave "that place", but never states specifically where she was. However, no other evidence of John's wife, if he had one, has been found.

In that same letter, Marie refers to assistance in finding work which John had given to Thomas Brooks, husband of Delia Gibbons Brooks, while John was selling books in Shasta, California, in the northern part of the state. Marie was very hopeful that all six siblings and their families, including Billy Gibbons, would soon be living together in California. Later in the letter, she states, "You know I do not want to live in Texas."

The Family Line of John J. Gibbons

We now know the reason Billy Gibbons knew she did not want to live in Texas was because she had already tried living in Texas, on land which he had sold to her.

Billy Gibbons evidently was not too receptive to that idea of moving from Texas to a large city in California.

The obituary of his sister Winifred Gibbons Chapple Fennell, published in 1899 in the *San Francisco Chronicle*, mentions her late brother John J. Gibbons. The *San Francisco Chronicle* listed the death of a John Gibbons, age 50, a native of County Galway Ireland, on May 14, 1898, (Galway is very close to Westmeath and Roscommon). FindAGrave.Com has a John Gibbons buried in Holy Cross Catholic Cemetery in Colma, ID#107319422 on about that date. This is the same cemetery where many other Gibbons family members are buried.

Timeline for John J. Gibbons

1847 John J. Gibbons born in Athlone, Ireland
1859 Immigrated to America
1860 Moved with siblings to San Francisco
1865 Listed in San Francisco City Directory as canvasser
1887 Working as bookseller in Shasta County, California
1898 Died in San Francisco and is buried in Holy Cross Catholic Cemetery

Chapter Eight

The Family Line of Adelia Beatrice Gibbons

Adelia Beatrice Gibbons was born in the vicinity of Athlone, Ireland, in June, 1861, according to her obituary. Based upon a marriage date of 1872, and a birth date of the first child of 1873, Delia was born at least 15 years prior to 1872, or about 1857, rather than the 1861 which she usually stated, in keeping with the tradition of Gibbons Women.

She was much younger than her siblings, and therefore did not immigrate with them. Her date of immigration is something of an intriguing mystery. Part of the explanation is found in the *International Genealogical Index (IGI) Microfiche for County Roscommon in 1872*. There, we find the marriage of Delia (under the name Brigida Giblin) to Thomas Brooks in Cam and Kiltoom Parish on August 25, 1872.

According to the *IGI Microfiche*, the first child born to Thomas and Delia was Martin Brooks, born 30 October 1873 in County Roscommon, Ireland. No subsequent reference has been found for him. The 1900 census of San Francisco County states that Delia was the mother of 8 children, 7 of whom were still alive. The assumption is that Martin is the one who died. It also helps explain the 5 year gap between the marriage of Thomas and Delia, and the birth of Marie in 1877.

The 1910 Census of San Francisco County, California, is the source of some confusion. It clearly states her date of immigration was 1872, and the date of the immigration of her husband, Thomas Brooks, was 1884. The same census states that they had been married for 24 years, which would have made the marriage date 1886, which we know is incorrect. In this census, she was now the mother of only 5 children, all of whom were still alive. Conveniently, Thomas was still listed as age 50, and Delia was still age 40.

The 1900 census stated that Thomas and Delia had been in the United States for 12 years, which would be correct with an 1888 immigration, but Michael had been in the US for 14 years, which would have been impossible if he had immigrated in 1888. Both Thomas and Michael had Alien Naturalization, but Delia did not. The census also stated that Winifred Brooks was born in California in 1886, but how could that have happened if her mother did not immigrate until 1888, as stated in 1900? The numbers just don't add up between the two census years, but these date discrepancies were really not that unusual during that time.

The intriguing dates on the 1910 census are the 1872 date for Delia's immigration, and the 1884 date for Thomas' immigration. The 1876 City Directory of San Francisco lists a Delia Gibbons living at 220 3rd Street. She is not listed on any other San Francisco City Directories. A look ahead to the Obituary for Delia Brooks reveals more interesting facts. The *San Francisco Chronicle* dated August 23, 1929, states the following:

MRS. BROOKS DEAD
Mrs. Adela (sic) Brooks, 479 Fair Oaks Street, died yesterday at the Hahnemann Hospital, following a brief illness. She was a Pioneer resident of the Mission District, having lived there more than 40 years. Mrs. Brooks is survived by two daughters, Deputy Coroner Luella D. Pepper of Daly City and Miss Marie T. Elliott, and six sons, Raymond J. Brooks, George, Charles W., Milton, William, and J. J. Brooks.

This obituary clearly confirms that Marie Theresa Brooks Elliott is indeed the birth daughter of Delia Gibbons Brooks. As stated earlier, Marie was born in 1877, either in California according to most census records, or "Other Country", as indicated on the State of California Death Notice for Marie. It depends upon which version of her birth location you choose to accept. Delia's stated age was about 16 at the time of Marie's birth, but she had married in 1872 in Ireland, so she was probably at least 5 years older. Marie was not adopted by the Elliotts until much later: In 1877 they were farming in San Saba County, Texas, and they were soon to go to South America for several years. They did not adopt Marie Theresa Brooks until around 1890, soon after they returned from South America.

Delia did not appear in any US Census until 1900, unless she possibly appeared on the 1890 Census, copies of which no longer exist. If Marie was born in the US, did Delia return home to Ireland with Marie until her subsequent immigration back to the United States in 1888? This question leads one to believe that Marie was born in Ireland, as indicated on her California Death Index record. The scenario would then be Marie, John J., and Michael Edward all born in Ireland, followed by the immigration of the entire family in 1888.

The 1884 date for the first immigration of Thomas Brooks seems to validate some statements in the letter Marie Theresa Gibbons Elliott sent Billy Gibbons in 1888: that "Delia needs to join her husband and get away from that terrible place." If they were in Ireland in 1884 with three or four children, and Thomas immigrated ahead of the family, then the scenario exists that Delia and the children remained in Ireland until 1888, when Thomas returned to bring them back with him to the United States. But that scenario doesn't fit well with the birth date of Winifred Brooks in San Francisco in 1886. How could that happen if they did not immigrate until 1888? The conclusion of all this is that dates did not seem to be very important to them.

Thomas Brooks had difficulty obtaining and maintaining employment, as well as suitable living quarters, during his time in San Francisco. In her letter to Billy Gibbons, Marie Elliott referenced the issues Thomas had with employment, stating that their brother John had found good employment for Thomas in Shasta County, California, sometime around 1887 - 1888.

In the 1900 Census, Thomas was listed as a laborer, and was unemployed for two months of the previous year. In the 1910 Census, Thomas was listed as a dry goods salesman, and was unemployed for 22 weeks during the previous year.

The San Francisco City Directories give some insight into his work career:

1885 - Thomas Brooks, laborer, residence 512 Mission
1886 - Thomas Brooks, carpenter, residence 512 Mission
1887 - No Thomas Brooks (Probably when he was in Shasta County)

The Family Line of Adelia Beatrice Gibbons

1888 - No Thomas Brooks (Probably when he went back to Ireland)
1889 - Thomas Brooks, laborer, residence 1016 Twenty-sixth
1890 - Thomas Brooks, shoemaker, residence 1016 Twenty-sixth
1891 - Thomas Brooks, shoemaker, residence 1016 Twenty-sixth
1892 - Thomas Brooks, laborer, residence 1016 Twenty-sixth
1893 - Thomas Brooks, spring maker, residence 1016 Twenty-sixth
1894 - Thomas Brooks, spring maker, residence 1135 Twenty-sixth
1895 - Thomas Brooks, laborer, residence 1133 Twenty-sixth
1896 - Thomas Brooks, laborer, residence 314 28th
1897 - Thomas Brooks, laborer Gray Brothers, residence 314 28th
1898 - Thomas Brooks, laborer Gray Brothers, residence 214 28th
1899 - Thomas Brooks, laborer Gray Brothers, residence 214 28th
1900 - Thomas Brooks, laborer, residence 314 28th
1901 - Thomas Brooks, laborer, residence 441 Fair Oaks
1902 - Thomas Brooks, laborer, residence 441 Fair Oaks
1903 - Thomas Brooks, laborer, residence 441 Fair Oaks
1904 - Thomas Brooks, laborer, residence 441 Fair Oaks
1905 - Thomas Brooks, iron worker, residence 441 Fair Oaks
1907 - Thomas Brooks, laborer, residence 441 Fair Oaks
1908 - Thomas Brooks, laborer, residence 441 Fair Oaks
1909 - Thomas Brooks, cond, residence 441 Fair Oaks
1910 - Thomas Brooks, laborer, residence 479 Fair Oaks
1911 - Thomas Brooks, laborer, residence 479 Fair Oaks
1912 - Thomas Brooks, laborer, residence 479 Fair Oaks
1913 - Thomas Brooks, laborer, residence 479 Fair Oaks
1913 - Thomas Brooks, laborer, residence 2449 Fair Oaks
1914 - Thomas Brooks, laborer, residence 2449 Fair Oaks
1915 - Thomas Brooks, laborer, residence 479 Fair Oaks
1916 - Thomas Brooks, asphalt worker, Brd of Pub Wks, 479 Fair Oaks
1917 - Delia B. Brooks, wid of Thomas, 479 Fair Oaks

If Thomas did immigrate in 1884, leaving his family behind, it appears he was living at 512 Mission Street while working several jobs. Then in 1889, when his family had rejoined him, they moved to 1016 26th Street and then to various other residences. When the will of Winifred Chapple Fennell was settled, the Brooks family was awarded her residence at 441 Fair Oaks. Although they did change residences some, this was the period of greatest stability in their lives.

Thomas A. Brooks died on August 10, 1916, and is buried in the Holy Cross Catholic Cemetery in Colma, California. Delia B. Brooks remained living in the house at 479 Fair Oaks with her unmarried sons Charles Ward Brooks and Raymond J. Brooks until her death on August 22, 1929. She is buried beside Thomas.

There are eight children listed in the death notice for Delia, including Marie, all of whom survive her. William, Milton and J. J. Brooks do not appear on any of the censuses, but do appear in other records which identify them as children of Thomas and Delia. There are 12 children who are mentioned in official records as children of Thomas and Delia Brooks. The children of Thomas and Delia Brooks are:

Martin Brooks	b. Oct 1873	Ireland
Marie T. (Brooks) Elliott	b. May 1877	Ireland
John J. Brooks	b. 1878	Ireland
Michael Edward Brooks	b. Jan 1880	Ireland
Winnifred Brooks	b. Dec 1886	California
Orson Brooks	b. Mar 1891	California
George Edward Brooks	b. Apr 1893	California
William H. Brooks	b. Mar 1894	California
Charles Ward Brooks	b. Jan 1895	California
Luella Delia Brooks	b. Jun 1897	California
Raymond J. Brooks	b. Abt 1904	California
Milton Brooks	b. Unk	Unk

The following sections of this chapter will provide more detail in the life of Delia's children and their descendents.

Martin Brooks

There is little known about Martin Brooks, other than that he was listed on the *IGI Fiche* for County Roscommon, Cam and Kiltoom Parish. The registers state he was born on October 30, 1873, the first child of Thomas and Delia Brooks. Since no further references to Martin have been located, it is assumed he is the child who died prior to the 1900 Census of San Francisco.

Marie Theresa Brooks Elliott

Much has already been said about Marie Theresa Brooks Elliott earlier in this chapter. Information regarding her early life was secretive, and her date and place of birth often had conflicting data. Although she usually claimed that her date of birth was June, 1881, the California Death Index and her obituary both state her date of birth to be May 9, 1877. Her tombstone in the Holy Cross Catholic Cemetery in Colma, San Mateo County, California, does not list a birth date, as is the custom in that cemetery. Census records indicated she was born in California, but the California Death Index lists "Other Country" for place of birth. Following the example of her namesake and adoptive mother, Marie Theresa Gibbons Elliott, she usually took a few years off her age at census time.

She does not appear in a U. S. Census until 1900, when she is listed as a 19 year old daughter of Orson and Marie Elliott. However, it is possible she was listed on the 1890 census, but that census was completely destroyed in a fire. She also appears on the 1930 census of Daly City, San Mateo County, California, living with her sister Luella D. Brooks Pepper, this time with a birth date of 1889.

After her mother's death, contention arose between the daughter Marie and her adoptive father, over her mother's will, naturally. On Sunday, June 8, 1902, on page 15 of *The San Francisco Chronicle* it was reported that Maria Teresa Elliott, 22 years old, sued Orson H. Elliott to recover property on Fair Oaks Street near Twenty-sixth, which she conveyed to him without consideration in March, 1901. The article states that Maria was not formally adopted by Orson but had been "regarded" as his daughter. (This isn't in the article, but in his will Orson repeatedly calls Maria his "adopted" daughter.) The newspaper article says she was regarded as his daughter since 1890. According to the article, Maria received the property in February and claims that Orson promised he would provide for her support during her life if she would convey the property to him. After she did that, she claims that he went back on his promise and ordered her to leave his home.

The Family Line of Adelia Beatrice Gibbons

Adopted daughter Maria Theresa Brooks Elliott and father Orson Elliott

The matter was resolved with the death of Orson Hyde Elliott on September 5, 1909, in San Diego, California. In his will, which was probated in December, 1909, Orson Hyde Elliott left his adopted daughter Maria Theresa Elliott certificates being held by a bank in Argentina. The implication is that the certificates were related to the property she had signed over to him. Here is a ship manifest list showing Maria's trip to Argentina in September, 1910 to retrieve the certificates:

Maria Theresa Elliot
New York Passenger Arrival Lists (Ellis Island), 1892-1924
Name: Maria Theresa Elliot
Event Type: Immigration
Event Date: 05 Oct 1910
Event Place: Ellis Island, New York City, New York, United States
Residence Place: U. S. A.
Sex: Female
Age: 28
Marital Status: Single
Nationality: US Citizen
Birth Year: 1882
Departure Port: Buenos Aires
Ship Name: Verdi

Marie Elliott married Harry Victor Roden on October 18, 1916, in Alameda County, California, as determined from his draft registration in 1917. She was listed as spouse, with their home address of 85 4th Street in San Francisco. This was not to be a long lasting marriage, as the 1930 Census referenced above lists Marie Elliott as divorced.

As has already been related, Marie Theresa Brooks Elliott died in 1955, and is buried with many of her Brooks and Gibbons relatives in the Holy Cross Catholic Cemetery in Colma, San Mateo County, California.

Michael Edward Brooks

Michael Edward Brooks was the first son of Thomas and Delia Brooks. He was born January 20, 1880, based upon the *IGI Fiche* for County Roscommon, Ireland. He immigrated with his parents in 1888, and became a naturalized citizen in 1900.

Edward, as he was called, married Sarah Adelia March on October 18, 1911, in Willetts, Mendocino County, California. Edward and Sarah were listed on the 1920 Census of San Francisco County with their two children, Robert, age 7, and Austin, age 3. On the 1930 Census, Sarah had divorced Edward, and was living with her brother, J. Edwin March, and his family, still in Mendocino County. Robert was living with her, but Austin was not mentioned in this census. Austin later reappears on the 1940 Census for Santa Clara County. He died in 2007 in San Jose at age 91, a well respected family man in the community.

In 1930, Edward appeared on the San Francisco County Census, living alone, and working as a Houseman at a Golf Club. On July 31, 1939, he married again, this time to Florence E. Conton. Edward relocated to El Paso, Texas, about 1946, and retired. According to the Texas Death Index, he died in El Paso on June 28, 1949, from heart failure, and his body was sent back to California for burial.

John J. Brooks

John J. Brooks was born in Ireland in about 1878. According to the 1910 Census, John immigrated in 1890, and was married to Florence Brooks, who was born in California. They had three sons: William, age 10; Thomas, age 9; and John F., age 7. John's occupation was house painter.

By the time of the 1830 Census, John and Florence had divorced, and he was living alone. However, this census does indicate he immigrated in 1888, and was naturalized. That immigration date makes much more sense than 1890, since his parents and brother did immigrate in 1888.

John died on May 18, 1933, and is buried in the Holy Cross Catholic Cemetery in Colma, California. In the *San Francisco Chronicle* dated September 30, 1933, there appears this notice:

BROOKS - Estate of John J. Brooks, on petition of William Brooks; heirs Thomas J. Brooks, et. al.; Value $10,000.

There no indication why the petition was filed, but the names do verify that John J. Brooks, son of Thomas and Delia Brooks, did die in 1933, therefore the identification of his burial location is correct.

Winifred C. Brooks

My wife, a great granddaughter of Billy Gibbons, often says, "I come from a long line of strong willed women." After reading the preceding story of Marie Theresa Gibbons Elliott, as well as that of Marie Theresa Brooks Elliott, and the following story of Winifred C. Brooks, it is easy to see where some of that strong will comes from.

Winifred Brooks, the second daughter of Thomas and Delia Brooks, was born in December, 1886, in San Francisco, California. Or maybe it was 1888, or even 1892. The dates seem to change on a whim. According to the marriage license, on November 24, 1908, at age 19 (making her date of birth 1888), she was married to Edward C. Lasswell, whose family were old pioneers of San Mateo County, California. They had three children: a son Bertram J. Lasswell, born September 5, 1910; a daughter, Ida May Lasswell, born January 26, 1916; and a daughter, Edna, born April 12, 1918 (although her tombstone indicates 1920).

She was left a widow very early on when Edward died on November 23, 1917. His obituary lists only the first two of their children. Evidently, Winifred was already pregnant at the time of his death. An article in The *San Francisco Chronicle*, July 29, 1918, tells the story of what happened next in Winifred's life:

YOUNG WOMAN IS CORONER
The Vistication Valley car tragedy in San Francisco, which killed eight persons and injured many others, brought into prominence Mrs. Winifred Lasswell – pretty and young – who was the Deputy Coroner of San Mateo County who conducted the inquests following the accident. Eight months ago her husband died and she succeeded him in the undertaking business and as deputy coroner. It was her first big case. "I've been working among the dead since I was 17", Mrs. Lasswell told an interviewer. "I was married then (which would make her date of birth 1891). At first I watched my husband out of girlish morbid curiosity. I thought I could never handle the work. But I soon got over that. Then my husband died. I was ready to take his place.

"I have handled a number of suicides. I fear nothing. I go everywhere," she added to the question. "A while back there was a murder on Salada Beach. An old man was found with a bullet through his head.

He was found in a tumbledown shack on the beach. I went after his body after midnight. It didn't frighten me a bit.

"I know you will not understand. Few people can. It takes time to get the viewpoint that this work is beautiful. I consider the two greatest works to be that of a doctor who brings life into the world and the person who sends life back to the grave. Few agree with me and that's what makes this profession so hard. The world makes it hard.

"I believe also that this is a woman's work. A woman is so much more artistic, and sympathetic and has a much better understanding than a man."

Winfred's sister, Luella Delia Brooks Pepper, was also studying under her brother-in-law Edward Lasswell, and when he died, she continued her apprenticeship under Winifred. Luella also became an embalmer and obtained her embalmer's license in 1918, which she maintained current until 1976. When her husband died, Winifred needed more time to care for their three children than was possible if she continued to work both as a funeral director and as a coroner. Winifred asked her sister to manage the funeral home on Mission Street while Winifred continued her role as deputy coroner. Winifred continued to make headlines, working on many attention-grabbing cases as a female deputy coroner.

Then when Winifred remarried, she didn't just remarry: she eloped, and made headlines again.

San Francisco Chronicle July 19, 1924
WOMAN CORONER ELOPES WITH S. F. UNDERTAKER
Mrs. Winifred C. Lasswell, San Mateo County's only woman deputy coroner and funeral director of Colma and Daly City, eloped to Watsonville Thursday night with Walter A. Leonetti, also an undertaker, connected with Halstad and Co., San Francisco. The couple are honeymooning in Santa Cruz. Mrs. Lasswell continued the undertaking business of her husband, Edward C. Lasswell, upon his death seven years ago.

Unfortunately, Winifred, like her first husband Edward, died an unexpected and early death.

San Francisco Chronicle January 7, 1926
"DEPUTY CORONER OF SAN MATEO DIES
Mrs. Leonetti is Victim of Pneumonia
Mrs. Winifred C. Lasswell Leonetti, deputy San Mateo coroner, with offices in Daly City, died early yesterday morning in San Francisco Hospital here of pneumonia induced by an attack of influenza. She was taken ill two weeks ago and brought to the hospital a week ago when her condition took a turn for the worse.

"Mrs. Leonetti was not only one of the best known women morticians in California, but was also reputed to be adept at criminal investigation in connection with her office. She took part in the investigation of the Hightower case, the trunk murder of more than a year ago, and many other baffling mysteries. Funeral arrangements have not been made yet."

Her obituary appeared in the *San Francisco Chronicle* the next day:

"In this city, January 5, 1926, Winifred Lasswell Leonetti, dearly beloved wife of Walter A. Leonetti, loving mother of Bert, May, and Edna Lasswell, daughter of Adelia and the late Thomas Brooks, sister of John, Milton, Orson, George, Charles, and Raymond Brooks, Marie Elliott, and Mrs. L. D. Pepper, a native of San Francisco, Cal. Funeral Services will be held today (Friday) at 9:45 o'clock a. m. from the chapel at Halstad and Co., 1122 Sutter St., thence to Saint Maximus' church, Daly City, where a solemn requiem high mass will be sung for the repose of her soul, commencing at 10:30 a. m. o'clock. Entombment Holy Cross Mausoleum."

Her sister Luella Pepper continued her role as manager of the funeral home and added the role of deputy coroner. Winifred's two daughters, Edna and Ida, also became embalmers, and joined Luella at the funeral home. According to FindAGrave.Com, Ida and Edna promoted themselves as "pioneer lady embalmers" in advertisements in the *Yellow Pages* and in trade journals. Winifred had always hoped to build a beautiful new mortuary facility, but was unable to achieve that goal due to her early death. The building was subsequently built by her family, and named in her memory, the W. C. Lasswell & Co. Funeral Home, which continued in business for many more years, until around the year 2001.

Winifred is buried in the Holy Cross Catholic Cemetery, a cemetery she was very familiar with through her mortician's role. Her tombstone indicates a birth date of December 1892, which is as good as any she provided over the years.

Orson Brooks

Orson Brooks appears on the 1900 Census of San Francisco County, and is one of the 8 children born to Delia Brooks by that date. He was born in California in 1891, but does not appear on any other verifiable government record found to date. Delia stated on that census that she had given birth to 8 children, 7 of whom were still alive, therefore, Orson had to be one of the 7 since he was listed on the census.

Orson is listed in the 1926 Obituary of Winifred Lasswell Leonetti as one of the children of Thomas and Delia Brooks. He was not listed in Delia's 1929 Obituary as one of the surviving children, so he conceivably could have died in the time period between the two obituaries.

One bit of speculation regarding his name: Delia immigrated to the US from Ireland in 1888, and Marie and Orson Elliott returned from South America at the same time. In 1890, Marie and Orson "adopted" Delia's daughter Marie Theresa Brooks, and a year later Delia's newborn son was named after Orson Elliott, possibly in gratitude for adopting teen-aged Marie Theresa Brooks, who appears to be one of those strong willed Gibbons women.

George Edward Brooks

The next child of Delia and Thomas Brooks was George Edward Brooks, Sr., born April, 1893, in San Francisco. He was living in the household of Thomas and Delia Brooks in both the 1900 and 1910 San Francisco County Census.

George married Ethel Mae Creamer on September 5, 1914, in San Joaquin, California. His occupation at the time of their marriage was listed as a telephone installer. Both George and Ethel were living in San Francisco at the time of the marriage, although the ceremony took place in San Joaquin County.

George and Ethel had two children, George Edward Brooks, Jr., born in 1922, and Kathryn Brooks, born about 1928. All were on the 1930 Census of Daly City, in San Mateo County. George Sr. was employed as a Stationary Engineer in office buildings. His obituary also mentions that he was a member of the Chauffeurs Union.

George, Jr. married Hazel M. Toma in 1982, and they had one child, Dennis G. Brooks. They lived in some of the more remote areas around Sacramento.

Kathryn married Carney Campion, who was the General Manager responsible for overseeing the Golden Gate Bridge operations as well as the San Francisco Bus and Ferry Divisions. Kathryn and Carney raised a large family of six children, and had a long, successful 63-year marriage when he passed away in 2015.

George E. Brooks, Sr. passed away on May 28, 1959. His obituary, as printed in the *San Francisco Chronicle*, dated May 31, includes the following: "George E. Brooks, Sr., beloved husband of Ethel Creamer Brooks, loving father of George E. Brooks, Jr. and Mrs. Carney Campion; devoted brother of Raymond J. Brooks, Sr., Austin Brooks, and Mrs. Luella Mudersbach."

William H. Brooks

William H. Brooks was born March 19, 1894 in California. He was never listed on a census which included Thomas and Delia Brooks, but he is listed in her obituary as one of her six surviving sons. Where was William for the 1900 census, when he was only 6 years old?

Another intriguing possibility is the 1910 census of San Saba County, Texas. Here is the census for that date:

1910 Census San Saba County

William H Gibbons	M	62	1846	Ireland	Married	Head
Mary V Gibbons	F	59	1851	Alabama	Married	Wife
John W Gibbons	M	22	1888	Texas	Single	Son
Will B Brooks	M	20	1890	California	Single	Boarder
(Father and Mother both born in Ireland)
Theodore Short	M	26	1884	Texas	Married	Boarder
Jake G Miller	M	24	1886	Texas	Single	Boarder
William H Bingham	M	68	1842	Rhode Island	Single	Boarder

In this instance, boarder probably means ranch hand, since the Gibbons Ranch was too far from town to be used as a traditional boarding house. It is also very typical for Gibbons nieces and nephews to go on extended visits with their relatives.

In addition, when William died in El Paso, Texas, on July 19, 1964, his Texas death notice included some pertinent information:

Name:	William H Brooks
Sex and age:	Male, 70
Death Date and place:	16 Jul 1964, El Paso, El Paso, Texas, United States
Normal place of residence:	El Paso, 45 years
Marital Status:	Single
Occupation:	Real Estate
Father's Name:	Thomas Brooks
Mother's Name:	Delia Giblin
Birth Date and place:	19 Mar 1894, California

William Henry (Uncle Billy) Gibbons

Informant:	Ray Brooks, San Francisco (Youngest brother)
Place of Burial:	Evergreen Cemetery, El Paso, TX

The death notice proves conclusively that William H. Brooks is the son of Thomas and Delia Brooks. When he died, he had been living in El Paso, Texas more than 45 years, so it is not too farfetched to assume that he moved to San Saba County to work on his Uncle Billy's ranch in his late teens, and stayed in Texas for the rest of his life.

Charles Ward Brooks

Charles Ward Brooks was born January 15, 1895, in San Francisco. He remained single most of his life, living with his mother and his youngest brother, Raymond J. Brooks, at her house at 479 Fair Oaks until her death in 1929.

Following her death, Charles and Raymond continued to live at 479 Fair Oaks until Charles finally got married, at age 42, to Eleanor Callan, in 1937. At that time, Charles and Eleanor moved to Van Ness Avenue.

Charles was a salesman all his professional life, mostly in real estate. He worked at many different real estate companies in San Francisco over the course of his career. He took a break from his salesman role during World War I, enlisting in the US Naval Reserve Force on August 6, 1918. He was discharged August 7, 1819, shortly after the war was over.

Charles and Eleanor had been married only four years when he died at the very young age of 46, on May 12, 1941. They had no children. Because of his service during the war, Charles is buried at the San Francisco National Cemetery.

Luella Delia Brooks

Luella Delia Brooks was born March 15, 1898, in San Francisco, according to the 1900 Census, taken when she was age 2. By the time of the 1910 census, she had lost two years, and was only 10, stating that she had been born in 1900. However, by 1930, she was only 25, and another 5 years were gone. The Fountain of Youth continued - on the 1940 census, she lost 3 more years, and was now only 32. Reality set in however, and when she died in 1994, her death notice had a birth date of 1897 - probably one year older than when she started life. It is ironic that someone who spent a lifetime at a mortuary where dates are carved in stone played so loosely with her actual date of birth.

Luella married young, at age 15, according to the 1930 Census. Her husband was Spencer Pepper, a machinist in a garage, who was about eight years older than she was. He was 25 when they married in about 1920, more or less. They had no children, and were divorced in 1938. Actually Luella was 22 in 1920.

Two years later, on December 9, 1939, Luella remarried, this time to William Mudersbach, a car salesman. This marriage lasted until his death in 1965.

Luella was studying to become a mortician under Edward Lasswell, Winifred's husband, when he died suddenly in 1917. She continued her apprenticeship under Winifred, and obtained her embalmer's license in 1918, which she maintained current until 1976. At the time, Winifred was working both as manager of the funeral home as well as performing as a Deputy Coroner.

Being the mother of three small children became too much while working two jobs, so Winifred asked Luella to assume the role of Manager of the Lasswell Funeral Home. When Winifred died in 1926, Luella also assumed the role of Deputy Coroner. Following in her sister's footsteps, Luella Pepper was treated as a celebrity by the *San Francisco Chronicle* while working in her Deputy Coroner role. So many of her cases were covered closely in the newspaper that her name became a household word in the San Francisco area.

After Luella retired, according to newspaper sources, she and William operated Applejack's, an out-of-town bar in a remote part of San Mateo County, in the town of La Honda. The bar still exists, is popular with bikers and is known as one of the 'best dive bars' in California.

Luella died on June 4, 1994, and is buried in the Holy Cross Catholic Cemetery. On her tombstone is the birth date in 1897, finally settling the question of what her date of birth really was.

Deputy Coroner Luella Pepper investigating a suspicious death scene

Raymond J. Brooks

Raymond J. Brooks was the baby, the last of Delia's 12 or so children. He was born about 1903 in San Francisco. Raymond and his older brother, Charles Ward Brooks, continued to live with Delia after the death of Thomas in 1916, until her own death in 1929.

Raymond married Eleanor Callan in 1930, and Charles remained in the house, living with Raymond and his family. When Charles married in 1937, he moved to his own home.

Raymond J. Brooks, Jr., was born about 1933. Raymond and Eleanor continued to live at 479 Fair Oaks until 1937, when he, the final Gibbons descendent to live at that address, moved out. This house was the final Gibbons-occupied house on this block of Fair Oaks, which had been continuously occupied by a Gibbons since 1867.

Surprisingly enough, Raymond J. Brooks, Sr. was employed in the mortuary business as well, serving as a driver and chauffer for the family funeral home and the deputy coroner's office. Raymond continued in that role until he retired around 1946.

Raymond died on April 2, 1973, and is buried in the Holy Cross Catholic Cemetery in Colma, San Mateo County, California.

Milton Brooks

Milton Brooks is the real mystery man of Delia's family. He never appears in a census with Delia, at least he never appears under the name Milton. However, he is consistently mentioned as a surviving child in the obituaries for Delia and some of her other children. No defining information has been found.

Timeline for Adelia Beatrice Gibbons Brooks

1857 Adelia Beatrice Gibbons born in Athlone, Ireland (Calculated from 1900 census, actual date is at least five years earlier)
1872 Thomas and Delia (Brigida) married in County Roscommon Delia's first immigration date listed on 1910 Census
1873 Martin Brooks born in Ireland
1877 Marie Theresa Brooks born in Ireland
1878 John J. Brooks born in Ireland
1881 Michael E. Brooks born in Ireland
1886 Winifred C. Brooks born in California
1888 Immigration date listed on 1900 Census
1891 Orson Brooks born in California
1893 George E. Brooks born in California
1894 William H. Brooks born in California
1895 Charles W. Brooks born in California
1896? Milton Brooks born in California, perhaps
1897 Luella D. Brooks born in California
1900 Listed on 1900 Census of San Francisco County
1901 Delia inherited house at 441 Fair Oaks from Winifred T. Fennell
1903 Raymond J. Brooks born in California
1910 Listed on 1910 Census of San Francisco County
1916 Death of husband Thomas A. Brooks
1920 Listed on 1920 Census of San Francisco County
1929 Death of Adelia B. Gibbons Brooks

Chapter Nine

The Family Line of William Henry Gibbons

Immigration to the US

William Henry (Billy) Gibbons was the second son and fourth child of Michael and Mary Gibbons, born October 4, 1846 in Athlone, Ireland. He did not immigrate to America with his older brother and sisters, but initially worked as a clerk for his father, Michael Gibbons, a prosperous merchant in the city. W. H. began to hear of the financial successes enjoyed by his siblings, especially in the real estate field, and decided to seek a new life in the United States.

According to a document produced by one of his great-granddaughters, Marcia Miller McNeill, W. H., at age 19, was given $500 by his father, and set sail for New York with a $35 ticket in steerage.

A possible record of his immigration may be contained in the following entry from FamilySearch.Org:

Name	Wm Gibbons
Sex	Male
Age	21
Immigration Date	1867
Immigration Place	New York City, New York, United States
Birth Year (Estimated)	1846
Birthplace	Ireland
Nationality	Ireland
Ship Name	City of London
Travelling in Steerage	

In any case, McNeill reported he arrived in Boston on August 4, 1867. From Boston, he traveled west to visit his siblings in San Francisco and Box Elder County, Utah, near Salt Lake City, where his sister Marie Theresa and her husband Orson Elliott lived.

In 1870, his brother Charles was not yet married, and lived with his sister Winifred Chapple and her husband Thomas in the San Francisco Mission District. Charles and Thomas had both been in the jewelry business when they first arrived in San Francisco, and the 1870 Census indicated both were involved in some form of book sales. At the same time, both men were beginning to become involved in real estate, and according to the San Francisco City Directories for 1867-68, Thomas even owned his own company, Thomas Chapple Real Estate.

There is no indication that the third brother, John J. Gibbons, was still in San Francisco after 1865, when the City Directory had him listed as a Book Canvasser, or book peddler, living at the same address as Charles Gibbons, and Orson and Marie Elliott.

Marcia Miller McNeill indicates that Billy Gibbons probably visited San Francisco first, and then went to Utah to see Orson and Marie Elliott. While in the Salt Lake City area, he became fascinated with the ongoing construction of the Mormon Temple, and worked for a time on the project. The Mormons were probably hiring any help they could, since they broke ground in 1853, but did not complete the temple for 40 more years.

Gone to Texas

Billy Gibbons returned to the East Coast soon after his visit in Utah, and sailed from Boston to the port in Galveston, Texas, arriving in 1871, according to the latest immigration date listed on the 1910 Census of San Saba County. The census also included a date of 1878 when he became a Naturalized Citizen. The immigration date of 1871 is repeated on the 1920 Census.

From Galveston, he went first to Austin and then to San Antonio, where he worked for two and a half years as a clerk at the historic Menger Hotel. On all these temporary jobs, he was saving as much money as he could.

While in San Antonio, he met an Englishman, William H. Bainbridge, who had some of the same ranching goals, so they decided to pool their resources. In his article "Richland Springs Rancher Put $500 in Sheep and They Have Builded Large Fortune", published in the *San Angelo Standard-Times* in 1929, Sam Ashburn stated Gibbons and Bainbridge bought 1500 Mexican sheep about 80 miles southwest of San Antonio, all ewes, for 85 cents a head, and began to drive them north through open range, while they walked behind them. According to Mrs. Edgar T. Neal, in her article "Gibbons San Saba Ranch Grows Fine Blooded Stock", Gibbons and Bainbridge were on the road for 18 months with their sheep.

Nedrah Stringfellow Magnan, in her article "WILLIAM HENRY GIBBONS: An Early Friend of Boys", states that they went from Uvalde through Fredericksburg to the eastern portion of San Saba County, northeast of Cherokee, a distance of about 200 miles. Eighteen months on the road would have gotten them to their eventual destination around 1876. They initially lived in tents and sheared their own sheep, taking the wool to market in Austin. Billy Gibbons even became adept at shearing with either hand.

The first record of the presence of W. H. Gibbons in San Saba County was on June 16, 1877, when he requested a survey be done on this land, confirming the probable arrival date in the county by 1876. Billy Gibbons and W. H. Bainbridge each acquired 80 acres of land, with the north side of the Gibbons tract abutting the south side of the Bainbridge. The map below, although mislabeled Gibson instead of Gibbons, shows the location of this land. The two tracts were located on the east central side of San Saba County, adjacent to the northwest corner of the present day Colorado Bend State Park.

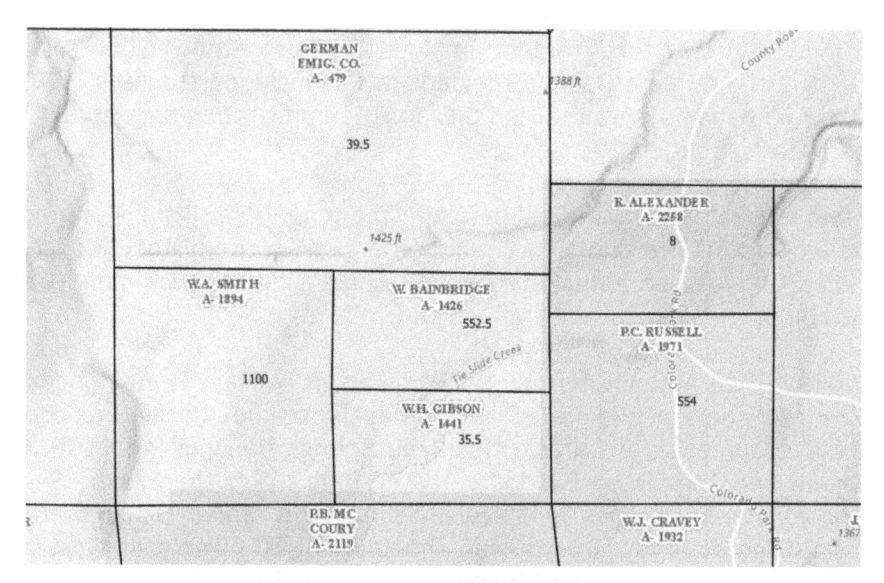

The Gibbons/Bainbridge Land
The darker section is the Colorado Bend State Park today

The purpose of the survey was to allow him to sell his 80 acres to his sister and brother-in-law, Marie T. and Orson H. Elliott. W. H. Bainbridge did a similar request for his 80 acres. The Texas General Land Office File 2509, Abstract 1441, is the official record of the transfer, and a partial transcription is located in Appendix E.

In summary, the file includes an affidavit of the fact that O. H. Elliott has occupied and improved the same as a homestead for the period of three consecutive years beginning the 16th of June 1877, that he is married and that he makes this affidavit for the purpose of obtaining a title to the same as a homestead under an act for the benefit of actual occupants of the Public Lands. The date of the transfer was April 25, 1881. The Elliotts were in San Saba County from June, 1877 until January, 1883, when he received a passport in Galveston which allowed them to relocate to South America where they resumed their bookselling activities.

William Henry (Uncle Billy) Gibbons

By the 1880 San Saba County Census, Billy Gibbons and William Bainbridge were out of the tent and living as boarders with the Roundtree family:

Robert Roundtree	M	45	1835	SC	Married	Raising Sheep
Sarah J Roundtree	F	38	1842	TN	Married	Keeping House
Robert T Roundtree	M	24	1856	TX	Single	Farming
Giles M Roundtree	M	20	1860	TX	Single	Raising Cattle
Lonzo Roundtree	M	14	1866	TX	Single	Working on Farm
Mittie Roundtree	F	6	1874	TX	Single	
Lawrence Roundtree	M	5	1875	TX	Single	
Ross M Roundtree	M	3	1877	TX	Single	
William Gibbons	M	35	1846	Irelnd	Single	Raising Sheep
Garrett Burk	M	19	1861	TX	Single	
William Bainbridge	M	30	1850	Eng	Single	Sheep Herder

On May 24, 1880, Billy Gibbons came upon a tragedy involving the Roundtree family. A few feet from the Roundtree home, there was an entrance to a cavern which contained a lake inside. While the three adult men of the family were away delivering wool to market, a terrifying wind and electrical storm blew in, and two ladies and all the children, fearing a tornado, sought shelter in the cavern. A river of water suddenly rushed into the cave, sweeping the family deep inside. The two youngest children, Lawrence and Ross Roundtree, drowned, and the ladies and other children were barely able to crawl outside.

Billy Gibbons was the first upon the scene, and began rescue efforts and called for help. After the water subsided, it took about an hour to find the bodies of the boys. More detail about this incident is in Appendix B.

The Move to Brady Creek

In 1876, Texas still had about 56,000,000 acres of unappropriated public domain and 20,000,000 acres of public land allotted to schools (School Lands). An influx of Southerners following the Civil War created pressure for new land. The Civil War had also left the state with financial troubles; so, to lower its debt, the legislature began to sell the unappropriated public domain and the School Lands as quickly as possible. The "fifty cent" act, passed in 1879, provided for the sale of public land in fifty-four West Texas counties at $.50 an acre. A limit of 640 acres per person was put on this land.

About the same time, fencing had come to the region, and the freedom of movement for Gibbons' large flock of sheep was becoming restricted. According to Mrs. Edgar T. Neal, Billy Gibbons did not have to buy land when he first came to the region, but he knew that was about to change. Billy Gibbons began to take advantage of the sale of public domain land and School Land to begin his acquisition of large tracts of land. He acquired a section of land south of Richland Springs with a good waterhole for $1 an acre, but he didn't patent it.

In the 1880 census, the land which the Elliotts bought from Billy Gibbons and William Bainbridge was in Precinct 4, near the town of Chappel. The Rowntree home, where Billy Gibbons was a boarder in 1880, was in Precinct 2, around Richland Springs, confirming that Billy Gibbons had disposed of his early holdings near the Colorado Bend State Park and relocated to the vicinity of Brady Creek and the San Saba River.

Then, according to Marcia Miller McNeill, he bought land in the Wolf Springs area, about two miles south of where he later built his permanent home. He had found his spot on Brady Creek where it joins the San Saba River. The first house he built was of lumber which had to be hauled 138 miles from Austin on an oxcart. This house no longer exists, but ruins can still be found on the location.

On a Texas General Land Office map, the Rowntree Property is shown to be connected at the southeast corner to a section of land owned by W. H. Gibbons, so it would have been easy for him to work his land, and board with the Rowntrees.

Also during that period, W. H. Bainbridge became ill, sold his share of the partnership to Billy Gibbons, and returned to England. When he had recovered, Bainbridge went to Australia, where he became wealthy. He had the desire to wander some more, and ended up in British Columbia, Canada.

W. H. Gibbons continued to acquire land whenever he could, building a solid block of 36,000 acres. Of that land, over 7,000 acres are documented acquisitions of School Land, as shown on the Texas General Land Office web site. His first acquisition of School Land is dated March 30, 1893.

As W. H. Gibbons' early land holdings grew, he started putting down roots in an area near the junction of Brady Creek and the San Saba River. He was beginning to prepare for the next major change in his life.

Wedding Bells

W. H. Gibbons and W. H. Bainbridge arrived in San Saba County with their sheep in 1876. Coincidentally, another family arrived the same year: the James Kaneer Taylor Family from Alabama. James K. Taylor was one of the earliest settlers and a prominent rancher in San Saba County. The family left Wetumpka, Coosa Co, Alabama in November, 1869. They sailed by boat from Mobile, Alabama to Galveston, then by train to Chappell Hill in Washington County, Texas, then by mule teams to Hill County, where they lived from 1870-1873. They then moved to Ellis County, near Waxahachie, finally moving to Richland Springs in November, 1876. Mr. Taylor was a wheelwright – he made wheels and the things that rode on them, such as carts, wagons, buggies and coaches. He brought with him a large family: On the 1880 San Saba County Census were four sons and three daughters. More detail on the Taylor Family Line can be found in Chapter Ten.

One of those daughters became of special interest to Billy Gibbons. The first documented evidence of that interest was two small handwritten notes in tiny envelopes. Mary Adelia Gibbons McGregor, the daughter of Billy and Mollie Gibbons and my wife's grandmother (MaMac to her grandchildren) had those notes in her possession when she died, and they were passed down to us. Wow. Formal requests for a date to go to church. How times have changed. A scan of the two notes, in Billy Gibbons' handwriting, can be found in Appendix G.

The first one, dated June 11, 1881 had written on it:

> Compliments of W. H. Gibbons to Miss Mollie Taylor and Soliciting the pleasure of your company to "the Singing" Next Sabbath Morning
>
>   Respectfully
>   W. H. Gibbons
>
> Seven(?) Oak Cottage
> June 11, 1881

The second one, in similar fashion, had written on it:

William Henry (Uncle Billy) Gibbons

Compliments of W. H. Gibbons to Miss Mollie Taylor &
Soliciting the pleasure of your company to Church next
Sabbath morning

      Respectfully
      W. H. Gibbons

June 24, 1881

The notes must have been effective: They were married in Richland Springs four months later, on October 27, 1881. Richland Springs at that time wasn't much, consisting only of a post office, a few log houses, and a church made of logs. The wedding occurred in a log house, followed by a dance and a feast. It was a love affair that lasted for the rest of their lives.

William Henry Gibbons   **Mary Virginia Taylor Gibbons**

Family and Fortune

After the marriage, W. H. Gibbons continued to increase his stock and landholdings. He bought other acreage whenever it became available, and never sold any of his land until at one time he possessed approximately 40,000 – 50,000 acres. Regardless of where in that range the total acreage falls, it is still a massive amount of land which made him the largest landholder in San Saba County.

As his family grew, he replaced his original house with a modern, well-built house, architecturally prominent for the times. The lumber now came from Brownwood, much closer than Austin. His sons grew up working on the ranch, and continued to do so all their lives. As they married and had children, two more fine houses were built close to the home of Uncle Billy and Aunt Mollie.

Marcia Miller McNeill wrote, "Uncle Billy Gibbons contended that sheep and cattle worked just fine side by side, and that was the way the Gibbons Ranch was operated. From the original flock of ewes, he improved his herd with breeding, but he never needed to purchase additional mama sheep. Williamson County and fine Ohio bucks were added to improve his flocks. His first sheep each sheared three pounds of wool a year. The upgraded flock of later years sheared 12-15 pounds per year. Additionally, Gibbons developed an outstanding herd of Hereford cattle, goats and horses including fine polo and race horses."

In addition to the vast increase in his ranching operations, Uncle Billy and Aunt Mollie, as they were known to everyone in the area, began their family as well. Sadly, their first two children, twins, died at birth, probably in about 1882. Billie McGregor Adams, granddaughter of Billy Gibbons, remembers visiting the Big Uncle Cemetery with her mother, Mary Adelia Gibbons McGregor, who pointed to a section of the cemetery and said, "That's where the twins were buried." The Big Uncle web page on Rootsweb has the Gibbons Twins listed with a birth date of 1883. An email from Louann Hall, who worked on the cleanup of Big Uncle Cemetery in 1999, stated that the two Gibbons babies were moved to the Richland Springs Cemetery, probably around 1920. However, they are not listed on the FindAGrave.Com web page for the Richland Springs Cemetery.

The first set of twins is not listed in the Gibbons Family Bible, either on the Births page or on the Deaths page. The other five children were listed on the Births page, and the final set of twins were both also listed on the Deaths page. See Appendix D for a copy of the Family Bible pages.

James Edward Gibbons, the first surviving child, was born on December 12, 1883. More detail about his life and the lives of the other surviving children will be covered in later sections of this chapter.

John William, Mary Adelia, and James Edward Gibbons

The next births were another set of twins; this time both survived. John William and Mary Adelia Gibbons were born March 14, 1886. Mary Adelia, better known to her descendents as 'MaMac', said she was told by her mother that they were so small at birth that they had to be kept alive in shoe boxes placed on the old pot-bellied stove.

The final children born to Billy and Mollie Gibbons were another set of twins, born March 19, 1890, a girl and a boy. The daughter died the same day she was born, and was not named; the son, who was named Patrick Henry Gibbons, lived for about two weeks before passing away on April 3. They are all buried in the Richland Springs Cemetery.

In 1914, the slowdown of growth in the livestock market began to be a concern to Billy Gibbons. On February 29, 1914, he placed this ad in the *San Angelo Standard Times*: "FOR SALE – 500 good bred ewes to reg'stered rams; 350 muttons and yearlings – one of the best flocks in San Saba County; will shear 9 lbs wool this spring; will commence to bring lambs about March 22. My reason for selling, I am getting old and want to quit the business. If sold in the next 30 days will take $4.00 per head, delivered at R. R., Richland Springs. Write or phone to W. H. Gibbons, Richland Springs, Texas."

This trend was continued in 1919, when Billy Gibbons sensed that a slump in the industry was coming, and he began to diversify. He continued to lower his livestock inventory, and to invest in real estate in El Paso, Brady, Fort Worth, Richland Springs, and elsewhere. He became a stockholder and president of the First State Bank of Richland Springs, as well as stockholder in the banks in Brady and Fort Worth, in addition to other institutions. This diversification helped him survive livestock market slumps whenever they came.

According to the Texas State Historical Marker outside the bank in Richland Springs, "John M. Burleson (1870-1933) founded the Burleson Bank in 1910 to expand his business interests and provide financial services to the community of Richland Springs. In 1913 Burleson reorganized his institution as the First State Bank; in 1919, W. H. Gibbons became the new director when Burleson left the bank. During Gibbons' tenure, in 1928, the bank was robbed at gunpoint. The First State Bank was renamed the People's State Bank, ruled and protected by federal law, in May 1933. The People's State Bank continued to uphold the standards set by its founder and to serve the community until May 8, 1958, when it was liquidated by the Texas Banking Commission. (1998)."

Mary Virginia (Aunt Mollie) Taylor Gibbons died on December 11, 1930, at her home on the Gibbons Ranch, according to her obituary published in the *Richland Springs Eye-Witness*. The obituary stated "Many of the friends were unable to be seated and stood in the rear and in and about the building during the address by Rev. J. M. Lewis of the Methodist Church. The beautiful floral tributes were quite the largest we have ever seen and spoke in glowing terms of the esteem and love in which she was held over this part of the state. The school was closed, the bank was closed and every business house in the town closed their doors to show their love for her. But none could equal that paid by the husband of almost fifty years. He too is in the sunset of life, but possessing every faculty that has made him one of the most wonderful businessmen of the state. His eyes filled with tears as he told us what a great mother and wife she had been – how to her was due a larger part of his success."

Uncle Billy and Aunt Mollie Gibbons

Billy Gibbons remained active attending to his ranching and other businesses until his death on March 18, 1932. According to journalist

Sam Ashburn, he rode into town nearly every day in his horse drawn buggy. At the time of his death, his net worth in 1932 was well in excess of a million dollars.

His last trip was to attend a cattleman's convention in El Paso. He was enroute home with a stopover in Fort Worth when he became ill. The Blackstone Hotel called the house doctor, but he could do nothing to save W. H. Gibbons from heart failure.

According to the obituary in the *Richland Springs Eye-Witness*, "Funeral services were conducted by Father John Quinlivan of Brady at the ranch home in the presence of one of the largest funeral crowds ever assembled in this county. People came from almost every town and village within a radius of 60 miles and some came more than 100 miles to pay their respects to the memory of a man they loved."

He was buried in the Richland Springs Cemetery next to the woman he loved so much.

W. H. Gibbons Family
Left to right Ed, Uncle Billy, Mary Adelia, Aunt Mollie, John

James Edward Gibbons

James Edward Gibbons was the eldest son of Billy Gibbons, born December 12, 1883. Like all of his siblings, he was born on the Gibbons Ranch, and in his case, he lived there all his life. Along with his brother John, Ed learned from his father before becoming successful in their own ranching careers. Ed and John ran the Gibbons Ranch after the death of Billy Gibbons, carrying on his excellent ranching heritage. Ed was a lover of fine motor cars, while John was a lover of horses. Their homes were on the ranch, and their families were reared there.

Ed married Nettie Caledonia Brown, daughter of Mr. and Mrs. Newton C. Brown, on October 31, 1906. Ed and Nettie had two children, Marjorie Virginia and James Harold. Marjorie was born on June 19, 1911, and died on her second birthday, June 19, 1913. She is buried in the Richland Springs Cemetery.

Harold was born March 6, 1909, on the Gibbons Ranch, and he led a short, but busy, life. His first wife was Anne Sue Miller, and they had two children: Elizabeth Ann Gibbons, born in 1931, and Mary Darlene Gibbons, born in 1932. The marriage did not last long. As indicated by the 1940 Census, Anne had already remarried and was living with their two daughters and her new husband, Alton Beck, in Brown County, Texas.

Harold married his second wife, Helen Herberg, in August, 1941. Seven months later, he enlisted in the US Army for the duration of World War II. He was stationed at Chanute Field, Illinois, when his father Ed Gibbons died in February, 1943. Less than three weeks later, Harold's son William Edward Gibbons was born on March 16, 1943. Helen and Harold didn't stay a happy family long: In September, 1946, Helen sued for divorce. Helen was later married to William Portwood, Jr., who adopted William Edward Gibbons. William assumed his new father's name and became William Gibbons Portwood. When William Gibbons later had a son, he carried on the Gibbons name by naming his son William Gibbons Portwood, Jr.

Harold was married a third time to Delphia Inez Gibbons. When Harold died of a heart attack in Fort Worth on September 28, 1948, he was listed as married and Delphia Gibbons signed his death certificate as an informant. She is buried next to him in the Richland Springs Cemetery.

According to Ed's Obituary, published March 1, 1943, in *The San Angelo Standard-Times*, "James Edward Gibbons, one of the larger ranch operators in West Texas, died suddenly last night in a Fort Worth Hospital where he was taken for treatment some days ago, according to word received here today....With his brother John, Mr. Gibbons operated the 50,000 acre ranch the two inherited from their father, the late pioneer W. H. 'Uncle Billy' Gibbons. It is considered the largest ranch holding in San Saba County. In addition to having it well stocked with cattle and sheep, the Gibbons brothers also pastured much stock on the Plains and in Kansas. They were heavy lamb buyers, which were pastured through the winter and marketed in the spring."

Ed Gibbons died in a tourist court in Fort Worth, Texas, on February 27, 1943. He was taking treatments in Fort Worth and Dallas after having been released from the hospital in Brady, Texas, where he was being treated for pneumonia. He was buried in the Richland Springs Cemetery. Nettie was buried beside him after her death on January 7, 1968.

When James Edward Gibbons died in 1943, his portion of the Gibbons Ranch which had not been sold was passed on to Harold Gibbons' daughters, Elizabeth Ann Gibbons Perryman and Darlene Gibbons Farnsworth.

John William Gibbons

John William Gibbons, and his twin sister, Mary Adelia Gibbons, were born on March 14, 1886, on the Gibbons Ranch, where John learned the ranching business from his father and lived his entire life.

John married Jennie May Walters on December 27, 1913, in Raton, New Mexico. John and Jennie May had two daughters. Virginia Katherine Gibbons was born January 5, 1915, in San Saba County. She married Maxwell Hugh Miller, of Haynesville, Louisiana, on April 12, 1936, in San Saba County. They returned to Haynesville to live. The Millers had three children, Marcia Ann Miller, born 1939; Sandra Sue Miller, born 1943; and William Gibbons Miller, born 1944. Marcia Ann Miller married Jerry McNeill, and her work on the life of Billy Gibbons has been quoted several times in this book. Sue Miller married Billy Joe Appling, and Gibby Miller married Roxann King. Virginia Gibbons Miller passed away on July 30, 1996, and is buried in the Old Town Cemetery in Haynesville, next to her husband Maxwell, who died in 1989.

The second daughter of John and Jennie May Gibbons was Mary Elizabeth Gibbons, born July 15, 1918, in San Saba County. She married George Buford Mays on May 11, 1941, in San Saba County. Buford and Elizabeth had two sons, Myron Daryl Mays, who married Patsy Patrick; and Glennon Buford Mays, who married Cynthia Jeanne Parker. Elizabeth Mays passed away July 9, 1988 and is buried on the Gibbons Ranch. Her husband Buford, died January 29, 1994.

John William Gibbons died on April 23, 1950, in a tragic automobile accident on the Gibbons Ranch. The prominent ranchman was found in his badly burned automobile, which had crashed into a tree. The vehicle left the road at a bend where it failed to negotiate a turn about 100 yards from his Gibbons Ranch home, located four miles south of Richland Springs. Dr. J. B. Woodall of Richland Springs said he had Mr. Gibbons under supervision for over a year for a chronic heart condition. He is satisfied that John William Gibbons had suffered a heart attack.

According to Marcia Ann Miller McNeill, after the death of John Gibbons, the land passed to his two daughters, Virginia and Elizabeth. Virginia Gibbons Miller's children are partners in Virginia Gibbons Properties, which owns the western segment of John Gibbons' land. The heirs of

Elizabeth Gibbons Mays own and operate the eastern segment of John's land. The Mays sons were reared on the ranch and were practicing veterinarians in the area, as well as experienced stockmen. The Mays Ranching Company is operating the ranch as a progressive modern cattle raising system; and has now leased grazing rights from the other heirs, operating the majority of the W. H. Gibbons Ranch as one unit again.

Mary Adelia Gibbons

Mary Adelia Gibbons, the twin of John William Gibbons, was born March 14, 1886, on the Gibbons Ranch. As the only daughter, she did not spend time working the ranch with her father, a privilege enjoyed by the two sons, but instead learned about life as a rancher's wife and mother from her mother. However, she wanted to be a boy, to get to have the "fun" of ranching. She wanted so badly to be a boy that she asked the ranch's blacksmith to turn her into a boy. The blacksmith told her he could not do that, but, if she could kiss her own elbow, she would be turned into a boy. She tried; but, alas, it was not to be. (Can you kiss your elbow?) This story was related to her granddaughter Donna Adams Wigley, who tried in vain to kiss her own elbow.

Life on a working ranch was anything but easy, even for the wives and daughters. According to a "bit of history" at the Gibbons Ranch, told by Billie McGregor Adams and recorded by her daughter, Mary Katherine (Mary Kate) Adams in May of 2000, Mary Adelia (MaMac) and Miss Bertha were responsible for all the domestic chores including the preparation of three hot meals daily. Miss Bertha, whose husband Ray Sullivan was also employed on the Gibbons ranch, was the domestic employee on the ranch. The ladies arose early every morning to prepare breakfast in time for all the men to eat and be mounted and ready to ride by daylight. Their day continued with their preparations for lunch and then for a hot supper, often walking to the corn patch, each of them picking a sack of corn, and then walking back up the hill to the house to continue the day's chores.

Among the hands being served the hot meals was Forrest Edwin McGregor, who would ultimately become MaMac's husband and the love of her life. MaMac and Grandad McGregor met when she was a girl living at home and he was employed as a hand on the Gibbons Ranch. He had a wide-spread reputation as an excellent horseman and horse trainer.

"(Copied from another picture, notes written by Mary McGregor):
Presented to Mary by Forrest & Emma McGregor August 1, 1901

Thursday we went down to Mr. McDaniels to the infare dimmer of Frank and Alice McDaniel

I might add this is about the time Forrest and I started our courtship ha"

As Billie Louise McGregor Adams recounts to Mary Kate, "Granddad McGregor had great compassion for the heavy work load MaMac had and vowed that when she became his wife she would never again have to prepare a hot supper. An interesting note here: When Granddad McGregor and MaMac were living on and working their own ranch, Granddad left on many days taking both of his sons, Uncle Mac and Uncle Dutch, with him to work on the ranch, leaving MaMac at home to prepare a hot lunch for them. I suspect we all can appreciate the humor of this story Mother (Billie) tells: MaMac of course cooked on a wood burning stove, and at one time had run completely out of wood in the wood box. She had repeatedly asked Granddad and the boys to cut wood, but to no avail. So one day the men came in from the pastures for lunch and nothing was on the table. Upon being questioned about the whereabouts of lunch, MaMac replied 'It's on the stove.' And it was...but waiting in an uncooked state in various pot and pans for wood to be brought in to the wood box so that MaMac could build a fire to cook. She was never again without cooking wood in the wood box!"

As to the marriage of MaMac and Granddad McGregor, that union was first met with disapproval by Granddad Gibbons. Grandmother Gibbons did not hold that same view and Granddad Gibbons apparently changed his view to be more tolerant as MaMac and Granddad McGregor were married in her parents' home on the Gibbons ranch on December 11, 1905.

The marriage announcement from the *Richland Springs Eye-Witness* published the next day has a wonderful description of the newly-weds: "The bride and groom are known by everybody in this part of the country, and a couple with more friends and admirers would be hard to find.

"The bride and groom have been sweethearts since they were young children, and the happy result of their admiration for each other is a source of much gratification to hosts of friends, who hope and believe their married life will be peaceful, prosperous, and pleasant."

Forrest and Mary had five children: John Clarke, Taylor Gibbons, Mary Forrestine, Fanora Mae, and Billie Louise. The first two children were born on the Gibbons Ranch, and the others on the McGregor Old Home

Place near Algerita. The story of Forrest McGregor and his children and their families will follow in the chapter on the McGregors.

The Old Home Place was given to Mary Adelia by Billy Gibbons, for her and Forrest to make a living for their growing family. It consisted of about two sections of land, located east of Richland Springs, with the southern end on the San Saba River. Billy Gibbons had acquired the land on January 2, 1905, the same year that Forrest and Mary Adelia were married in December. He always kept his eye out for available land which he could purchase. He bought this tract from Richard Bludworth Taylor and his wife Ola – Dick Taylor just happened to be the son of Dr. Job Taylor and a nephew of Mollie Gibbons.

Using the San Saba County Deed Records, 1131 acres were gifted by Billy Gibbons to Mary Adelia Gibbons McGregor on November 20, 1911. The acreage was slightly less than 2 sections because 11 acres were sold for railroad right of way, and Billy Gibbons kept 160 acres for his own purposes. Forrest handled ranching on the land himself, until the two sons were old enough to help him out. Originally, it was called the Mary McGregor Dry Creek Ranch, or as locals called it, the McGregor Ranch.

While they were living near Algerita, Forrest McGregor was a member of the Baptist Church there. According to a story told to Mary Kate Adams by Billie McGregor Adams, Forrest was churched (removed from the church roll) from that congregation because he helped construct a platform for a political rally, and later that platform was used as a dance floor at the rally. It didn't matter that he was just doing a job for a salary, it was still a dance floor. He later became a member of the First Baptist Church in Richland Springs.

Part of the family took a break from ranching for a few years, starting in 1926. John Clarke, the oldest son, was attending Draughan Business School in Abilene, and the entire family relocated to Abilene while he was in school there. Forrest kept the ranch going without much help from the two boys, since they were in school. Forrest went back and forth between the ranch and Abilene whenever he could. John Clarke graduated from Draughan, and T. G. McGregor graduated from Abilene High School in 1927. The family relocated to Central Texas shortly after that. The following picture shows the family in Abilene:

Forrest McGregor Family
Left to Right - MaMac, Billie Louise, John Clarke, Forrestine, Taylor Gibbons, Fanora Mae, Forrest

The family returned home to the ranch near Algerita in about 1928. By the time of the 1930 Census, John Clarke and his wife Cora were living in the Old Home Place in Algerita, along with John's brother, Taylor Gibbons McGregor, better known as 'Dutch'. Forrest, Mary, and the three girls also had a house in Brownwood, on Rogan Street. Forrest managed to get himself counted twice on the census that year, with Mary when the census was taken in Brown County on April 8, and two days later he showed up again with John, Cora, and Dutch on the San Saba County census.

Toward the end of 1930, an unexpected tragedy struck the Forrest McGregor household. Forrest Edwin McGregor died suddenly at the very young age of 50 at his home near Algerita about 8:00 PM on

September 15, 1930. He had complained of feeling bad during the afternoon, but kept working. He ate a hearty supper and retired. In a few minutes he told his wife he couldn't see and felt like he was going to faint. He drew two or three short breaths, and then was dead. Dr. Nelson was summoned but could do nothing to revive him. Forrest McGregor's funeral service was conducted at the Community Tabernacle and he was laid to rest in the Richland Springs Cemetery.

Mary lost not only her husband in 1930, she had also lost her mother about three months later when Mary Virginia Taylor Gibbons died on December 11. Then her father, William Henry Gibbons, died 15 months later, on March 18, 1932. His two sons inherited all the ranch land because Billy Gibbons felt that sons should inherit the land. According to the *Richland Springs Eye-Witness*, Mary McGregor, as the only daughter, came into possession of much real estate in Richland Springs and Brady, as well as other places around the state. She became closely identified with Richland Springs business and social life, as well as being very active in her charitable and church life.

Mary Adelia Gibbons McGregor and some of her descendents

After the death of Forrest, Mary McGregor moved back into the town of Richland Springs to the permanent home she would live in. In the 1940 San Saba County Census, she was living there with her youngest daughter Billie Louise, who was actually away at college at the time. All her other children had married and moved away by that date. With the help of her sons, she continued to operate the ranch, along with commercial property in Richland Springs, Brady, and possibly Brownwood.

Mary Adelia Gibbons McGregor passed away August 30, 1962, in a hospital in Brownwood, Texas, and is buried next to her husband in the Richland Springs Cemetery. Following the death of MaMac, her estate, including the Old Home Place, was inherited in equal portions by all five children.

On March 3, 1966, John Clarke McGregor bought the McGregor Ranch from Dutch and Maxine, Nelson Rushing (Forrestine McGregor Rushing had already passed away by then), Fanora Mae and Ed Taylor, and Billie and Dean Adams. On that same day, Fanora Mae Taylor and Billie McGregor Adams bought from John Clarke McGregor his interest in 82 acres of the original land which fronted on the San Saba River. Since that date, Fanora Mae sold her share of the land to the children of Billie Adams. Billie then deeded her share of the land to her children, Dean Adams, Jr., Mary Katherine Adams, and Donna Louise Adams Wigley. That tract of land continues to be owned and operated by those descendents of William Henry Gibbons.

The ranch land on the San Saba River, officially The Adams Wigley Adams Ranch, but more commonly called simply The River, has become a very special location in the lives of Billie and Dean Adams, and their descendents. Because of a river bottom filled with native pecan trees, it was operated as a pecan farm for several years, but primarily it was used as a getaway from city life for the families of the three children. Many fond days have been spent fishing, hunting, camping, swimming, and playing Pinochle with Uncle Dutchie and Aunt Maxine.

There is no truth to the rumor that I was bribed into marrying Donna by the prospect of trot-lining for catfish there for the rest of my life. Even so, the highlight of my fishing career was when my two sons and I pulled a gorgeous, 66-pound yellow cat from the San Saba River on Mother's Day in 2000. Happy Mother's Day, Donna!

John Clarke McGregor

John Clarke McGregor, Uncle Mac to his nieces and nephews, the first child of Forrest and Mary McGregor, was born on November 11, 1906, on the Gibbons Ranch. The place of birth listed on the birth certificate was near Richland Springs, Texas, and the doctor who did the delivery was Dr. James Job Taylor, Mary McGregor's uncle. John Clarke was named after his Uncle John Gibbons, and his grandfather James Clarke McGregor.

Clarke attended Draughan Business College in Abilene, Texas. After graduating from Draughan, he moved to Cisco where he was employed at the Acorn Stores, Inc. He soon met and married Cora Loretta Rupe, born September 23, 1902. The marriage took place in Cisco, Eastland County, Texas, on July 8, 1928. The wedding notice itself, published in a Cisco paper, has a classic headline: "Marriage of Cisco Couple a Surprise: Quite a pleasant surprise took place Sunday morning when the marriage of Miss Cora Rupe and John Mcgregory (sic) was solemnized in the Presbyterian Church of Eastland. Miss Rupe is the daughter of Mr. and Mrs. J. G. Rupe, and was employed as a cashier at Kleiman's Department Store. Mr. McGregory of Cisco, and is the son of Mr. and Mrs. John McGregory of Abilene." Though the McGregor names are in error, the marriage was real!

The happily married couple notified his parents of the wedding by a telegram from Meridian, Texas at 4:30 PM the same day: "Married this morning leaving for Galveston Please send your Congratulations."

The next telegram was sent by John and Cora from Cisco with a message of sadness and grief, dated October 11, 1929: "Cora is resting Baby is Dead Come". The baby, a boy, was still born.

Clarke and Cora returned to Richland Springs where he went into ranching at the Old Home Place, and banking at The People's State Bank of Richland Springs. They were listed on the 1940 San Saba County Census, living on Marion Street in Richland Springs, where his occupation was stated as Bank Cashier. The February 24, 1944, issue of the *Richland Springs Eye-Witness* has a column covering a Proclamation from the Mayor of Richland Springs, John Clarke McGregor, declaring February 27 through March 4 as Texas Week.

Cora Rupe and John Clarke McGregor

Then came the good news from John Clarke and Cora McGregor that they were the parents of a new baby girl. Sheila Faye McGregor was born October 12, 1942, in Temple, Texas. Sheila married Jackie Wayne Carroll on August 10, 1963, in Richland Springs. Jack and Sheila both graduated from Richland Springs High School. Jack attended Texas Tech University and earned a degree in Range and Wildlife Management. Sheila attended Hendrick Hospital School of Nursing, and has a B.S.N. from Angelo State University and an M. Ed from Hardin-Simmons.

The Family Line of William Henry Gibbons

Sheila and Jack have been blessed with three sons, John Clayton Carroll, Monte Rey Carroll, and George Thomas Carroll, and many grandchildren. Sheila and Jack were living in Mimbres, New Mexico, where Jack was employed by the Forest Service, when their first two sons were born. They relocated to Brownwood, Texas, where Jack worked in real estate until his retirement. Sheila worked as a nurse until her retirement.

John Clarke McGregor died on March 29, 1970, at his residence – the Old Home Place, near Algerita. Cora died on April 16, 1995, in Brown County, Texas. Both are buried in the Richland Springs Cemetery.

Cora and Sheila inherited the Old Home Place when Clarke passed away, and Cora then gave her interest in the ranch to Sheila, which she and Jack still own and operate as a ranch. It is now called The Yellowjacket Ranch, based on a story told to Sheila by her Uncle Dutchie (Taylor Gibbons McGregor) after her father died. Uncle Dutchie said that when he and John Clarke were young boys, they used to ride their stick horses across Dry Creek. They would always encounter lots of yellow jackets, so the boys called it The Yellowjacket Ranch. After hearing the story, Sheila and Jack renamed the ranch to honor that tradition.

Thanks to the efforts of Sheila and Jack, in 2017 The Yellowjacket Ranch was designated by the Texas Department of Agriculture as a Texas Land Heritage Farm and Ranch, an honor for families who have owned and operated a continuous agricultural operation for 100 years or more.

Taylor Gibbons McGregor

Taylor Gibbons McGregor's birth soon followed that of his brother. He was born January 10, 1909, on the Gibbons Ranch, according to his birth certificate. He was named using the surnames of his maternal grandparents, Mary Virginia Taylor and William Henry Gibbons, and grew up working on both the Gibbons Ranch and the Forrest McGregor Ranch.

Taylor Gibbons (Dutch) McGregor was married on October 21, 1937, to Lucy Maxine Doran, born October 21, 1916 in San Saba County, the daughter of Worth and Clara Doran of Howell Doran Funeral Home, the largest funeral home in San Saba County. Unfortunately for Dutch, he was good friends with the editor of the *Richland Springs Eye-Witness*. Here are the headlines from the marriage announcement:

"Rent Collector McGregor Marries Undertaker's Girl
Horse Trader Married in last Thursday Morning's Ceremony"

Taylor Gibbons and Maxine Doran McGregor

On the 1940 Census, Dutch and Maxine were listed living in Richland Springs City, and his occupation was Manager, McGregor estate. In 1949, John W. Gibbons brought Dutch back to his portion of the Gibbons Ranch as a foreman. Dutch moved his family to live on the Gibbons Ranch in 1949. When John Gibbons was killed in a car accident in

1950, Virginia Gibbons Miller, who inherited half of the John Gibbons land, retained Dutch as the manager of her portion of the ranch until his death.

Dutch and Maxine's first child, Dorianne, was born on December 30, 1940. Dorianne married Ross Land, Jr., on December 28, 1962, in the home of Taylor and Maxine. Ross was serving on active duty at the time, so their first home was in El Paso, Texas. Ross and Dorianne had three children: Quinnell Land, Bruce Land, and Marthann Land.

Dorianne attended Tarleton State University and graduated from a cosmetology school. She was a cosmetology instructor and later, while living in Arlington, was a public relations director. Ross was a manager for Vought Aircraft. Some time after their divorce, Dorianne moved to Arkansas, where she passed away in Arkansas on December 16, 2011, and is buried in the Richland Springs Cemetery; Ross died December 28, 2020, and is buried in the Dallas-Ft. Worth National Cemetery.

The second child of Dutch and Maxine, also a daughter, was Mary Jo McGregor, born November 8, 1942, in Scott and White Hospital, Temple, Bell County, Texas. Mary Jo and Arnold Holley were married on October 21, 1962, in Richland Springs. Both were attending Howard Payne College in Brownwood at the time. Mary Jo and Arnold had two sons, Keith Gregory Holley and Brent Worth Holley.

Mary Jo has a BA degree from Hardin-Simmons University, and an MA from West Texas State University. She is a CPA, and was an Accountant for the Treasury Department. Arnold was a pastor for various churches around the state.

Mary Jo and Arnold divorced in 1988, and her work moved her to Washington, D.C. and other cities, until she returned to Texas to work in Dallas. She met Casey Weldon in Dallas. Casey was an explosives expert and engineer in oil fields for Halliburton, both onshore and offshore. They were married January 4, 1997, in Wood County, Texas, and they lived in the small town of Alba in Wood County, very close to Lake Fork. Casey passed away on January 1, 2012, in Wood County. After his death, Mary Jo coordinated McGregor Family Reunions on Lake Fork until the Covid-19 Pandemic forced a temporary halt to those wonderful occasions. Mary Jo has since relocated back to her roots in San Saba County.

The final child of Dutch and Maxine, and only son, was Forrest Edwin McGregor, born June 25, 1944, in Temple, Texas. He married a San Saba native, Sylvia Ann Millican, May 14, 1964 in Concho County, Texas. Their first child, Gregory Edwin McGregor was born in Brown County, Texas. The next two children died at birth in 1969 and 1970, respectively. Their final child, Cathy Renee McGregor, was born in Dallas, Texas. Forrest attended Howard Payne College in Brownwood, where he earned a BBA Degree.

Like his father, his grandfather, and his great-grandfather before him, Forrest has spent much of his working life in ranching, in and near San Saba County. In addition, he began his working career at Sears in Dallas, and also served many years as a Baptist minister. Sylvia worked at a San Saba bank for many years.

Taylor Gibbons McGregor passed away on May 2, 1973. He is buried in the Richland Springs Cemetery. Maxine Doran McGregor received her BA and MA in 1969 from Howard Payne University in Brownwood, and was a teacher until her retirement. She passed away in San Saba on September 7, 2000, and is buried in the Richland Springs Cemetery, next to her husband, Taylor McGregor.

Mary Forrestine McGregor

Almost five years after the birth of Taylor Gibbons McGregor, on May 17, 1914, the first daughter of Forrest and Mary was born: Mary Forrestine McGregor. The name is derived from the names of her parents. The address where they were living was listed as Algerita, Texas.

Forrestine attended public school at Richland Springs, Abilene, Brownwood, and then back to Richland Springs where she graduated from W. H. Gibbons High School. After graduation from high school, she attended the College of Industrial Arts in Denton, which later became Texas State College for Women, now Texas Woman's University, or TWU. CIA became the first institution of higher learning to establish and maintain a department of music. Forrestine loved music and was an exceptional pianist. The family always said if you hummed a few bars, she could play it.

Forrestine married Stanley Nelson Rushing, born March 9, 1912, to Millard and Annie Rushing in Eastland County, Texas, on December 31, 1933, in Goldthwaite, Mills County, Texas. Their first child, Stanley Nelson Rushing, Jr., was born on August 14, 1937, in Brady, McCulloch County, Texas. Scott Bradley Rushing soon followed January 10, 1939, also in Brady. Their first and only daughter, Karen Rushing, was born April 23, 1942, in Brady as well.

Other than a brief period of residence in Hobbs, New Mexico, Forrestine spent her whole life in Central Texas, where she devoted her time to being a homemaker, wife and mother, and as an active member of the Baptist Church, where she was a pianist extraordinaire. Forrestine and Nelson, along with Stanley and Bradley, were listed on the 1940 San Saba County Census, where it states that Nelson was the operator of a truck line.

The family was living in Cranfills Gap, Texas, when the two boys graduated from high school. Nelson was in the ranching business there. When Bradley and Stanley enrolled at Howard Payne College, Forrestine followed the lead of her mother and relocated to Brownwood while the boys were in school. Karen graduated from Brownwood High School while they were living there.

Bradley, Karen, Forrestine, Stanley, and Nelson Rushing

Forrestine and Nelson were ranching in Erath County, near the town of Hico, when Forrestine was found dead at home around midnight on February 13, 1964. She was almost the exact age of her father when he suffered an equally sudden death. She was buried in the Richland Springs Cemetery. Nelson was living back in Richland Springs when he died at his home on January 31, 1979. He was buried in the Richland Springs Cemetery as well.

Stanley, the oldest son, never married. He was a rancher in the Central Texas area for most of his working life. Like his mother, he died at age 49. He was in Harris Hospital in Fort Worth at the time of his death from leukemia on November 16, 1986. Services were held in First Baptist Church of Richland Springs, and he was buried in the Richland Springs Cemetery.

Bradley married Rebecca Blue in Cranfills Gap on June 17, 1961, and they had two sons: Scott Bryan Rushing and Bruce Kevin Rushing. Bradley worked for Montgomery Ward, and lived in various cities around the country. He divorced Rebecca in 1982, and married Susan Ziehe, a nurse, on April 4, 2004, in Clark County Nevada..

Karen Rushing married Bill Yousey, an aeronautics engineer, in her parents' home, December 21, 1963, and they had two daughters: Leslie Forrestine Yousey and Renee Michele Yousey, born in Fort Worth. .

Karen and Bill were divorced in 1983. Karen worked as a secretary and a kindergarten teacher for a brief time, and married William Newsom, an aviation engineer, on December 26, 1984 in Azle, Texas. Karen lived the majority of her adult life in Azle, where she was an active member of First Baptist Church in Lakeside. She died in Fort Worth on December 4, 2007, and her obituary in the *Fort Worth Star-Telegram* sums up her life well: "Her life was dedicated to Christ, family and friends. She lived for love, laughter and nurturing others. She was 'Mim' to her beloved nine grandchildren and 'mom' and friend to many." Karen Rushing Newsom was buried in the Richland Springs Cemetery.

Fanora Mae McGregor

The next child was born to Forrest and Mary Adelia McGregor three years to the day after her sister Forrestine, on May 17, 1917. The new baby daughter was Fanora Mae McGregor, also born in Algerita. Her somewhat unusual name was derived from the names of three of Mary McGregor's friends: Fanny, Nora, and Mae.

Fanora Mae graduated from W. H. Gibbons High School, and she attended Texas State College for Women and Howard Payne College. She married Charles Edward Taylor, born March 15, 1916, to Thomas and Myrtle Taylor in Brownwood, Texas, on December 31, 1937. On the 1940 Brown County Census, they were living with Dr. and Mrs. Thomas H. Taylor, Ed's parents. Dr. Taylor was the long time president of Howard Payne College, where many of the descendents of W. H. and Mary Gibbons received their higher education. Ed's occupation at the time was listed as a canner of food products.

Ed enlisted in the US Army Air Corps, and he and Fanora Mae were stationed in California, conveniently enough, near Billie McGregor Adams and her husband, Dean Adams who was at March Airfield, near Riverside, California. When Ed was released from active duty, he and Fanora Mae moved to Richland Springs where he owned a tailor shop until about 1960, when they moved back to Brownwood, where he worked for the US Postal Service. While living in Richland Springs, their daughter, Suzanne Taylor, was born on October 21, 1950, and their son, Charles Thomas Taylor was born on September 25, 1954.

Suzanne married Bill Faircloth on October 21, 1972, in Brownwood, Texas. Bill and Suzanne had two sons, Brandon Taylor Faircloth and Forrest Baker Faircloth. Bill worked in Texas public schools as a teacher, and later as an administrator. Suzanne has worked as a social worker for many years.

Tommy Taylor never married. He had a long career as a car salesman, doing business in many cities of north central Texas. He died of a heart attack while battling cancer in Sherman, Texas on June 13, 2018. He is buried in the Richland Springs Cemetery.

Fanora Mae Taylor died in Brownwood on July 18, 1996. Ed, who missed her terribly, passed away less than a year later, on May 18,

The Family Line of William Henry Gibbons

1997. Both are buried in the Richland Springs Cemetery, next to their son, Tommy.

Fanora Mae and Ed Taylor, Billie McGregor Adams

Billie Louise McGregor

The fifth and final child born to Forrest and Mary McGregor was Billie Louise McGregor, born November 4, 1919, at the Old Home Place in Algerita. On May 31, 1969, she became my mother-in-law. Her name came from the name of the heroine in a book MaMac was reading when it came time to decide the name for the new baby.

Billie was almost 11 when her father died. She graduated from Richland Springs High School, or W. H. Gibbons High School, as it was known then, in 1936. She was an excellent student, but, rumor has it, she did not graduate as valedictorian or salutatorian – intentionally. She did not want to give any kind of speech, so her senior year, she took just enough courses to graduate, but not quite enough to qualify for those honors. Another strong-willed woman in the Gibbons line.

She attended Texas State College for Women, studying Library Science. Between her junior and senior years, she took a semester off so that she and MaMac could take a long vacation by train, enjoying the scenery in California and the American west. She then returned to TSCW and completed her degree in 1940. In the 1940 Census of San Saba County, Billie and MaMac were listed together in MaMac's home in Richland Springs. The census was taken in April, with an indication that Billie was away at college, but listed with her mother as her permanent residence.

After graduation, Billie worked in the People's State Bank of Richland Springs, then taught English for a year at Seymour High School. She then returned to Richland Springs to teach English at W. H. Gibbons High School. In 1943, *The Richland Springs High School (W. H. Gibbons High School) Alumni Association and Graduates* publication recorded the following: "Class of 1943 – Everyone enjoyed and loved R. J. Powell, Agriculture Teacher, and Billie (Adams) McGregor, English Teacher. They were class sponsors. The senior trip was a 'Fun Day' at Ellis Crossing on the San Saba River...Billie McGregor gave the class a senior party in her mother's home with refreshments and games that were enjoyed by all."

In 1943, a momentous event took place at the movie theater in Richland Springs. According to Billie's future husband, Norman Dean Adams, he and Pancho Miller went to the movie theater, and observed two ladies sitting together, unaccompanied. Dean said to Pancho, "I'll take the teacher, you take the other one." They sat down beside the respective ladies, and the rest is history.

Billie McGregor and Dean Adams April 1943

Dean, born June 2, 1923, to W.G. and Kate Adams in San Saba County, Texas, was inducted into the US Army Air Corps as an Aviation Cadet on May 11, 1943, at Abilene, Texas, fulfilling his lifelong dream of flying. He was called to active duty on May 18, 1943. He completed his Advanced Flying School at Luke Field, Phoenix, Arizona, on November

19, 1944, and was assigned to the Lincoln Army Air Field in Lincoln, Nebraska, until he would be given his next training assignment.

During Dean's transit to Lincoln, he and Billie were married on December 11, 1944, in Richland Springs. Dean left immediately to report to Lincoln. Billie said, "I'll come join you right after I celebrate Christmas with my mother – just like I always do." Dean was ultimately assigned to March Field near Riverside, California, to complete his army aviation training. Coincidently, Billie's brother-in-law Ed Taylor was assigned to a base near Riverside at the same time, so they were able to enjoy California together. MaMac came in September, 1945, to visit both couples and to take some sightseeing trips with them. The war was already winding down, and at the end of November, 1945, Dean was discharged and he and Billie returned home to Richland Springs.

In the fall of 1946, Dean enrolled in veterinary school at Texas A&M. On November 11, 1946, their first child, Donna Louise Adams, was born in the St. Joseph's Hospital in Bryan, Texas. At the end of the semester, Billie and Dean made the decision to move back home to Richland Springs with their new baby girl.

Dean was the owner of a local feed store, as well as working as a farmer. In 1947, they moved into their new house which Dean had built. The next year Mary Katherine Adams was born, on September 23, 1948. When Mary Katherine was about to be born, Billie Adams told her mother-in-law, Kate Adams (AKA Big Mama), that if the baby were a daughter, she was going to name the baby Mary Kate after her and the baby's other grandmother, Mary Adelia McGregor. Big Mama responded, "Pete and Kate, sounds like a pair of mules. I hate that name!" So Billie, thinking that Big Mama didn't care about the baby being named after her, named the daughter Mary Katherine. When Big Mama heard the name, she said, "Katherine! Where did that name come from? I thought you were going to name her after me." Billie somehow managed to keep from shooting her mother-in-law, and Mary Katherine has been called Mary Kate ever since.

Then some earth-shaking events took place in their family. In Billie McGregor Adams' own words, written in her Memories Book documenting the events: "Friday, January 28, 1949, Donna was standing on her stool at the kitchen cabinet, helping Mommie grate cheese. When Daddy came home for lunch, Donna started to climb down, but somehow slipped and fell, and in falling, the double boiler of soup and water spilled on Donna. Daddy grabbed her up and took off her pajamas; we poured foille on her and rushed her to San Saba where the Dr. gave her first aid. On his advice, we brought Donna to Brady Hospital, Room 109, and placed her under the care of Dr. James P. Anderson. She received plasma Friday afternoon, Saturday & Sunday. On Wednesday she was given a transfusion (Daddy's blood) which gave her a big boost. Penicillin everyday."

She had second degree burns over a lot of the lower part of her body, with some third degree on her left leg. She was bandaged with sterile Vaseline strips, which were removed after a week, and then re-bandaged. Thursday, February 10, she was free of fever, and released from the hospital, still in bandages, on February 15. She returned to the hospital every 4 days for bandages.

Then, in June, while Donna was still in bandages, the next disaster struck. Billie was diagnosed with polio. In July and August, she was in rehab at Warm Springs Rehabilitation Hospital in Gonzales, Texas. Dean was left with a daughter still in bandages from devastating burns, a baby daughter less than a year old, and a business to run so the family could survive financially. Thankfully, MaMac and Fanora Mae came to the rescue and cared for Donna and Mary Kate while he was working. Mary Kate charmed Uncle Ed so much that he wanted to keep her when Billie came home from Warm Springs. She was walking with a limp, but she survived and she was walking. When the Polio Vaccine came out, the doctor in Brady called Billie to bring the children, and Donna, Mary Kate, and Dean Jr., were the first in line for the shot.

About the time the Adams household was recovering from the events of 1949, their third and final child was born. Their first and only son, Norman Dean Adams, Jr., was born on April 19, 1951, in Brady. At age 7 months, he was taken deer hunting for the first time, and he has loved to hunt since that day.

The three children all attended the Richland Springs public schools, until 1963, when they commuted to Brownwood to attend Brownwood Schools. Billie then moved to Brownwood to live while Dean continued to try to make a living in Richland Springs. Eventually, he too moved to Brownwood for work. He was able to fly again, and worked as a flight instructor. He began to work as a crop duster, and soon had his own company: Dean Adams Flying Service, which he operated for the rest of his life.

While attending Brownwood High School and performing with the high school band, Donna met her future husband, Donald Burt Wigley, born March 22, 1947, to Albert and Bonibel Wigley in Waco, Texas. They dated through high school, and continued to do so while she was in Lubbock going to Texas Tech, where she obtained her BA in 1968. They were married on May 31, 1969. Don had the joy of graduating from Howard Payne College, getting drafted, and getting married, all within one week.

They moved to Houston, where Donna was already working for IBM. Don went into the US Army in November, so they relocated to Fort Lee, Virginia, for about 10 months. Don was next assigned to a NATO base in Naples, Italy, where their first child, Jeffrey Burt Wigley, was born. Jeff got to travel all over Western Europe, but doesn't remember a thing about it! After almost two years in Naples, Don was discharged from the army, and went to work in Information Technology at Texas Power and Light Company in Dallas, Texas. He retired from one of their sister companies in 2018.

Jeff Wigley has never married, and has no children. After receiving a BA from Baylor University, he has worked as an IT Professional, primarily in the medical field, most of his working life. On a family trip to Ireland, Jeff was intrigued by the number of people who still spoke Irish as a primary language instead of English. When we returned home, he took classes in Irish, and now teaches the language for an Irish club. I'm sure Billy Gibbons would approve of that effort.

Their second child, Devin Adams Wigley, was born in Dallas. Devin never married. He worked for Albertson's and in the Dallas County Courthouse till his death from Pulmonary Fibrosis on September 16, 2018. He is buried in the Adams Cemetery in San Saba County.

Their third child, and only daughter, Manda Greg Wigley (the Greg is a derivation of McGregor), was born in Dallas. She went to Texas Tech and even lived in one of the dorms her mother had lived in. She met Fred Lee Salinas while at Tech, and they were married December 29, 2001, in Dallas. Fred was in the US Navy at the time, and they were stationed in Pascagoula, Mississippi. Despite all the hurricanes, they love living on the Gulf Coast, and remained after Fred was discharged. They have two beautiful children, Maisie Fidela and Ryker Lane Salinas, our only grandchildren.

Mary Katherine Adams (Mary Kate) never married, so her dogs were her children. Lots of dogs, mostly red ones. Like her Aunt Forrestine, Mary was a very accomplished pianist. She played for churches all around the Central Texas area, taught piano, tuned pianos, and accompanied a well-known professional singer in the area in countless concerts. Mary had to deal with many health and physical issues in her later life, including severe arthritis, heart problems, and advanced kidney disease. She passed away in Dallas on February 12, 2021, and is buried in Adams Cemetery.

Dean Adams, Jr. married Judy Muehlbrad on June 8, 1969. Dean, Jr. and Judy have two children, Shahala Deann Adams, and Norman Dean Adams, III, born in New Braunfels. Shaye married Johnny Sanchez on September 16, 2000, in New Braunfels, Texas, and they have one son, Johnny Dean Sanchez, or JD. Dean III married Edward Howard Harris on July 6, 1996, in Houston, Texas.

Norman Dean Adams, Sr., beloved Grandad to all of his grandchildren, died of a stroke on January 20, 1982, in Brownwood, Texas, at the relatively young age of 58. He is buried in Adams Cemetery, near Richland Springs. While living in Brownwood, Billie finally got to utilize her degree in Library Science by working at the Brownwood Public Library. When the head librarian retired, Billie assumed the job of head librarian until her retirement. After retirement, she moved back to Richland Springs to the house Dean built in 1947, sharing it with Mary Kate. Despite a serious bout with polio, she lived a long and fruitful life, passing away at the age of 87 on October 25, 2007. She is buried in Adams Cemetery next to Dean, Sr., Mary Kate, and Devin.

Chapter Ten of this volume will provide more information regarding the McGregor ancestry of Forrest Edwin McGregor, son-in-law of Billy Gibbons.

The Legacy of William Henry (Uncle Billy) Gibbons

When you think about the legacy that a highly successful man leaves behind, you ordinarily think of wealth, property, and possessions. In the case of Billy Gibbons, he did leave behind all those material things in great abundance, but his true legacy is so much more.

Throughout his life, his generous nature led him to share much of what he had accumulated during his lifetime, especially in his later years. Schools, the Boy Scouts, churches, and the community were recipients of his generosity. C. H. Bentley, the editor of the *Richland Springs Eye-Witness* stated it well, when he wrote in an editorial after the death of W. H. Gibbons: "The hardships he endured in acquiring the nucleus of his wealth left him considerate of all men. He loved Richland Springs and the people of this section where he made his start and on more than one occasion said to the writer: 'I help these people because they are my people, when I know that investment elsewhere will bring a greater return'...The Irishman had come to the new world, made his fortune, and shared it with others, especially young people."

One of the churches helped immensely by the generosity of Billy Gibbons was the First Christian Church in Richland Springs, the church Ed and Nettie Gibbons attended, as well as the family of Dean and Billie McGregor Adams. The church, which had been organized in 1901, was severely damaged by a storm in May, 1923. In August, 1928, Billy and Mollie Gibbons deeded to the church the land which was necessary to rebuild the facility, and the current frame building was erected.

As Marcia Miller McNeill writes in her document on the life of Billy Gibbons, "The discovery of an elaborate underground cavern on the ranch created another opportunity to give the people of the region a playground and financial boost. A deal was made with the Piper and Pate Amusement Company to develop and operate the Richland Springs Magic Cavern. Recreation opportunities offered included a swimming pool, cabanas, camping sites, and a clubhouse. The cavern was still being developed when World War II and the death of Lon Piper caused its closing."

Uncle Billy did everything he could to provide the children of Richland Springs with what they needed for schools, including requesting that some of his property be moved to the Richland Springs taxing district so that the school would benefit from the increase in funding, even though the higher tax rate was more costly to him. Other special needs, including loans for teacher salaries, were met out of his own pocket.

Shortly after his death, school trustees, because of his efforts to develop the community and maintain the schools of the district, voted to designate the high school of the district for all time to come to be known as W. H. Gibbons High School. Evidently for all time doesn't really mean forever, because the school was unfortunately later renamed Richland Springs High School by a different set of school trustees.

In 1930, Billy Gibbons gave verbal permission to the Boy Scouts of America for them to camp on a site near the junction of Brady Creek and the San Saba River. Heavy rains which flooded the camp site and damaged equipment forced the camp to be rebuilt. Ed Gibbons, who inherited the land the Boy Scout camp was on when his father died, gave the Boy Scouts a 25 year lease on the land.

Subsequent to the lease, the property south of Brady Creek was sold. The new owners, because trespassers were causing problems at the site, insisted the Boy Scouts relocate. The family gave the Boy Scouts a financial settlement, and John W. Gibbons and his wife gave a tract of 103 acres, four and one-half miles upstream from the original site, for the Boy Scouts to use. The camp is dedicated to the memory of Billy Gibbons, and will be known as Camp Billy Gibbons for as long as the Boy Scouts choose to use the property.

In the article "Hill Country Roots Run Deep For Rancher-Veterinarian Mays", by David Bowser in *The Livestock Weekly*, Myron Mays, great grandson of Billy Gibbons, is quoted as saying: "He made lots of loans. There are people still alive that remember when they would come with their daddies to see old Billy Gibbons at his home to borrow money to buy cows with.

"When the Depression hit, a lot of people near Richland Springs owed Gibbons money for livestock loans. He told them to forget it until the bad times had passed.

"Some of the people told him they just wanted out from under their loans. They'd bring him their cows or mules or whatever. There's one pasture on the ranch that to this day is called the Depression Pasture. He'd tell them to go over and dump it out in the pasture. That pasture was plumb full of goats, hogs, horses, mules, cattle, everything in the world."

The true legacy of Billy Gibbons was not the financial wealth and status he attained, but in the difference he made in the lives of his family, friends, and neighbors through his continuing support and generosity.

Timeline for William Henry Gibbons

1846 William Henry Gibbons born in Ireland
1867 W. H. Gibbons arrived in New York, sailed on to Boston
1868 Traveled to San Francisco to visit siblings
1869 Visited sister Marie in Utah, worked on Mormon Temple, Salt Lake City
1871 Returned to the East Coast and sailed to Galveston in May
1871 Worked at Menger Hotel in San Antonio for 2 ½ years
1873 Met W. H. Bainbridge in San Antonio; bought 1500 ewes together
1876 Arrived with their sheep in San Saba County
1877 Billy Gibbons requested survey of 80 Acres in San Saba County
1877 Maria and Orson Elliott cultivated 160 acres in San Saba County
1878 Gibbons and Bainbridge transferred 80 acres each to the Elliotts
1880 Orson and Maria Elliott on 1880 Census San Saba County Precinct 2
1880 On 1880 Census San Saba County boarding with Roundtree Family
1880 Gibbons holdings now in western San Saba County, southwest of RS
1881 W. H. Gibbons marriage to Mary Virginia Taylor
1881 Orson Elliott patented the Billy Gibbons land in San Saba County
1882 Birth and death of first set of twins
1883 Orson Elliott applied for a passport to go to South America
1883 Birth of James Edward Gibbons
1886 Birth of John William and Mary Adelia Gibbons
1887 Maria Elliott received letter from Billy Gibbons while still in Chile
1888 Elliotts in Argentina where Marie wrote letter to Billy Gibbons
1890 Birth and death of third set of twins
1919 Sensed a slump in livestock markets and diversified
1928 Deeded land to Richland Springs First Christian Church
1930 Committed to use of ranch land as a Boy Scout Camp
1930 Death of Mollie Gibbons
1932 Made a deal with developers of Richland Springs Caverns
1932 Death of Billy Gibbons in Fort Worth

Chapter Ten

The Ancestry of Mary Virginia Taylor Gibbons

Mary Virginia Taylor Gibbons was a member of another pioneering family to San Saba County. She was the daughter of James Kaneer (sometimes spelled Kanier or Kneer) Taylor and Ann Elizabeth Norman Taylor. According to the *San Saba County History* book, the Taylor family, consisting of James K. and Ann Elizabeth plus all of their ten children, sold their land and left Wetumpka, Coosa County, Alabama, in November, 1869, carrying all their household goods on a flat-top boat down the Coosa River to Mobile. Two of the children were already married, and brought their families on the journey, making a very large contingent.

They took a larger boat from Mobile to Galveston, Texas, and then a train to Chappel Hill in Williamson County. From Chappel Hill, the Taylors were forced by heavy rains to hire men to hitch four mules to each wagon to pull them through the mud to Hill County, Texas. From Hill County, they moved a little further to Ellis County. Sarah Margaret Jane Taylor Lewis, daughter of James K. and his first wife, Sarah Ann Delaney, and her husband, William Hampton Lewis, remained in Williamson County with the rest of their family when the Taylors moved on to Hill County. The Lewises later rejoined them in San Saba County around 1876. Dr. James Job Taylor, the other child who was already married, along with his wife Missouri Massey Taylor, and their 2 year old daughter Roxie, went to Hill County with James K. Taylor and party.

The Taylor family is listed on the 1870 Hill County census. At the time of the relocation from Alabama, James K. Taylor was 65, and Ann Elizabeth was 54. This was quite a move at their age, but their children were old enough to be a big help. The family, as listed on that census, were:

James K Taylor	Male	65	1805	North Carolina
Annie Taylor	Female	54	1816	North Carolina
James W Taylor	Male	21	1849	Alabama
Thomas H Taylor	Male	19	1851	Alabama
Richard H Taylor	Male	16	1854	Alabama
Elbert N Taylor	Male	14	1856	Alabama
Mary V Taylor	Female	22	1848	Alabama
Susan M Taylor	Female	11	1859	Alabama
Annie E Taylor	Female	8	1862	Alabama

The John Job Taylor family was listed in a different household on the same census.

James K. Taylor by profession was a wheelwright. He made the wheels as well as the carts and wagons that ran on them. He made his own wheels and wagons, bought some large mules, and in 1876, moved himself to San Saba County, settling in the northwest portion of the county, around the town of Richland Springs.

All the Taylors and in-laws arrived in San Saba County the same year Billy Gibbons arrived. Aunt Mollie had come to San Saba County to meet Uncle Billy.

James Kaneer & Ann Elizabeth Norman Taylor, granddaughter Rosie

Davenport Family

At the same time, another large family had plans for a move to Texas, and ultimately San Saba County, as well. Robert S. Davenport married Sarah Ann Brown in Kentucky in 1846, and they had nine children: Flavious R., Lutitia, John R., Luther C., Newton M., Septimas A., Sophia, Luella Amazon, and Aura Jane. Lutitia and her mother died, and Robert married Elizabeth Rusk Mann, a widow with two children, Granvell and Sarah.

Children born to this second marriage while they lived in Kentucky were Eudora, Kelbert, Victoria, Annie, and Fernando. Fernando died while they still lived in Kentucky. Robert and Elizabeth Davenport and their fourteen children decided to make the move to Texas. The two children from Elizabeth's previous marriage, Granvell and Sarah Mann, also traveled with the Davenports. Several other families and some young men who wanted to go west joined their party, and they left Kentucky in a wagon caravan on September 23, 1873.

The caravan arrived in Ellis County on November 8, 1873, and remained there for two years. All the Davenport party except Flavious, who had married and wanted to stay in Ellis County, left Ellis County in December, 1875, and arrived at Richland Springs shortly before the end of the year. They located about two miles southwest of town.

The Taylor party arrived in the area less than a year later, and settled within half a mile of the Davenport place. As might be expected with such a large group of young people living so close to each other, a lot of intermarrying took place. There were three marriages between the Taylors and Davenports: Richard Henry Taylor married Aura Jane Davenport, Elbert Taylor married Eudora Davenport, and Susan Taylor married Luther Davenport. In the second generation, James Hampton Lewis, the son of William Hampton and Sarah Jane Taylor Lewis, married Victoria Louise Davenport, who was the daughter of Robert S. Davenport, and one of the first generation of Davenports.

Several other close neighbors also got into the act: Robert Rowntree married Ann Eliza Taylor, and Mary Virginia Taylor married W. H. Gibbons. Then finally, John R. Davenport couldn't find any more Taylors to marry, so he had to settle on marrying another Davenport, his first cousin, Susan Davenport Davenport.

Almost all of the Taylors remained in San Saba County for the rest of their lives.

Sarah Margaret Jane Taylor Lewis married William Hampton Lewis before the Taylors left Coosa County, Alabama. Not only are they buried in the Richland Springs Cemetery, but also many of their descendents are buried there as well.

Dr. James Job Taylor, the first son of James K. and Elizabeth, was an important figure in the history of Richland Springs. He became a self-taught physician during the Civil War.

Dr. James Job Taylor and Family

According to his obituary published at his death on July 8, 1915, in the *Richland Springs Eye-Witness*, "Dr. Taylor was a pioneer physician and served his fellowman in that capacity when the country was infested with Indians and when the buffalo trails were the highways of travel. How much the community owes him and such as he." Dr. Taylor and his wife, Missouri Elizabeth Massey, had 14 children, most of whom married, raised families, and remained in San Saba County or nearby.

William Henry (Uncle Billy) Gibbons

Much has already been written about Mary Virginia Taylor, who married W. H. Gibbons in Richland Springs in 1881. She remained a much loved and respected resident of Richland Springs, living on the Gibbons Ranch for the rest of her life. She is buried beside her husband in the Richland Springs Cemetery.

John William Taylor was born in 1848 in Wetumpka, Alabama, and came to Texas with his family. In the 1880 census, he was listed with the James K. Taylor family, age 30, single, and employed as a freighter. He died in 1911 and is buried in the Richland Springs Cemetery.

Thomas Hardaman Taylor was born in 1851 in Wetumpka, Alabama, and moved to San Saba County with his family. He moved a little further west, to Concho County, where he was a long-term resident. He had nine children, and is buried in the Burr Oak Cemetery in Concho County.

Another prominent son was Richard Henry Taylor, who came to Richland Springs with the family and never left. He bought farm land about two miles southwest of Richland Springs, and continued to add to his land over time. He was born in Alabama in 1853, and died in Richland Springs in 1939. He and Aura Jane Davenport had eleven children. Most of his children were lifelong residents of San Saba County, and are buried in the Richland Springs Cemetery.

Elbert Neal Taylor was also a farmer in the same area as his brother Richard Henry. He also married a Davenport daughter, Eudora. They had fifteen children, twelve of whom lived to maturity. In the mid-1890s they left San Saba County because of a severe drought, and moved to Norman, Oklahoma on a train. A year later, the drought struck Oklahoma, and they moved back to Richland Springs. Most of the children spent the rest of their lives in or near Richland Springs.

Another Taylor who married a Davenport, Susan Mariah, had also found her permanent home. She and her husband, Luther C. Davenport, had nine children. Their daughter Anna, who died at age two months in 1882, was the first person buried in the Richland Springs Cemetery. Most of the Luther and Susan Davenport family were also eventually buried there.

The youngest child of James K. and Ann Elizabeth Taylor was Ann Eliza, who also married a neighbor, but this time it was a Rowntree. She and Robert Thomas Rowntree had five children. They did not stay in the Central Texas area, but moved north – way north. Ann Eliza and Robert ended up in Amarillo, where they are buried in the Llano Cemetery, but two of their children moved on to what was Indian Territory at the time, Chickasaw, Grady County, Oklahoma. Another son moved to the Temple, Texas area, and the last one to California. America was becoming much more mobile.

James Kaneer Taylor and Ann Elizabeth Norman Taylor both died in Richland Springs just before the turn of the century: he died on September 24, 1894, and she passed away on June 15, 1898. They are buried in the Richland Springs Cemetery, surrounded by their children and grandchildren.

John Taylor

The father of James Kaneer Taylor was Colonel John Taylor, born October 11, 1775, in North Carolina. His wife and James K.'s mother was Margaret Caroline Bludworth (or Bloodworth, as it is often spelled), who was born March 14, 1770, in Alabama. Colonel John Taylor has been listed as a Colonel in the Revolutionary War, but that is extremely unlikely since he was 8 years old at the end of the War. He may have been in the War of 1812, but no evidence of that has been found. John and Margaret came to Montgomery County, Alabama, in 1818, and spent most of their lives there. They were staunch Presbyterians; he was of Scotch, and she of Irish, descent.

The John and Margaret Taylor family birth and death dates are provided on the Hannon Family Register, page 78. A copy of the page is shown in Appendix F. They had the following children:

Jean Elizabeth Taylor, born 1800 in Wilmington, North Carolina, and died in 1866 in Coosa County, Alabama. She was married to Thomas Earle Hannon on January 24, 1821, in Coosa County. She had moved with her parents to Montgomery, Alabama, in 1818.

The Hannons had 8 children, one of which, George P. Hannon, was killed at Seven Pines during the Civil War, and another, Joseph B., was severely wounded at Gettysburg, but survived. One son-in-Law, John Milton Collins, husband of Margaret Caroline Hannon, was severely wounded at Baker's Creek, and suffered throughout his life from the severe pain from the wound. Thomas and Jean, and many of the rest of their family, are buried in the Friendship Cemetery in Elmore County, Alabama. Elmore County was created from a portion of Coosa County, so the Hannon Family did not actually relocate.

The second child of John and Margaret Taylor, and first son, was John Bludworth Taylor, born September 15, 1803, in North Carolina. He married Sarah Smith, and they had eight children. They were living in Mobile, Alabama, when he died in 1870. The Hannon Family Register confirms a death location as Mobile, but no date is listed.

The third child born to John and Margaret was James Kaneer Taylor, born in 1805 in North Carolina. He married Ann Elizabeth Norman in 1841, and all of their children were born in Wetumpka, Coosa County, before they left in 1869 to move to Texas. The ancestry of the Norman family will be traced later in this chapter.

Maria Margaret Taylor was the fourth child, born in February 19, 1808 in North Carolina. She became the second wife of William K. Oliver on December 22, 1842, and two years later, on March 10, 1844, she gave birth to her only child, John T. P. Oliver. He was killed at Chattanooga during the Civil War, November 3, 1862. He is buried in Wall Cemetery in Titus, Elmore County, Alabama. Margaret died February 22, 1894, and is also buried in Wall Cemetery.

Richard Henry Taylor was the youngest son of John and Margaret Taylor. He was born December 24, 1811 in Georgia. He married Nancy, and they had five children, as listed in the 1850 Census of the Hatchet Creek District of Coosa County, Alabama:

Richard Taylor	39	M	GA
Nancy Taylor	29	F	GA
Andrew Taylor	13	M	AL
Aaron Taylor	11	M	AL
William Taylor	9	M	AL
Margaret Taylor	6	F	AL
John Taylor	2	M	AL

The death location indicated on the Hannon Family Register is Montgomery County, Alabama, but no date was listed.

John Taylor, the father of James K. Taylor, and his wife, Margaret Bludworth, were listed on the 1830 Census of Montgomery County, Alabama. John was listed as 50-60 years old, which is consistent with a birth date of 1775. Margaret is shown as 50-60 also, again, consistent with her date of birth of 1770. Their daughter Jean was already married, thus she does not appear on this census. The same is probably true for their oldest son John Bludworth Taylor. The ancestry of the Bludworth family will also be traced later in this chapter.

James Kaneer Taylor, age 25, is shown in the bracket of males 20-30 and Richard Henry, age 19, is shown as a male age 15-20. The final child, Maria Margaret, is the only questionable one on this census: She is 22, but the only female child shown on the census is in the age 15-20 range; close, but not exact.

William T. Taylor

According to ObjGenealogy.Com, William T. Taylor is the father of Col. John Taylor. William was born in Virginia in 1749, and was married to Sarah Garrett Foster in Henry County, Virginia, in 1773. Sarah was born in Orange County, Virginia, also in 1749.

William and Sarah had 10 children, according to the McDade Family Tree on Ancestry.Com:

John Taylor	1775 – 1830
George Thomas Taylor	abt 1775 – 1838
Nancy Taylor	1779 – 1815
William Taylor	1780 - 1850
Zachariah Taylor	1782 – 1807
Joshua Taylor	1788
Jesse Riley Taylor	1791 – 1862
Richard Taylor	1792
Thomas Andrew Taylor	1793
James Taylor	1800

At this time in history, children were often named after relatives, meaning that parents, grandparents, aunts, uncles, cousins often had the same or similar names, which can be very confusing when trying to explain a family tree. The Taylors are no exception to this plight, as is evident in the information below.

William T. Taylor and his brother, Richard Lee Taylor, were the sons of Zachary Taylor, the grandfather of President Zachary Taylor. Richard Lee was born April 3, 1744, and married Sarah Dabney Strother August 20, 1779, in Rapidan, Orange County, Virginia.

Richard Lee and Sarah Taylor's son, Zachary Taylor, was born November 24, 1784, in Barboursville, Orange County, Virginia. Zachary Taylor fought in the War of 1812, and vanquished the Seminoles in Florida. After the Mexican War began in May, 1846, he commanded the American forces at the Battle of Palo Alto and the nearby Battle of Resaca de la Palma, defeating the Mexican forces, which greatly outnumbered his own. These victories made him a popular hero, and within weeks he received a brevet promotion to the rank of Major General and a formal commendation from Congress. The following September he inflicted heavy casualties upon the Mexican defenders at the Battle of Monterrey, and then prevailed again at the Battle of Buena Vista in February, 1847. Remaining at Monterrey until November, 1847, he returned to Louisiana, receiving a hero's welcome in New Orleans and Baton Rouge.

Having never revealed his political beliefs or previously voted, in 1848 he received the nomination for President as a member of the Whig Party, and selected New Yorker Millard Fillmore as his Vice Presidential running mate. The ticket went on to defeat Lewis Cass, the Democratic candidate, and Martin Van Buren, the Free Soil candidate. He was inaugurated as the 12th US President in 1849. He died on July 9, 1850, five days after he became ill while attending a July 4th celebration at the Washington Monument. He was the second President to die in office.

He was first buried in the Congressional Cemetery, Washington D.C., July 13, 1850. His remains were shipped back to his home in Louisville, Kentucky, on October 25, 1850. There they remained in the family vault in the Zachary Taylor National Cemetery until he and his wife were moved to their final resting place on May 6, 1926, in the newly constructed Taylor mausoleum nearby.

Richard Lee and William's father, Zachary Taylor, was born April 17, 1707, in King and Queen County, Virginia. He married Elizabeth Lee in 1737. Zachary, father of Richard Lee and William Taylor, was the son of James Taylor II, Junior or the Younger. His father, James Taylor I or James Taylor the Elder, was the first of the Taylor line to come to the Colonies.

James Taylor the Elder

The first record of James the Elder in the Colonies is in December, 1675, when he purchased 200 acres of land from Thomas Reynolds. Some genealogy sources have reported that James Taylor the Younger was born in Orange County. This was a later name for the area where the family lived at the time of James' birth, since Orange County was not created until 1734. His place of birth is more than likely New Kent County, although there is no proof of where James Taylor the Elder was living in 1674 when James the Younger was born.

James the Younger was a surveyor in the Spotswood expedition (Knights of the Golden Horseshoe) exploring the Piedmont area. This land surveying expedition, which had crossed the Blue Ridge Mountains into the Shenandoah Valley, took possession of the land between the Blue Ridge and the ocean in the West in the name of King George I of England. Those who had been part of the expedition then began to stake out claims to the land that had been surveyed, James Taylor being among them.

In 1721, Ambrose Madison (President James Madison's grandfather) married Frances Taylor, the daughter of James Taylor the Younger. Thus, the Taylors were ancestors of future Presidents Zachary Taylor and James Madison.

James Taylor, Jr., helped build a 13,500-acre estate. In 1723, Taylor probably pointed out some of the best acreage for his two sons-in-law, Thomas Chew and Ambrose Madison, to patent jointly. This land would become part of the Madison estate, which was originally called Mount Pleasant. When James Taylor's son, another James Taylor, moved onto another portion of his father's estate, the Taylor, Chew, and Madison families became a small community in themselves, all living within a few short miles of each other.

Today, there is a historical marker with an inscription about Bloomsbury, the estate of James Taylor: "A mile north is Bloomsbury, estate of the pioneer, James Taylor, ancestor of Presidents James Madison and Zachary Taylor. He was a member of Spotswood's expedition over the mountains in 1716."

The Norman Family

Ann Elizabeth Norman Taylor was a member of another one of those families who were pioneers in the westward expansion of the United States. She was the daughter of Job Norman, a memorable character in the early days of Alabama, and Job's wife, Rebecca Chilcutt.

Job Norman (1783-1864) was born in Greensboro, North Carolina; he probably was a large baby because as an adult he grew to be 7 feet tall and weighed 400 pounds. He was one of four children of Charles Wesley Norman (1756-1818) and Rebecca Caffey Norman (1767 - unknown). Charles was born in Virginia and moved to North Carolina shortly after the Revolutionary War ended. Job married Rebecca Elizabeth Chilcutt, alternately spelled Chillcott, (1790-1834), in 1808; her parents were Elkannah and Anna Chilcutt.

Job's brother, John, died in 1817, and his father, Charles, in early 1818. After the death of his father, Job and Rebecca Elizabeth moved to Alabama in late 1818 with their five children and his nephew, Hiram, age 8. Hiram was one the three sons of Job's deceased brother John. Job's mother, Rebecca Caffey Norman remained in North Carolina with an unnamed son and the widow of John, Fannie Deer Norman. Also accompanying Job to Alabama was the family of his first cousin, Thomas Caffey and the families of their good friends the Wallers.

Job and Rebecca settled in the vicinity of the closed Harrison School on the Southern Bypass in Montgomery. They owned land from the current bypass to Catoma Creek. Job had built bridges in North Carolina, and was called upon to build the first bridge over Catoma Creek in Montgomery County. He agreed to build the bridge with his slaves; the bridge would help him visit the Caffey and Waller families who had settled in Athens, Alabama (Athens became Ramer in 1851 when application for a Post Office was submitted). The bridge that Job built is still called the Norman Bridge, as is the road from there which leads directly to the Alabama Capitol Building, the Norman Bridge Road (although it has been renamed Union Street as it nears the capital).

The children of Job and Rebecca Norman are:

Rebecca   (1808-1835)
Anna   (1810- unknown)

Riley   (1812-1857)
Henderson H.   (1814-1864)
Ann Elizabeth   (1816-1898)
Thomas Webb   (1819-1874) – first Job Norman child to be born in Alabama
James   (1821-1836)
Sarah E.   (1824-1849)
Mary   (1826- unknown)
Margaret J.   (1829-1853)
Emily Maria   (1831-1864)
Elizabeth   (1834-1834)

After Job's wife, Rebecca, died in 1834, he married a widow, Mary Edwards, in 1836. Mary had been previously married to Jesse Edwards, with whom she had a son and daughter. Mary Edwards also had another prior marriage, this one to John Shelby. John and Mary had two sons, who became step sons of Jesse Edwards. When Job and Mary married, they became the guardians for the two Shelby boys. Mary died in 1838, leaving Job a widower for the second time; so Job became the sole guardian for all four of Mary's children in 1839.

In early 1864, Job's third grandson, William Riley Norman enlisted in the Confederate Army. He arrived in Georgia as General W. T. Sherman was fast approaching Atlanta. Upon Norman's arrival, he immediately discovered that his two older brothers, John and Thomas Norman had died in the war. Job ultimately had 10 children, as well as two grandsons, and two wives who predeceased him.

Job Norman died on August 9, 1864. He was buried near the house where his two wives and many of his children and grandchildren were buried. Eight months later, in April 1865, those still living at the "old home site" faced Union troops approaching from the west. In fear, they abandoned the farm that had provided for the Normans for 46 years. They removed to Ramer to be with the Caffey, Waller, and Norman families of that community. General James H. Wilson's raiders encamped at the outskirts of Montgomery on Job Norman's property. When the Union troops left, they burned the house and barns to the ground. They destroyed all the livestock and most hurtfully, they destroyed the grave markers and scavenged the family gravesites. It is no wonder so many of the family left for Texas in 1869.

Ann Elizabeth Norman was the fifth child of Job and Rebecca. She married James Kaneer Taylor (1805-1894) on February 10, 1841, at the home of her parents. James K. Taylor's brother, Richard, owned the property adjoining that of Job Norman. James and Ann raised their family in Wetumpka, but left Alabama with other Normans for Texas in 1869. As stated earlier, they first traveled to Mobile, then via ship to Galveston, Texas, by train to Chapell Hill, Texas, and then drove a mule team 150 miles to the Boz/Bethel communities, just eight miles southwest of Waxahachie, Texas.

Thomas Webb Norman, the sixth child of Job and Rebecca Norman, had married Permelia Ann Myrick in 1842, in Montgomery County. Thomas Webb and Permelia Ann Norman raised a large family of eleven children in Alabama, farming over 400 acres. After losing two sons in the Civil War, and seeing his father's farm and home destroyed, the family made a decision to move to Texas in 1869. Immediately after the marriage of their son William Riley Norman to Mary Elizabeth Williams, the families moved to the Boz/Bethel communities in Ellis County, Texas.

There they were met by the James K Taylor family. Thomas, Permelia, and their families remained in Ellis County when the Taylor contingent moved to San Saba County two years later.

Bludworth Family

Margaret Caroline Bludworth, the mother of James K. Taylor, was married to Col. John Taylor sometime prior to 1800, when their first child, Jean Elizabeth Taylor, was born in New Hanover County, North Carolina. Margaret was born March 14, 1770, in North Carolina. According to the Hannon Register referenced earlier, Margaret had an older brother, Thomas Bludworth, Jr., who was born September 1, 1768. The fact that he was Thomas Jr. implies that their father was Thomas Bludworth, Sr.

Based on the above information, it is believed Margaret descends from Timothy Bloodworth, who was born 1686 in England. He came to this country in 1698, in connection with a land grant. Robert Beverly was the receiver of the grant for transporting eleven persons, including Timothy. Robert Beverly was a member of the Virginia Company in England, as was Thomas Bloodworth, Lord Mayor of London.

Timothy Bloodworth married Jane Amistead in Elizabeth City County, Virginia. She was the daughter of Major William Amistead. Their children were Susannah, Mary, Elizabeth, and Ann Bloodworth, all born in Elizabeth City County. Jane Amistead Bloodworth passed away, and Timothy moved to New Hanover County, North Carolina, and married Margaret Evans.

Their children, all born in New Hanover County were:

John Bloodworth, b. 1730 d. 1808
Timothy Bloodworth, b 1736 d. 1814 (Served in the NC Legislature
    and represented his state in the Congress of the Confederation
    1784-1787. He opposed the ratification of the Constitution).
David Bloodworth, b 1740
James Bloodworth, b. 1740 d. 1799
Sarah Bloodworth
Thomas Bloodworth, married Sarah Rooks

Thomas and Sarah Rooks Bloodworth had at least two children, as documented in the Hannon Family Register. The first was Thomas Bloodworth, born in 1768, and the second was Margaret Caroline Bloodworth Taylor. Evidently, Margaret and Thomas came together to Montgomery County, Alabama. Thomas died in December 2, 1835, in the nearby city of Wetumpka, Coosa County, Alabama.

Conclusion of the Taylor Ancestry

The Taylors, Normans, and Bloodworths encompass many of the key components of early American history: They immigrated very early to a new land full of opportunity, but also full of risk; they were part of the rebellion against a powerful mother country, and persevered despite the odds; they participated in the creation of a new style of government, setting up and governing through a democracy; they lived and fought through a harsh period of a near break-up of that new democracy; and they continued the constant push westward to Texas and ultimately to the west coast – from sea to shining sea. What a marvelous heritage.

Chapter Eleven

The Ancestry of Forrest Edwin McGregor

Immigration

The immigrant ancestor of Forrest Edwin McGregor, husband of Mary Adelia Gibbons McGregor, and son-in-law of William Henry Gibbons, was Bartlett McGregor of Scotland. Bartlett McGregor came to Montgomery County, North Carolina, in the mid-1700s, along with his brothers, the Rev. William McGregor, a Baptist Minister (sometimes referred to as William the Preacher to keep him separate from all the other William McGregors), and John McGregor. Andrew McGregor was a possible fourth brother, but no verification is available. Bartlett McGregor was born about 1730, and William the Preacher about 1734, both in Scotland. No records have been found verifying exactly when they immigrated to America, but it was probably around 1770.

According to *The Quaich*, a clan Gregor research magazine published by the Clan Gregor centre in Edinburgh, they were said to have come from Scotland in 1773 or 1774, settling in Montgomery County, North Carolina. There is a report that Rev. McGregor was from the Isle of Skye and had brothers Bartlett and John. *The Quaich* states that Rev. William McGregor was from the Minginish area of the Isle of Skye. It also states that William's brothers were Bartlett and John, and there was an Andrew who was in the 1790 census of North Hampton County, NC. Other sources indicate he was from Glen Ossian, which is near the town of Glencoe in the Scottish Highlands, and that John was not his brother. However, John's will, probated in 1797 in Northampton County, North Carolina, references his brother, William.

Searching the parish registers in Scotland reveals perhaps a better possibility for the family of the three McGregor brothers. This information comes from the Scotland Births and Baptisms, 1564-1950 database, on FamilySearch.Org. The William McGregor family of the Inveresk and Musselburgh Parish, Midlothian, Scotland, near Edinburgh, had sons that match nicely with the three brothers who came to the Colonies around 1770. The members of the family, with all records coming from Inveresk with Musselburgh Parish, Midlothian, Scotland are:

> William McGregor, father, born July 25, 1693, married Oct 21, 1718
> Margaret Scot McGregor, mother, born April 3, 1698, died Dec 28, 1736
> Helen McGregor, daughter, born October 15, 1719
> Jean McGregor, daughter, born November 18, 1721
> Margaret McGregor, daughter, born September 27, 1724
> Janet McGregor, daughter, born February 25, 1728
> James (Bartlett) McGregor, son, born April 23, 1730
> William McGregor, son, born January 19, 1733
> Katharine McGregor, daughter, born November 2, 1734
> John McGregor, son, born October 3, 1736

According to the same source, William McGregor, the father, was the son of Peter McGregor and Isabell McDigall. Peter was born in 1670 and died in 1710. Isabell was also born in 1670, and her death date is unknown.

Bartlett McGregor

Very few records remain in this country for the Immigrant Bartlett McGregor, but he is mentioned in some of the earliest censuses taken in the United States. He is listed on the 1787 State Census of North Carolina, taken on July 3. The census is barely legible, but the name Barlet Mc— appears as individual #100, appearing next door to #101 Wm McGrice, both in Montgomery County. These are undoubtedly Bartlett and William the Preacher. Penmanship and spelling were not highlights of the census taking profession at that time.

The first US Census was taken in 1790, and once again Bartlett and William are listed in Montgomery County:

Megrigler, William   Salisbury District, Montgomery County
                                3WM>16 2WM<16 3WF
Megrigler, Bartlett   Salisbury District, Montgomery County
                                1WM>16 1WM<16 2WF

The male greater than 16 is Bartlett, the Immigrant, and the male less than 16 is his son Bartlett, born about 1775. After the death of Bartlett the Immigrant, his son Bartlett is usually referred to as Bartlett, Sr., and his son Bartlett, is Bartlett, Jr.

By the time of the 1800 Census, Bartlett the Immigrant and his wife were no longer in the picture. The size of the family indicates Bartlett, Sr. may now have had a combined family with some of his father's other children. Bartlett, Sr. had married Anne Harris, born about 1770 in Pennsylvania, sometime around 1790. Bartlett and Anne had four children prior to the 1800 census, but the census shows seven children in the household. William the Preacher was now about 68 and still preaching, and William, Jr. now appeared with his own family:

Megreger, William Sr.
   2WM16-26 1WM 45+ 1WF45+
Megriger, William Jr.
   2WM<10 1WM 26-44 2WF<10 1WF10-16 1WF26-44
Megriger, Bartlett
   2WM<10 1WM 10-16 1WM 26-44 2WF<10 2WF10-16 1WF 26-44

Bartlett, Sr. and his descendents will be covered in a later section of this chapter, entitled The Descendents of Bartlett McGregor the Immigrant, in much more detail.

William (The Preacher) McGregor

William The Preacher first appears in North Carolina in 1771 on the Bute County North Carolina tax roll, and he was mentioned as a messenger from the Fishing Creek Church in the Kehuky (or Kehukee) Baptist Association minutes in 1774. The Kehukee Baptist Association was formed in the eighteenth century by Baptist churches in eastern North Carolina. These churches had previously belonged to the Charleston Baptist Convention, but decided, because of distance and divergent interests, to form their own association. The actual date of the formation is now accepted as 1769.

William was ordained to preach in June, 1776, in Bute County (Bute County was abolished and the area became part of Franklin County in 1779), and was the organizing pastor of Mouth of Uwharrie Baptist Church in 1780, in Montgomery County, North Carolina.

William purchased land in Anson County, lying southwest of the Pee Dee River near the mouth of Attaway Branch, in 1778. In 1779, Montgomery County was formed from part of Anson County, so William's land was now in Montgomery County. He paid taxes in 1780 and 1782 for five hundred acres of land in Montgomery County in the same location. The land is on the west side of the Yadkin River, about one mile from the falls. The land is now part of Morrow Mountain State Park in western Montgomery County.

William the Preacher's wife is often listed as Sarah Flowers McGregor, the daughter of Ransom Flowers. Her date of birth is approximately 1755, but that is the same year stated as the birth year of his oldest son, William McGregor, Jr., so she would obviously not have been his first wife. Also, William, Jr. was born in Scotland prior to immigration, therefore Sarah Flowers McGregor could not be his mother. There is a gap of over twenty years between the birth of William, Jr. and the birth of his next child, Ava, or Avery, who was born in 1778; therefore, it is a probability that Sarah was a second wife, and that he had at least one more child by her, which would be Avie (Ava or Avery).

William, Jr. was the oldest child of William the Preacher, and was born in Scotland, prior to the immigration of the McGregor brothers. He also was a Baptist preacher. He was married to Mary Jane (sometimes known as Martha) Stiles in Montgomery County in 1780, but William

Jr. was not listed on the 1790 Census of North Carolina. He probably remained a part of his father's household until the 1800 Census, when he is listed as a head of household with a wife, three daughters, and two sons.

The best way to identify which children belong to which father is to visualize this by mapping the two households into the 1790 census and the 1800 census, assuming a combined household for both families in 1800. Those underlined belong to the William Jr. family.

	1790			1800						
	M 16+	M < 16	F	M < 10	M 16-25	M 26-44	M 45+	F < 10	F 10-15	F 26-44	F 45+
Sr.	3	2	4	0	2	0	1	0	0	0	1
Jr.	0	0	0	2	0	1	0	2	1	1	0
	Sr.		Wife				Sr.				Wife
	Jr.					Wm Jr.				Wife	
	Unk		Avie								
			Mary		Ezek				Mary		
		Ezek	Wife		Willis						
		Willis						Eliz.			
								Sarah			
				Richm							
				Jehu							

From this analysis, we can conclude that Avie, Ezekiel, and Willis are all children of William the Preacher and his wife, Sarah Flowers McGregor. William Jr., was the son of an unknown mother in Scotland before immigration. The Unknown Male on the 1790 census could be another son born before immigration from Scotland, or just someone else living in the household, which was not unusual for the time.

The other child who could be in question regarding which William was her father was Mary Ann McGregor, born in 1783. However, there is no young female listed on the 1800 census for the William the Preacher household, so Mary Ann must be the daughter of William, Jr.

Therefore, the conclusion is that the following are the children of William the Preacher McGregor, and his wife Sarah Flowers McGregor:

    Ava, or Avie, born 1788, married to Bennett Solomon
    Ezekiel (twin) born 1784, married to Sarah Jane Ware (twin)

Willis (twin) born 1784, married to Susannah Ware (twin)

Avie was born September 10, 1788, in Anson County, North Carolina, which became Montgomery County the next year. Sometime about 1795, when she was 17 or 18, she married minister, Rev. Bennett Solomon. Bennett Solomon, and his brothers William Jr. and Goodwin, were from Franklin County, sons of a William Solomon and Deana (or Diana) Gordon Solomon. Bennett's name is found in church records, often in conjunction with that of Rev. McGregor.

Bennett and Avie appear on the 1810 census of Montgomery County with 7 children under 16. There is no 1820 census available for Montgomery County. It was possibly burned in one of the many courthouse fires. By the 1830 Census, Ava McGregor Solomon was a widow and had migrated to Warren County, Tennessee, with most of her children, to live close to others in her family who were already there.

In the 1830 census, Ava was a widow, and living next to her brother, Ezekiel McGregor. She is the "Aby" in the census. Her second son, William Solomon, had taken over as shepherd of the flock of William the Preacher's church, following his father and grandfather into the ministry. As such, he remained in North Carolina to lead the congregation his forebears had founded. The congregation of The Mouth of the Uwharrie became Stony Hill, and the site of the old church is just down the road from the Kron House site at Morrow Mountain State Park. The church later moved a few miles down the mountain to a hill above Valley Drive, where it remains today.

In the tax record of Warren County, Tennessee, for the year 1836, Ava was the head of her own household, owning 80 acres of land, valued at $200. Her tax was $15. She was also charged for something called school land of 70 acres and a $100 value with a tax of $5. She had one slave, valued at $500 and taxed at $25, giving her a total State tax of $45.00. Her son, Willis, was listed next to her and taxed only at 1 white poll. By 1840, Ava had moved in with her son Willis, who had married Myrick Safley about 1838.

Ava "Avie" McGregor Solomon died on October 5, 1857, in Warren County, Tennessee, at the age of 79. Her tombstone is inscribed, "Wife of Bennett Solomon". She is buried at the Smyrna cemetery in Irving College, Warren County.

The known children of Bennett Solomon and Ava McGregor Solomon were:

1797 - Bennett Solomon II - Married Elizabeth Parker
1799 - Martha B. Solomon - Married George Bullen
1801 - William S. Solomon, Sr. - Married Tabitha Marks
1803 - Frances "Fanny" Solomon - Married a Russell
1805 - Sarah A. Solomon - Married Hardy Russell
1807 - Mary "Polly" Solomon - Married Michael Mauzey
1809 - Willis Lymon Solomon - Married Myrick Safley
1812 - Jane Solomon - married George Turner
1814 - Hickey or Hixie Solomon - married Charles Hutchinson

The twin sons of William the Preacher and Sarah were Ezekiel and Willis McGregor, born November 26, 1784, in North Carolina. The twin boys must have enjoyed being twins, because they married twins. Ezekiel married Sarah Jane Ware, the daughter of Roland and Temperance Ware, in 1805. Sarah Jane was the twin of Susannah Ware, both born on December 15, 1787, in North Carolina. Susannah married Willis McGregor after the McGregors and the Ware Family had relocated to Warren County, Tennessee, sometime before 1810.

The Ware Family had ties to both Northampton County and Montgomery County, North Carolina. According to FindAGrave.Com, Roland Ware "probably migrated to Northampton Co., N. C. by 1774 with Peter Ware. In 1778 he entered the service and fought in the Revolutionary War. While a resident of Montgomery Co., NC, he enlisted in 1778, and served at various times until the close of the Revolution, amounting to about 12 months in all."

Ezekiel and Sarah Jane, along with Willis and Susannah, moved to Warren County, Tennessee, sometime before 1806, when their first children were born in Tennessee. Amazingly enough, the first children of Willis and Susannah were twin daughters, Ahixoam (Hixie) and Ahinoam, born April 20, 1806. They went on to have eight more children. Here is the list of children:

    Ahixoam (Hixie), born 1806, married Philip Hoodenpyl
    Ahinoam (Hinie), born 1806, married Logan Dietz
    William Jefferson, born unk, never married

William Henry (Uncle Billy) Gibbons

Minerva (Myra), born 1812, never married
Sarah, born unk, married Anderson Safley
Mexico, born 1816, married James M. Ware
Nancy, born unk, married Peter Hunter
Vesta, born 1821, never married
Oroha, born 1822, married John W. Mitchell
Lavinna Anna, born 1824, never married
Cynthia Barnett, born 1827, married William Lane Swann

Ezekiel and Sarah Jane almost kept up the pace: they had nine children:

Temperance, born 1807, married James Allen
Willis Nard, born 1810, married Nettie Ellen Harrison
Jason, born 1813, married Margaret Pennington and Teresa Sims
Susan, born 1814, married Benjamin Huckabee
Jemima, born 1816, married William Huckabee
Wiley A., born 1818, married Sarah Ann Young
Avery, born 1819, married Benjamin Marks, then Bartlett Huckabee
Henderson, born 1821, married Martha C. Young, sister to Sarah who married his brother Wiley
Clinton, born 1824, married Phoebe Biles, Melgena Meyers, Mary Reese

In 1805 William the Preacher was still listed as the pastor of the Mouth of the Uwharry River Baptist Church in the Sandy Creek Association in Montgomery County, where he had been pastor since 1778. At this time, he would have been about 73 years old. He was still listed as pastor in 1806, and in 1807, was a messenger to the Collins River Baptist Church, along with his son, William McGregor, Jr. By 1809, all references had ceased.

William the Preacher died about 1807; it is not known when his wife died but probably around the same time as she was alive in the 1800 census. His home, along with an apple orchard and 294 acres of land, was purchased by Dr. Francis J. Kron on November 2, 1839. William (The Preacher) McGregor and his wife are buried in the cemetery above the Kron Cemetery which is called the McGregor Cemetery at the Morrow Mountain State Park. Shortly after his death, all of those with McGregor surnames in Montgomery County had relocated to Warren County, Tennessee.

After his father and mother passed away around 1808, William, Jr. relocated his family to Warren County, Tennessee, where he spent the remainder of his years. According to *Pioneer Baptist Church Records of South-Central Kentucky and the Upper Cumberland of Tennessee,* William McGregor, Jr. was a messenger from the Collins River Baptist Church to the Stockton River Association in the years 1808 – 1813.

William, Jr. was commissioned Justice of the Peace of Warren County in 1817. He was also a trustee of the Quincy Academy, and helped Rev. Jesse Dodson start the Head of the Collins River Church.

William, Jr. and Mary Jane had the following children:

> Mary Ann, born 1783, married to Robert Stiles, III
> Elizabeth, born 1789, no further information
> Sarah, born 1792, married to Elijah Dodson, 6 children
> Richmond, born 1794, married to Mary Myers, 4 children
> Jehu, born 1800, married to Sarah Dodson, 9 children
> William, born 1805, married Mary Unknown, 11 children

William the Preacher McGregor was an influential presence in Montgomery County, North Carolina, but after the death of their patriarch, no McGregors from his family remained in the county, other than Bennett and Avie Solomon, and their family. They assumed leadership in the church to which William the Preacher dedicated a lifetime of faithful service. The church where he ministered to the area is still active, although under a different name and in a different location.

Timeline for William (The Preacher) Mcgregor

1770   Rev. William and Bartlett immigrated from Scotland to North Carolina

1771   Rev. William on tax rolls of Bute County, NC (Bute created 1764)

1774   Rev. William was a messenger to Kehuckee Association from Fishing Creek Church in Bute County, NC

1774   Rev. William was a delegate to Kehuckee Assoc. Sandy Creek BC, Franklin County, NC

1776   Rev. William Given License to preach in Franklin County (Still Bute County until 1779 when Bute abolished and divided into Franklin and Warren)

1778   Rev. William bought land in Anson County (Montgomery County formed 1778 from Anson County – wakespace.lib.wfu.edu; Abstract of deeds 1Jul 1778, Henry Mounger Esq. of Anson Co. to William McGrigger, the same)

1780   Montgomery County Records – William McGreger 500 Acres

1782   Taxpayer Montgomery County

1784   Twin Sons Willis and Ezekiel born in Montgomery County

1787   On NC State Census Montgomery County

1790   On US Census Montgomery County 3WM>16 2WM<16 3WF

1800   On US Census Montgomery County 2WM16-26 1WM 45+ 1WF45+

1800   Held Revivals in Montgomery County

1805   Still listed as pastor of the Uwharry Baptist Church

1806   Delegate to Sandy Creek Association, Pastor of then Mouth of Uwharry, Mont. Co.

1806   Probable death date of William the Preacher McGregor

John McGregor

John McGregor, the brother of William the Preacher McGregor and Bartlett McGregor, was born about 1736 in Scotland. The best evidence found that he is their brother is stated in John McGregor's will (see below), when he references a sorrel mare he bought from his brother William.

According to the publication *The McGregor House, Rutherford County, Tennessee*, "The first generation of the McGregor family had immigrated to the United States in 1761. John and Margaret (Thomson) McGregor, departed Scotland with their infant daughter Helen (b. 1761), and settled in Northampton County, North Carolina by 1762. In North Carolina, the McGregors had two more children – twin boys Lewis and Flowers (b. 1762).

"The Revolutionary War and the subsequent political battle over North Carolina's western territory shaped the McGregor family's experiences. Arriving in the American Colonies on the brink of the American Revolution, the McGregor family quickly undertook the cause of their new homeland. As a new immigrant, John McGregor mustered into the 2nd Continental Artillery Regiment in 1778 for three years of service. Although the specific details of John's personal life remain unknown, it is clear that he returned to North Carolina following his military service, where in 1790 he recorded fifteen persons in his household – two white males, four white females, and nine enslaved individuals.

"Before and during the Revolutionary War, the area known today as Tennessee was an uncultivated frontier. At the conclusion of the French and Indian War, King George III issued the Proclamation of 1763, which appropriated the land west of the Appalachians as Native American territory, thereby prohibiting settlement by colonists. Despite this proclamation, colonists moved west over the Appalachian Mountains in search of new fertile farmland. The defiant nature of these early trans-Appalachian settlers led to their support for a large-scale rebellion against the British. Thus, the western territory of North Carolina became a pro-independence region.

"Following the conclusion of the war, this same group sought statehood from Congress. The earliest attempt at forming an independent state was in 1784; however, North Carolina and Congress refused to recognize the new state and it dissolved by 1789. After North Carolina ceded its western territory to Congress in 1790, settlers attempted statehood once again. In 1796, Tennessee became the 16th state in the Union.

"Although John and Margaret McGregor established roots in North Carolina, their children would soon leave and head for the newly admitted state of Tennessee. Just four years before John McGregor's death in 1797, his son Flowers McGregor departed North Carolina and became the first of the McGregor family to settle in Tennessee. On October 5, 1793, at thirty-one years old, Flowers married his wife Polly Payne in Sumner County. Together they had three children – John (1794 – 1836), Ransford (1801 – 1882), and Albert (1803 – 1860)."

The book quoted above has some very interesting information, but at the same time, has a few discrepancies. There is no mention of William the Planter McGregor, who is mentioned in John's will as a son. And, along those same lines, there is no twin brother of Flowers named Lewis who is mentioned in the will. Helen, the baby daughter who came with John and his wife when they immigrated, is not mentioned in the will, and neither is a wife named Margaret, but they could have been deceased by the time John wrote his will. As is seen in some of the deed records below, a wife named Elizabeth signed some of the land records, and a wife named Mary is named in the will. In short, the historical perspective of the document is accurate, but the individuals should be researched further. The source of the information regarding individuals appears to come from Ancestry.Com, with no indication of further references.

The first official record of John McGregor's presence in North Carolina is from *Deed Book - Northampton County North Carolina 1759-1774*:

#1168	Nov 30, 1772	Ransford Flower of Northampton County to John McGregor of same 150 acres on south side of Beaver Creek Pond
#1216	Jan 18, 1773	John Brewer and Baker White of Northampton County to John McGreggor (Megriger) of same 100 acres

Deed Book - Northampton County North Carolina 1774-1780:

#332	Jan 9, 1778	John Catoe to John Hardin... John Mcgreger witness
#76	Mar 4, 1776	John Megreger and wife Elizabeth to Wm Megreger planter of Warwick County VA (Hereafter referred to as William the Planter) 287 acres which John Justice sold to John Megreger on Jack Swamp
#77	Mar 4, 1777	Robert Little to John Megreger 270 acres
#94	Nov 30, 1777	Samuel Wornom to Henry Mason 100 acres - John Megregs and Ransford Flowers witnesses
#164	May 16, 1777	John (x) Megreger to Jessee Mitchell 150 acres - also signed by Elizabeth (x) Megriger - witness Ransford Flowers

In 1780, he was listed as a taxpayer in Northampton County, and on the 1786 Northampton, North Carolina state census:

```
McGrigger, John    2WM 21-60    3WM <21 or >60    5 WF
                   John         William           Mary
                                Flowers           Sarah
                                                  Frances
                                                  Cynthia
                                                  Jean
```

Record of Estates Northampton County, NC Vol I and Vol II
#62   Jan 22, 1788   John McGregor to Norwood Bond to make a title to land
#564 Dec 10, 1789   Listed as a buyer in the estate sale of Ransford Flowers

On 1790 Northampton North Carolina, US census
```
McGregor, John      1 WM>16    1 < 16      4 WF     and 9 slaves
McGregor, Flower    1 WM>16                         and 2 slaves
McGregor, William   1 WM>16    3 WM<16     3 WF     and 2 slaves
```

John McGregor is said to have married Mary (Polly) Flowers, daughter of Ransford Flowers, a close neighbor in Northampton County. This easily could be consistent to having brought a wife named Margaret with him from Scotland, because a wife named Mary is referenced in his will. It is also consistent with John having a first wife named Elizabeth, as shown in official records in North Carolina. John's brother William the Preacher also is said to have married a Flowers daughter, Sarah.

John McGregor and Mary's children are listed in his will shown below. They are:

> Sarah, born unk, married Unk Williams
> Frances, born unk, married John Sandifer, 5 children
> Cynthia, born unk, married Robert Sandifer, 6 children
> Flowers, born 1762, married Mary Payne, 8 children
> Jean, born unk, married unk Brown
> William, born 1755, married Nancy and Anne

John died in 1794 in Northampton County, North Carolina. The following is his last will and testament, probated in 1797.

Last Will and Testament of John McGregor

Anson County, North Carolina
Will Book A, Page 68, July 1797
In the name of God - amen.
I John McGregor of Northampton County being sick and weak of body but thanks be to God of sound mind and memory do ordain this to be my last will and Testament in manner and form following court. I give to my wife Mary McGregor one negro girl named Ely, her choice of my beds, two cows and calves, and my sorrel mare that I purchased from my brother William McGregor to her and her heirs and assigns forever.
I give to my daughter Sarah Williams one negro wench named Sarah, one bed and furniture, two cows and calves which are in her possession to her and her heirs and assigns forever.
I give to my daughter Frances Sandifer one negro girl named Judy, one bed and furniture, two cows and calves which are in her possession to her and her heirs and assigns forever.
I give to my daughter Centhey Sandifer one negro named Rachel, one bed and furniture, two cows and calves which are in her possession to her and her heirs and assigns forever.

Then I give to my son Flowers McGregor one negro boy named ???, one bed and furniture, two cows and calves which are in his possession to him and his heirs and assigns forever.

Then I give to my daughter Jean Brown one negro boy named Jacob, one bed and furniture, two cows and calves which are in her possession to her and her heirs and assigns forever.

Then I give to my son William McGregor one negro boy named Aron and all the land and cows in the County of Northampton, only that my wife is to have the one third for life as heretofore mentioned to her and her heirs and assigns forever.

Then I give to my daughter Elizabeth McGregor one negro wench named ??? and her child named Charity and their increase to her and her heirs and assigns forever. Then I give to said daughter Elizabeth one negro girl named Mary and her increase to her and her heirs and assigns forever.

My will and desire is that all the rest and residual of my estate which is not heretofore given away be sold and after (payment of) my debts the remainder if any be equally divided among all my children.

I hereby appoint my son in law John Sandifer my executor to this my last will and testament, revoking all former wills heretofore by me made.

In witness I have hereunto set my hand and affixed my seal this 3rd day of August, one thousand seven hundred and ninety four. In presence of

Jno Rives, Adam Lockhart, Betsy Kelly   July Court 1797

William the Planter McGregor was born about 1755 in Scotland, and came with his parents to Northampton County, North Carolina, when they immigrated in 1761.

William the Planter's first appearance in official records was in 1776 in the *Northampton County NC Deed Book 6 1774-1780*:

<u>#76</u> John Megreger and wife Elizabeth to Wm Megreger planter of Warwick County VA 4 Mar 1776 287 acres which John Justice sold to John Megreger on Jack Swamp.

Jack's Swamp begins in north Northampton County and flows northeast into Virginia where it becomes Fountains Creek, identified in early maps by Byrd in 1728. There was a Jack Swamp community on Jack's Creek in north Northampton County from about 1775, when a Quaker Meeting House was built there, until about 1812, by which time most of the people had moved to central North Carolina and Ohio. This would place Jack Swamp in the far northwestern corner of Northampton County.

By 1781, William the Planter had relocated to Warwick County, Virginia, where he was employed in a foreman role by Hudson Allen, a large plantation owner in the area. In 1781 in York County, Hudson Allen claimed a loss of 554 British pounds due to the British Invasion. The National Historic Site at Yorktown has a marker on the Allied Encampment Tour which commemorates the location of the Hudson Allen Plantation House.

The Charles Parish York County Virginia History and Registers records the baptism of McGregor, Elizabeth, daughter of William and Anne, born September 29, baptized Dec 3, 1781 (Of Warwick County).

In the 1782 the Warwick County, Virginia Census lists William McGregor with 7 White 12 Black persons. Also, the corresponding 1782-5 Personal Property Tax List for Warwick County, Virginia lists William McGregor with 1 Free Men 12 Slaves 4 Horses and 40 Neat Cattle.

After the death of Hudson Allen, the 1784 Warwick County Census lists Wm McGregor as head of the household of 10 White Souls on the Hudson Allen Estate consisting of 1 dwelling and 7 other buildings (from the Hudson Allen will dated 1784 York County VA).

The York County 1786 Census listed William McGregor with no slaves, and no cattle or horses. Shortly after this census he returned to Northampton County.

In 1788, he was referenced in the will of Ransford Flowers, Northampton County; NC as grandson William McGregor. He received one Negro named George.

Record of Estates - Northampton County NC Vol I
#564 William McGregor was listed as buyer on account of sale of estate of Ransford Flowers Dec 10, 1789.

William McGregor was counted on the 1790 Northampton County, NC census:

1 WM > 16   3 WM < 16   3WF   2 Slaves

In July, 1797, he was referenced in will of John McGregor, Northampton County, NC.

The Northampton County, NC census 1800 lists:

William McGregor
1 WM < 10 1 WM 45+ 1 WF < 10 1 WF 10-16 1 WF 16-26 1 WF 45+.

Will of William McGregor, Sr.

In the name of God Amen. I William McGregor of Northampton County and State of North Carolina being of sound and perfect mind and memory (blessed be to God) do this 6th day of April in the year of our Lord one thousand eight hundred and nine make and publish this my last will and testament in manner following that is to say-

Item 1st I lend to my beloved Wife Nancy McGregor the whole of my Estate both real and personal during her natural life or widowhood and at her death or marriage my will and desire is that one hundred Dollars be raised out of my Estate, which hundred dollars I give and bequeath to my son Anthony McGregor, to him and his heirs forever.

Item 2nd I give and bequeath to my Son William McGregor at my Wifes death or Marriage one negro boy named Moses and one still which I now have in use, to him and his heirs for ever--

Item 3rd I give and bequeath to my son Alexander McGregor at my wifes death or Marriage one negro man by the name of Billy, one Sorrel Alderman? Colt one gun and one feather Bed and furniture and all my land below the branch that runs into the south prong of Jack swamp just above the house- Beginning at the mouth of the branch where it empties in to Jack swamp thence up the branch to a white oak on the side of a path thence along the path until it comes into the road just below Robert Foxes Dwelling House to him and his heirs forever

Item 4th I give and bequeath to my two Daughters after my wifes death or Marriage, Nancy Williams and Frances McGregor my two Negroes Betty & Esther to be equally divided between them also all the residue of my land lying above the branch as before mentioned to be equally divided between my two Daughters before mentioned. But my will and desire is that my daughter Nancy Williams (after making an equal division of said land the line beginning at Jack swamp and running a north course) should have the upper part of said land to them and their heirs forever,

Item 5th My Will and desire is that in case either of my Children should die under age or without heir that all the property which has heretofore or may hereafter be devised to them should be equally divided between my three surviving Children to them and their Heirs forever--

Item 6th All the residue of my property which has not heretofore been devised away shall be sold and equally divided between Anthony McGregor William McGregor Nancy Williams and Francis H. McGregor to them and their Heirs forever—

And I hereby make and ordain my beloved Wife Nancy McGregor & my son William McGregor Executors of this my last Will and Testament in Witness whereof I the said William McGregor have to this my last Will and testament set my hand and Seal the day and year above written
his
William X McGregor Seal
mark

William died in December 1815.

The Descendents of Bartlett McGregor the Immigrant

It appears that Bartlett the Immigrant and his wife both died prior to the 1800 census. Bartlett, Sr. is listed there in the age range 26-44, but no male McGregor older than that is found in Montgomery County, North Carolina.

When William the Preacher died around 1808, all of the McGregors except William's daughter Avie McGregor Solomon left to go to the new state of Tennessee, admitted to the Union in 1796. Many settled in Warren County, in Middle Tennessee, southeast of Nashville. Bartlett, Sr. and his family kept going until they reached Stewart County, in the northwest part of the state. The motivation for relocation was readily available land in the new state.

Bartlett, Sr. married Anne Harris, born around 1770 in Pennsylvania, sometime prior to the 1791 birth of their oldest child, Nancy, in Montgomery County, NC. All of the rest of their children, with the exception of the youngest, Noah, were born in North Carolina. They settled in the town of Indian Mound in Stewart County, Tennessee. Many in the family were carpenters and stonecutters, and built many of the stone chimneys which still stand in and around Indian Mound. Bartlett McGregor, Jr. built the Methodist Church there.

The Bartlett McGregor, Sr. family arrived in Stewart County prior to the 1810 census. The actual census itself was lost, but was partially recreated through tax lists. Their children were:

    Nancy, born Feb 21, 1791 in NC, married John H. Hogan
    Harris Valentine, born Feb 9, 1794 in NC, married Elizabeth Ann Garrett
    John McGregor, born about 1794 in NC, married unknown
    Mary Lucinda, born April 16, 1800 in NC, married John Stone
    Joel, born about 1805 in NC
    Bartlett III, born about 1805 in NC, married Elizabeth Mann
    Lucy, born about 1807 in NC, married John Mann
    Arvilla (Avey), born about 1808 in NC, married William Morris
    Noah, born Jan 3, 1811 in TN, married Sarah Allen and Mahala Duncan

Bartlett, Sr. began buying land on March 3, 1810. According to the *Stewart County Deed Book 3 and Deed Book 4*, he bought 50 acres on that date, and another 50 acres adjacent to it on the same date. On May 4, 1811, he bought two more tracts of land – 100 acres on the first purchase, and another 50 acres on the second. He purchased another 125 acres on February 18, 1813. All the land he purchased was on North Cross Creek.

Two of the McGregor sons were involved in the War of 1812. John and Harris Valentine McGregor both served in Captain Thomas Gray's Company A, formed in Stewart County as part of Col. Richard C. Napiers regiment. They entered service 28 Jan. 1814 and were discharged 10 May 1814.

The 1820 Census for Bartlett McGregor, Sr. in Stewart County, Tennessee:

< 10	Males	1	Noah	Females	0	
10-16	Males	2	Joel, Bartlett Jr.	Females	1	Lucy
16-18	Males	0		Females	0	
18-26	Males	1	John	Females	1	Mary Lucinda
45+	Males	1	Bartlett Sr	Females	1	Anne

On the 1830 Census of Stewart County, Tennessee, the Bartlett McGregor, Sr. household consists of only three people:

1 Male 20-30 (Noah), 1 Male 60-70 (Bartlett), 1 Female 60-70 (Anne)

Nancy McGregor, the oldest child of Bartlett, Sr. and Anne, married John H. Hogan, the son of Edmund Hogan and Patsy Wilburn. Edmund Hogan was born June 17, 1762, in Pittsylvania County, Virginia, and led a very eventful life. He served with General George Washington in the Revolutionary War for four years, and then went to Kentucky with Daniel Boone in about 1795, where he remained for 10 years.

John and Nancy had three children:

> William C. Hogan, born April 21, 1817, married Crotia Ann Gouge
> E. A. F. Hogan, born Feb 19, 1830, died in 1848
> John McGregor Hogan, born Jan 31, 1832, married Adelaide Cherry

Nancy and John remained in Stewart County, where she died February 17, 1855, and is buried in the McGregor Cemetery in Indian Mound, Tennessee.

Harris Valentine McGregor, born in North Carolina in 1794, was the oldest son of Bartlett and Anne. As mentioned earlier, he and his brother John were involved in the War of 1812, when both were teenagers.

Harris married his first wife, Lucy Ross, soon after finishing his service in the war. He and Lucy had four children before she passed away in 1823. The children were:

> Aliza, born in 1815
> Tennifly, born in 1818, married to Asa Yarborough
> Frances, born in 1820
> John, born in 1823

Harris and Lucy were on the 1820 Census of Stewart County:

> 2 Males, age 0-10   Tennifly, Unknown
> 1 Male, age 26-45   Harris
> 1 Female, age 1-10   Aliza
> 1 Female, age 10-16   Unknown
> 1 Female, age 16-26   Lucy

After Lucy's death, Harris married Elizabeth Ann Garrett. Harris Valentine McGregor, Sr. moved his family to Trigg County, Kentucky by 1845, when his son, Harris Valentine McGregor, Jr., was born. His final son, Montague M. McGregor, was born in 1849, also in Trigg County.

The 1830 Census of Stewart County show Harris Valentine, Sr. with a family of six:

> Male 5-10   1   Unknown
> Male 10-15   2   Tennifly, John
> Male 30-40   1   Harris, Sr.
> Female 10-15   1   Frances
> Female 40-50   1   Elizabeth Ann (she was actually about 28)

The family was still living in Trigg County when Harris, Sr. died in 1854. Harris, Jr. was still living in Trigg County with his mother on the 1860 Census, but by the time of the 1870 Census, he had relocated his family to Upshur County, Texas. In 1900, the family was located in Dallas, Texas, where he died in 1907.

John McGregor was the second son of Bartlett, Sr. and Anne McGregor. He was born about 1794, so he conceivably could be older than Harris Valentine, Sr., or John and Harris, Sr. could be twins. In any case, the two were evidently very close in their younger years, and they served together in the War of 1812, at age 18. The only other information found regarding John were the birth of two sons, Andrew, born about 1830, and Gramm, born about 1835.

The next child born to Bartlett, Sr. and Anne was Mary Lucinda McGregor, born in North Carolina about 1800. She appeared on the 1820 Census of Stewart County as a female in the 16-26 age range. By the time of the 1830 Census, she was no longer living in the household. She is believed to have married John Stone prior to 1830.

The next children born to Bartlett, Sr. and Anne were two sons, born in North Carolina around 1805. They are Joel and Bartlett, Jr. The 1820 Census of Stewart County lists two males in the age range of 10-16, indicating they are not the same person, but conceivably could be twins. By the time of the 1830 census, they were no longer living in the Bartlett, Sr. household.

The 1827 Stewart County, TN Tax List indicates Bartlett, Jr. and Harris, Sr. had already established their own households. A neighbor, William Mann, was soon to become Bartlett, Jr.'s father-in-law. Bartlett, Jr. married Elizabeth Mann in December, 1827.

Name	Acres	Area	#White Polls
Bartlet McGregor	125	Cross Creek	1
Bartlet McGregor			1
Harris McGregor	200	Honey Fork	1
William Mann	80	Cross Creek	1

Very little additional information concerning Joel has been found, but Bartlett, Jr. left quite a few tracks. As the direct line ancestor of Forrest Edwin McGregor, Bartlett, Jr. will be discussed at the end of this section.

The seventh child born to Bartlett, Sr. and Anne McGregor was Lucy McGregor, born November 30, 1806, in Montgomery County, North Carolina. Lucy married John Mann in Stewart County, on November 19, 1928. Lucy and John had eight children, all born in Stewart County:

> William T. (Billy), born 1829, married Melissa Boyd, and Unknown Duncan
> Rebecca, born 1833
> Sara A., born 1835, married Marvin Wait Tucker
> Robert Noah, born 1838, married Elmira Blane
> Martha Burton, born 1840, married Joel Harvey Gillum
> Lucy Jane, born 1846, married William Thomas Vaughan
> Nancy Fredonia, born 1849, married William Reynolds

John Mann died at age 57, on October 21, 1863, and is buried in the McGregor Cemetery. Lucy lived almost 25 more years, passing away on August 16, 1887. Her burial location is not recorded.

Another daughter was born to Bartlett, Sr. and Anne: Arvilla Ann (Avey) Mcgregor, who was born about 1808 in Montgomery County, North Carolina. She married William Thomas Morris, born in 1804, also in North Carolina. Avey and William had seven children before he died a very early death in 1838. Their children were:

> Nathaniel Newton, born 1830, married Ann Reed
> Mary, born 1831
> Sarah, born 1832
> Enoch, born 1833
> Jasper N., born 1834
> Sophronia Ann, born 1835
> Narrard, born 1836?

Avey then married Uriah Tyson, a much older, but quite wealthy man. They had one child, Harriet F. Tyson, born 1839 in Tennessee.

Noah McGregor was the youngest child of Bartlett, Sr., and Anne McGregor, and the only one to be born outside of the state of North Carolina. He was born on January 3, 1811, in Indian Mound, Tennessee. Noah was very active in community affairs, starting with Grand Jury service when he was only 21.

In 1838-1839, when Noah was about 27, the Index to Volunteer Soldiers in Indian Wars and Disturbances lists him as having served in Wallace's Company of the 3rd Batallion of Tennessee Infantry in the Cherokee War. Some Indian tribes, especially the Cherokees, refused to leave their homelands east of the Mississippi River. In 1838, U.S. troops began forcibly removing the Cherokee Indians from their homes in North Carolina, Tennessee, Alabama, and Georgia.

Many of the Indians died of disease, starvation, or exposure. Because of the tragic nature of this journey, it was called the "Trail of Tears." By 1850 most of the Indians had been removed to the area that is now the state of Oklahoma.

On April 7, 1845, Noah McGregor was listed by the Stewart County Court Records as the administrator in the settlement of the Bart McGregor estate, following the death of his father. In this role, Noah was the author of my all time favorite legal statement in a probate document. From the *Stewart County TN Probate Records Roll #53 Vol E*: "Know all men by these presents that we Noah McGreggar, A. Wallace and James Wilson all of the County of Stewart and State of Tennessee are held and firmly bound with the gov in and over the state of Tennessee or his successors in office and the sum of Eight Hundred Dollars to be paid to the said governor or his successor in office or their assigns which payment well and freely to be made ... bound ourselves overheirs, executors and ... jointly and severally firmly by these presents sealed with our seals and on this second day of January 1843- the condition of the above assignation is such that if the above bound Noah McGreggar, Administrator of all and singlular the goods and chattles Rights and credits of Bartlett McGreggar, deceased do make and cause to be made a true and perfect inventory of all and singluar the goods and chattles Rights and credits of the deceased which———— **and so on, as written by lawyers who are paid by the word and say the same thing over and over.**" The document goes on to state that "It appears that no last will or testament was made by the deceased." It was signed for the January, 1843 Court by Noah McGreggar, James Wilson, and A. Wallace.

Noah was the only son to remain at the old home place in Stewart County, Tennessee when the rest of his brothers moved to Kentucky, Mississippi, and Texas.

Noah's first wife was Sallie Sarah Allen. They were married December 29, 1831, but unfortunately it was a short-lived marriage. Sarah died of cholera on July 29, 1834. By that date, Noah and Sarah had two children, William Bartlett McGregor, born September 30, 1832, and Priscilla Elizabeth McGregor, born May 20, 1834.

Sarah, her sister, Nellie, and the two children all had cholera at the same time. Sarah and her sister both died from the disease. The doctor had ordered that no water be given to those sick with cholera, but Noah disobeyed the doctor's orders, and gave water to his two children when they cried for water. When it was later determined that water was essential for recovery from cholera, Noah was credited with saving his children's lives.

William Bartlett McGregor married Ruth Ellen Shrader on December 20, 1853, in Montgomery County, Tennessee. William and Ruth had 13 children:

>   Leonora Isabella (1857 - 1859)
>   Charles Franklin (1860 - 1931), married Lavania Lewis
>   William Emmett (1861 - 1928), married Lucy Walker
>   Clarence Pinkney (1863 - 1956), married Louie Smith, Melinda Vaughn
>   Washington (1865 - 1868)
>   Elner Elizabeth (1866 - 1868)
>   Noah Lee (1869 - 1890), married Ellie Boyd
>   Dr. Hiram Chase (1871 - 1925)
>   Albert Leslie (1874 - 1933), married Lillie Green
>   Tilden Plummer (1876 - 1957), married Ora Lewis
>   Florence Ellen (1878 - 1952), married Joseph Harper
>   Clayton Haliday (1881 - 1962), married Ida Eldridge Smith
>   Cordia A. (1884 - 1887)

Priscilla Elizabeth McGregor married Alsey Fawcett on September 9, 1855. They had three children:

>   William Bradford (1856 - 1896)
>   Green Harris (1858 - ?)
>   Alsey Franklin (1860 - ?)

Twelve years after the death of his first wife, Noah McGregor married Mahala Duncan on March 29, 1846. Noah and Mahala had seven children:

    Daniel Chase (1847 - 1915), married Florence Rossiter
    Marion Franklin (1850 - 1855)
    Lucy Ann Savanna (1854 - 1929), married N. Elems Yarborough
    Manson Clayton (1856 - 1920), married Sallie A. Tippit, Ludie Equals
    Mary Leona (1859 - 1909), never married
    Noah Edward (1863 - 1893), never married
    Nannie Susan (1865 - 1903), married Willie Mann

Noah McGregor died August 4, 1885, in Indian Mound, Tennessee, and is buried in the McGregor Cemetery with so many of his family. Mahala died November 3, 1913, and is buried in the McGregor Cemetery as well.

Bartlett McGregor, Jr.

As stated in the previous section, Bartlett McGregor, Jr. and his family left Stewart County, Tennessee prior to the 1840 census. Tracing their route to Texas from there is not a straight-forward search, but some documents published in Brazos County, Texas, which became their permanent home, provides insight into the path they took.

The most complete reference comes from an obituary published in *The Texas Baptist* in 1860, the year of death for Elizabeth McGregor. It provides a lot of information concerning the history of the Bartlett, Jr. family, and has credibility since it was written down by the Clerk of the Minter Spring Baptist Church, who happened to be her son, Joel Henderson McGregor, (although it is a little flowery): "Sister Elizabeth McGregor is no more in our midst. Her pure spirit passed away from the earth on the 28th of July, 1860. She was the daughter of William and Patsy Mann, and was born in Halifax County, Virginia, on the 19th of February, 1807. She removed with her parents to Tennessee and was married to Bro. B. McGregor in Montgomery Co. (sic) in December, 1827. After remaining here three years they settled in Hinds County, Miss., where she professed religion and was buried in holy baptism in the spring of 1841, by that eminently devoted servant of God, Elder Moses Granbury. In 1843 she and her husband removed to Texas and united with the Washington Church, under the pastoral care of Elder Wm. M. Tryon, the great pioneer missionary. In 1856 she settled, with her husband, in this neighborhood, and in 1857, with nine others, united in the constitution of this (the Minter Spring) church and continued an active and useful member, till on the 28th of July, the Master said, "it is enough, come up higher." Her disease was dropsy of the chest. She bore her afflictions with great Christian fortitude. Her hopes hovered around the sweet promises of God, and she talked calmly about the child she was leaving behind, and her sweet home in the skies, even till her last hour. Resolved, therefore, that in the death of sister McGregor this church has lost one of its brightest gems, her husband an affectionate wife, and their six children a devoted mother and this community a good neighbor, who was loved more and more as she was better known. Resolved, that we deeply sympathize with our dear brother and his esteemed family in his sad bereavement; yet we bow in meek submission to Him who is too wise to err, and too good to do wrong, and he has said, "blessed are the dead which die in the Lord, from henceforth; yea saith the spirit that they may rest from their

labors and their works do follow them." Resolved, that these resolutions be spread on our minutes, and a copy of the same be sent to the Texas Baptist for publication, and that the Tennessee Baptist be requested to republish them. Done by order of conference, Minter Spring Church. Thomas Eaton, Moderator.
Joel H. McGregor, Clerk. Brazos Co., Texas, Sept. 9, 1860. Texas Baptist (Anderson), 27 Sept.1860, p.2."

This information provides a lot of search assistance in tracking the movement of the family, and matches subsequent censuses regarding Bartlett, Jr. and Elizabeth. They appear in the 1830 Census of Stewart County with a male less than five, Joel Henderson McGregor, who was born February 7, 1830, and will be more fully discussed in a later section of this chapter. Bartlett, Jr. is listed in the age range 20-30, and his wife, Elizabeth Mann McGregor, is in the same age bracket.

William Bartlett McGregor, the next son of Bartlett, Jr. and Elizabeth, was born in 1834, in Tennessee. Several months later, Bartlett McGregor, Jr. was given Land Grants in Madison County, Mississippi in 1834 and 1840, Issue Date: 10/9/1834
Land Office: Mt. Salus
State: MISSISSIPPI
Acres: 80.37
W[1/2]SW Section 15/ 7-N 1-E No Choctaw MS Madison

After the move to Mississippi, two more children were born, Sarah Martha McGregor, born April 4, 1835, and Eliza L. McGregor, born about 1840. The Bartlett, Jr. family remained in Mississippi until 1843, when they relocated to Texas to take advantage of the massive amount of readily available land there.

After arriving in Texas, the McGregor Family moved around quite a bit looking for their permanent home. They lived for about a year in Robertson County (Washington-on-the-Brazos and Independence), then moved to Burleson County, and lived there several years. John H. (Jack) McGregor was the first of Bartlett, Jr.'s children born in Texas. He was born in Burleson County in October, 1844.

By 1846, the family had once again relocated, this time to Washington County, where Bartlett, Jr. paid the Republic of Texas Poll Tax. In 1850, the family was listed on the census, still living in Washington County, Texas.

Joel Henderson McGregor went back to Burleson County, and brought a bride home with him. According to the *Burleson County Marriages Book, Volume 1*, Joel H. McGREGOR was married to Margaret J. GRIFFIN on Feb. 17, 1852 [groom: WashingtonCo].

Finally, around 1856, the family had moved one more time, and settled for good in Millican, in Brazos County. Bartlett, Jr. had received a pair of land grants in Brazos County patented in 1860, 640 acres total: Texas General land Office in Austin.

Survey	Blk	Grantee	Leag Section Abs
BARTLETT MCGREGOR		B. MCGREGOR	171
BARTLETT MCGREGOR		B. MCGREGOR	170

This grant was followed by two more grants, patented in 1861 and 1862, for an additional 640 acres. Two sections of land made Brazos County a great place to put down permanent roots.

The Brazos Genealogist - Vol 13 reported that the Minter Spring Baptist Church, Brazos County, was organized the 4th Lord's Day in September, 1857. Among the nine people who were first added into the organization on that Sunday were Bartlett McGregor, Joel McGregor, undecipherable McGregor (possibly Elizabeth), and Margaret McGregor (Joel H. McGregor's new wife). J. H. McGregor was elected as the first clerk of the church.

As written earlier, their joy at finding their new home in Brazos County was dampened significantly with the death of Elizabeth Mann McGregor, the wife of Bartlett, Jr., in July, 1860. Her burial location is unknown.

The 1860 Census of Brazos County listed a smaller Bartlett McGregor, Jr. family. Elizabeth had passed away, and Joel H. and Sarah Martha had both married and moved to their own households. William Bartlett, Eliza L., John H., and Madera A. McGregor were still living with Bartlett, Jr., along with Ann Simmons and Caroline Burk.

In 1865, Joel Henderson and William Bartlett McGregor each were listed on the Brazos County Property Tax Rolls as responsible for taxes of 320 acres each of the original Bartlett McGregor, Jr. land grants. Evidently Bartlett, Jr. had retired and passed his land on to his children.

Bartlett McGregor, Jr. passed away in Brazos County, Texas, between 1868 and 1870. His burial location is unknown. He fought in the Civil War with the Texas 4th Infantry, Company G.

Bartlett, Jr. and Elizabeth had a total of 6 children. The oldest was Joel Henderson McGregor, who is a direct line ancestor of Forrest Edwin McGregor, and will be discussed in the next section.

The second child born to Bartlett, Jr. and Elizabeth was William Bartlett McGregor, born about 1834 in Stewart County, Tennessee. William Bartlett went to Mississippi, and then ultimately to Brazos County, Texas, but very few records are left which reference his name. He appeared on the 1850 and 1860 Census of Brazos County, listing Bartlett McGregor as head of household, but his date of death and burial location are unknown.

Sarah Martha McGregor was one of the two children born in Mississippi to Bartlett, Jr. and Elizabeth. She was born April 4, 1835, in Hinds County, Mississippi, and is listed on the 1850 Census of Washington County, Texas, living in the Bartlett McGregor, Jr. household. She married Samuel D. Harlan in Washington County, Texas, on December 15, 1852.

The first two children of Sarah and Samuel Harlan were both born in Texas, Mary Elizabeth, born in 1853 and Samuel D. Harlan, born in 1866. The family then relocated to Chicago, where Samuel was in mining. Ada M. Harlan was born there in 1872. They returned to Texas for the birth of their last two children, Lillie, in 1874, and Robert in 1875. The family had returned to Chicago in time for the 1880 census.

Seven years later, in 1887, Samuel Dawson Harlan died in Waukesha, Wisconsin. His body was returned to Texas for burial in the Oakwood Cemetery in Austin. Sarah died in 1918 in Austin, and is buried beside Samuel in the Oakwood Cemetery.

Mary Elizabeth married a Guinard, and remained in Chicago until her death in 1924, when she was also returned to Austin for burial. Samuel, (who married Annie Mattinglee), Ada Harlan Bartholomew, and Robert were all living in Austin when they passed away, and are buried in Oakwood Cemetery with their parents and siblings. Lillie was married to W. C. Thompson when she died in Los Angeles in 1925, and once again, was brought home to Texas to be buried in the Oakwood Cemetery.

Eliza L. McGregor, the other child of Bartlett, Jr. and Elizabeth McGregor who was born in Mississippi, was on the 1850 and 1860 Census, living with her parents, but no further information has been found regarding her life.

John H. (Jack) McGregor, was born in Texas in October, 1844, the first child born to Bartlett, Jr. and Elizabeth in the Lone Star State. He married twice, first to Ann H. Rector Millican, the widow of Wesley J. Millican, on October 26, 1865, in Brazos County. The next year, they had their first child: Virginia (Jennie) McGregor, born August 24, 1866, in Brazos County. Virginia married James Farquhar in Brazos County in 1885, and over the next thirteen years they had six children:

    William Eaves, born 1885, married Ethel Camp
    Albert O., born 1889, no record of marriage
    Anna Belle, born 1892, no record of marriage
    Florence, born 1893, no record of marriage
    Essie, born 1894, married Ernest Lockett Kennard
    James Edward, born 1895, married Marjorie Echols

Virginia died March 2, 1898, and is buried in Minter Spring Cemetery.

Alice McGregor, born December 7, 1874, married Albert Sidney Grant on June 1, 1898, but there is no record of any children. Alice died December 20, 1945, and is buried in Oakwood Cemetery in Austin.

Emmett McGregor was born about 1877, but there is no further record found regarding his life.

Madora McGregor was the last child born to John and his first wife, Ann Rector Millican McGregor. She was born June 15, 1882, and never married. She died May 26, 1915, and is buried in Oakwood Cemetery in Austin.

Ann McGregor died sometime between the birth of Madora and 1886, when John married his second wife, Ella Dowling, on November 3, 1886. John and Ella had three more children:

Annie, born 1887, married W. C. (Dollie) Boyett, Ernest Seeger
Walter Bartlett, born 1889, married Ollie Ruth Steele
Dolly, born and died 1898, never married

Seven weeks after Dolly was born, the following announcement was published in the *Bryan Eagle:* "J. H. McGregor was here from near Wellborn yesterday and announced the serious illness of his wife. Their little daughter Dollie, age 1 month 21 days, died last Thursday and was buried Friday. They have the deepest sympathy from The Eagle." Less than two weeks later, the *Eagle* published another notice: "Mrs. Ella McGregor, wife of J.H. McGregor, died yesterday morning at 3:45 o'clock at the home of Mrs. M.L. Royall, near Bryan. She leaves a husband and two children and other relatives, as well as a very large circle of friends to mourn her loss. Mrs. McGregor was a member of the Baptist church and was born and raised in Brazos County, being much beloved by all that knew her. In her last illness all that loving care and medical attention could do were exerted in her behalf without avail. The funeral will take place this morning at 10 o'clock at Minter Spring near Wellborn."

This was a time of a great deal of sorrow in the life of John H. McGregor. Less than a year before, he had this notice placed in the *Bryan Eagle* concerning the death of not a family member, but a close family friend of many years:

"African American deaths in *Brazos County Newspaper*:
Mr. J.H. McGregor of Wellborn, one of Brazos County's oldest and best citizens, brings to the *Eagle* a request from numerous citizens of Wellborn and vicinity that the death of Ned McGregor, colored, be appropriately mentioned in view of the sincere regard for the deceased Negro's worth entertained by those who knew him. Ned McGregor was born March 5, 1830, and died Sept. 30, 1897. Mr. B. McGregor brought him to this state in 1843. He was a good servant until he was freed, when Mr. McGregor gave him a home. For 25 years he was a member of the Methodist Church, and he was all his life a good honest citizen, respected by white and colored people. Those whom he had served so faithfully administered to his wants in his last illness, and many attended

his funeral. He leaves a wife and four children." (weekly) *Bryan Eagle*, 7 October 1897.

John H. McGregor passed away May 19, 1906, and is buried in the Minter Spring Cemetery, beside his wife and other members of his family.

The youngest child of Bartlett, Jr. and Elizabeth was Madora A. McGregor, born about 1848. The only information available is a possible marriage to Samuel Burck in Galveston, Texas, on April 11, 1866, when she was 18 or 19. She died a year later, on August 16, 1867, and is buried in the Old City Cemetery in Galveston.

Joel Henderson McGregor

Joel Henderson McGregor was the first child born to Bartlett McGregor, Jr. and Elizabeth Mann McGregor. He was the grandfather of Forrest Edwin McGregor, husband of Mary Adelia Gibbons McGregor.

Joel was born February 7, 1830, in Stewart County, Tennessee. As mentioned earlier, he married his first wife, Margaret J. Griffin, on February 7, 1852, in Burleson County, Texas. Margaret was the daughter of Joseph B. Griffin, whose roots were in South Carolina, and his wife, Rebecca Jewell Griffin.

Joel was a Brazos County rancher, and served as a County Commissioner for eight years. He used these leadership skills in the Civil War, serving as a 1st Sergeant in Texas Waul's Legion Company A.

Joel and Margaret McGregor were very active in the Minter Spring Baptist Church. They were founding members in 1857, and Joel served for many years as Church Clerk.

The couple had three children. James Clarke McGregor was their first child, born in 1852. He was a direct line ancestor of Forrest Edwin McGregor, and will be discussed in detail at the end of this section.

The next child born to Joel and Margaret was another son, William Bartlett McGregor, born in 1854 in Brazos County. William Bartlett was a farmer, and lived his whole life in Brazos County. He was one of three young farmers listed on 1880 Brazos County census, age 26, in the household of C. D. Taylor. The third person listed in the household was A. L. McLeod, who later married William Bartlett's sister Mattie.

On December 16, 1885, William Bartlett McGregor and Theodocia Iris (Dosia) Jones, born in April, 1864, were married in Brazos County, Texas. She was the daughter of John Henry Jones, Jr. and Martha Elizabeth Johnson Jones. John Henry Jones, Sr., her grandfather, was one of the original pioneers of Brazos County. According to FindA-Grave.Com, "The town of Boonville, Texas was established in 1841 as the county seat of Navasota County by John Millican, John H. Jones, J. Ferguson, E. Seale, and Mordecai Boon whose name it bears. The name of the county was changed to Brazos in 1842. Boonville flourished until 1866 when Bryan was established on the railroad." In one of those historical coincidences, Mordecai Boon is my GGG-Grandfather, as recorded in an earlier book, *Advancing the Frontier – The Life of Hezekiah Boone and His Descendents.*

John H. Jones, Sr. was also referenced in BrazosCountyHistory.Org: "College Station, Texas – The Brazos County Historical Commission and the Texas Department of Transportation (TxDOT) are hosting a public dedication of the Providence Church Historic Site on Monday, April 21, 2008, at 1 p.m. The ceremony will be at the historic site at the intersection of Raymond Stotzer and Turkey Creek Road. The church members donated the land with the stipulation that the state would erect or create a memorial to the founders of the church who were the pioneers of the area.

"The last members of the Providence Memorial Baptist Church were descendants of John H. Jones, the original settler of the area. Jones received over 4,500 acres on which the church stood as a bounty grant for his service in the Texas Revolution and as an early Texas Ranger. Jones' descendants deeded their two acre church tract to the Texas Highway Commission in 1940. The land was being acquired by TxDOT for construction of Highway 60. By then, the church no longer had regular services and the building may have already been gone." The patriarch of the Jones family was truly one of the great pioneers of Texas and the Brazos County area.

William Bartlett and Dosia had three daughters, Willie, Minnie, and Laura Lillian. They were born in 1890, 1892, and 1894, respectively, all in Brazos County. Dosia died in 1904, and William Bartlett McGregor in 1919. They are both buried in Wheat Cemetery, in the town of Millican, Brazos County. In the 1910 Census of Brazos County, Willie McGregor was suddenly listed as a head of household, at age 20. The three daughters were living with an older couple, Richard and Mary C. Meredith, but there is no indication where William B. McGregor was living at the time of the census.

Willie McGregor married Unknown White, and, according to her sister Minnie's obituary, was living in Norfolk, Virginia in 1963. Willie died in 1975 and is buried in the Wheat Cemetery in Millican.

Minnie Bell McGregor married Robert Dewitt Crawford and they had four sons: Lewis Dewitt Crawford (1913 – 1977), William McGregor

Crawford (1918 - 2007), and twin sons, David W. Crawford (1924 - 2008) and Herbert Lee Crawford (1924 - 1992). Minnie died in Navasota, Texas in 1963, and is buried in the Oakwood Cemetery in Navasota, along with her husband and three of her sons.

Laura Lillian McGregor married George F. Goebel in Houston on December 22, 1919. Lillian and George had three children:

> Frances Irma (1920 - 1952), married David Sorelle
> John William (1922 - 1986)
> Lillian Marie (1924 - 1979), married John Wilson

Lillian was married to Thomas Pearl Noland at the time of her death, on November 20, 1966, in Houston. She and Thomas, who died in 1954, are both buried in the Wheat Cemetery, Millican, Texas, with many of their relatives.

Joel H. and Margaret McGregor's youngest child was Sarah Mattie McGregor. She was born February 2, 1857, in Brazos County. Mattie married Alexander L. McLeod on November 24, 1881 in Brazos County. Alex and Mattie had eight children.

Their first born was Walter William McLeod, born September 30, 1882, in Brazos County, Texas. He died January 11, 1917, and there is no indication he was ever married.

The second child of Alex and Mattie was Eva Byrd McLeod, born June 9, 1884, in Millican, Texas. She married Frank Elkna Loftin, Sr., on December 18, 1906, in Brazos County. They had two sons, Frank Elkna, Jr. (1909 - 1973), and Cecil L. Loftin (1910 - 1964). However, Frank, Sr., passed away in 1915, and is buried in Wheat Cemetery. Eva then married a Mr. Shanley, but in a few years was a widow again. She was listed on the 1940 Brazoria Census with an indication that she was a resident of Oklahoma in 1835, but no record is found of her in Oklahoma. She died October 9, 1961, and is buried in Wheat Cemetery.

Alex and Mattie had another son, Earnest LeRoy McLeod, born July 9, 1886, and he also died at a very young age. He died of consumption on March 20, 1915, and never married. He is buried in the Wheat Cemetery as well.

Samuel Harlan McLeod was born May 10, 1988, in Millican. He married Jenobia Byrd on August 13, 1913, in Burleson County, Texas. The first of the McLeods four children was Florence, born about 1916 in Texas. She married William Edward Gustavsen about 1936, and they had four children, Betty Wynne Gustavsen (1938), Robert Harlan Gustavsen (1940), William Edward Gustavsen, Jr. (1944), and John Edward Gustavsen (1948). Her second husband was Winton Edward Sims. The date and place of Florence's death is unknown.

The next child born to Samuel and Jenobia was Milton McLeod, born about 1920 in Texas. He was still living with his father, along with his two younger brothers, in 1940. Milton passed away on May 8, 1979, in Brazoria County, Texas. There is no record that he ever married.

William Jake McLeod was born to Samuel and Jenobia on August 13, 1925, and he married Bernice Sophrania Hughes, although the exact date is unknown. They had two sons, William David and Samuel Charles, born in 1955 and 1956 respectively. William Jake McLeod died June 17, 1968, in Angleton, Texas.

The last child born to Samuel and Jenobia was James Allen McLeod, born April 3, 1930, in Angleton, Texas. He married Carlyne Compton Walker, and they had two children. James died August 7, 2002, in Brazoria County.

The information regarding Alex and Mattie McGregor McLeod's next child is a little confusing: the 1900 Brazos County Census shows a daughter, Dolly, age 9. The 1910 Census does not have a Dolly listed, but does list a Girley M. McLeod, age 18. Since there is no daughter listed in 1900 close to age 8, the assumption is that Dolly and Girley are the same person. It appears that Dolly/Girley never married, and passed away on August 22, 1918, in Brazos County.

The last two children of Alex and Mattie were twins: Alex Earl and Mattie Pearl McLeod were born February 22, 1894. Their story is a very sad one, as both suffered from mental issues. Mattie Pearl married R. J. Lofton, and they had no children. Mattie Pearl died in the Austin State Hospital on December 12, 1939, from exhaustion from Psychosis; diagnosed as Manic/Depressive.

Likewise, Alex Earl McLeod married Minnie Lois Bennett in 1929, and they had one child, Bessie Bruce McLeod. Alex worked in the prison system as a guard, and he died from an apparent suicide, according to the coroner. His death occurred in 1953.

Moving back to the Joel Henderson McGregor family, Margaret J. Griffin McGregor passed away suddenly in about 1868, at the age of 35. Losing Margaret at such a young age left a big void in Joel's life, but he soon married his second wife, Emily Margaret Lawrence Gay, on November 19, 1868. Emily had previously been married to William Gay, of the Gay Family of Gay Hill, in Washington County. The settlement was first known as the Chriesman Settlement, in honor of Horatio Chriesman (1797–1878). In 1840, the Republic of Texas'established a post office and renamed it 'Gay Hill' in honor of Thomas Gay and William Carroll Jackson Hill, who owned the general store. William Gay was the son of Thomas Gay.

Emily and William Gay, a stockraiser, were married in 1860, and were listed on the census of Brazos County that year. William was serving with Company H, Border's Regiment of the Texas Calvary, when he took a 14 day sick leave at home in Brazos County, where he died of pneumonia, November 22, 1862.

Joel and Emily were married six years later, and she evidently brought with her to the marriage what is known today as the Gay-McGregor-Allen House. A Library of Congress web site, https://www.loc.gov/resource/hhh.tx0603.sheet/?sp=1, provides the following historical perspective on the house: "The Gay-McGregor-Allen House, one of the first houses built in Brazos County, is probably the only surviving house that predates the Republic of Texas.

"Thomas Gay, the founder of Washington-on-the-Brazos, first capital of the Republic, arrived in Texas from Georgia in May, 1830, with Stephen F. Austin's Second Colony. Gay bought this quarter-league (1107 acres) from Robert Matthews in July, 1834. Assessed value increased twelve-fold between 1834 and 1838, suggesting a construction date for the house. After his death in December, 1838 his widow Eleanor kept the Peach Tree property, which remained in the family until 1868 (the year Emily Gay married Joel McGregor). After forty years in the McGregor family, the land passed through several owners to E. E. Allen in 1927."

Verification that this is the same land which the Gay-McGregor-Allen House stands on comes from the 1888 Brazos County Tax Rolls – Joel H. McGregor was paying taxes on the 1107 acres, original grantee Robert Matthews, the person from whom Thomas Gay originally bought the land.

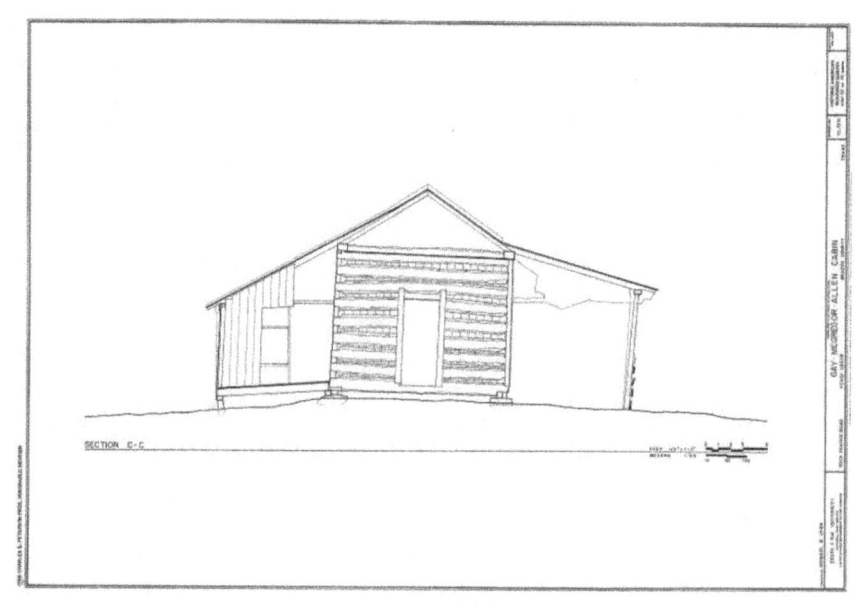

Gay-McGregor-Allen House Architectural Drawing

The marriage of Joel Henderson McGregor and Emily Margaret Gay McGregor produced three more children, with a 12-year gap between the youngest child of Margaret and the oldest child of Emily.

The first child born to Joel and Emily was Charles Bennett McGregor, born November 6, 1869. Charles married Carro Ellen Davis on February 18, 1894, in Brazos County. Charles and Carro had three children. Their first-born was a daughter, Cecile Bird McGregor, born in 1894. Sadly, she died at age three, and is buried in the Wheat Cemetery in Millican.

The next child was a son, Joel Ira McGregor, born June 26, 1896, in Brazos County. Joel Ira married Martha Louise Bobbitt on August 31, 1918, in Hill County, Texas. They had three sons, Joel Ira McGregor, Jr.

(1921 – 2018), Frank Bobbitt McGregor, Sr. (1922 – 2000), and Charles Bennett McGregor (1924 – 2017). Joel Ira, Sr. died in 1958, and Martha died in 1993. Both are buried in the Oakwood Cemetery in Waco, Texas.

Fanora Mae McGregor Taylor and Frank Bobbitt McGregor began correspondence, and shared some family history information in 1982, where much helpful genealogical information was exchanged. Because of the gap in ages between the two sets of Joel Henderson McGregor's children, there were essentially two separate families, and Frank provided some missing pieces which helped determine Emily Lawrence Gay McGregor's family background. Frank Bobbitt and Frank Bobbitt McGregor, Jr. had law practices for decades in the McGregor Building on the Courthouse Square in Hillsboro, which you can still see as you drive through on Highway 22.

The youngest child of Charles and Carro was another daughter, Ruth Emily McGregor, born November 19, 1899, in Brazos County. Ruth Emily married Jefferson Pettus Royder, Jr., with whom she had two children, Jefferson Pettus Royder, III and Gwendolyn Royder. Ruth died in Vancouver, British Columbia, Canada, in 1985, and is buried alongside her husband in the Wheat Cemetery in Millican. She was a retired teacher.

The Brazos Genealogist has an article entitled "Early Brazos County Methodist Churches", stating that when the Millican Methodist Episcopal Church was established, Charles was a church trustee when the land was purchased for the creation of the church in 1917. It is interesting that Joel Henderson McGregor and his son were both instrumental in starting new churches in small communities in Brazos County, but for two different denominations.

Charles Bennett McGregor died in Brazos County on February 24, 1947, and Carro Davis McGregor passed away 13 years later. Both are buried in the Wheat Cemetery.

The next child born to Joel and Emily was another son, Joel Algernion McGregor, born September 12, 1896. He married Martha Anna Smith on May 12, 1901, and they moved to Houston, where he was listed on the 1910 census as an assistant cashier for a newspaper. In 1920, he had become a bookkeeper for an iron works company. Eventually, he enjoyed a fine career as a tax assessor.

Joel A. and Annie had two children, Malcolm A., born in 1904, and Mildred L., born in 1906. Joel passed away on January 3, 1956, and is buried in the Brookside Memorial Park in Houston. Annie died soon thereafter, on February 12, 1960, and is buried beside him there.

The youngest child born to Joel H. and Emily McGregor was Robert Burke McGregor, born in Brazos County on April 29, 1880. He married Gertrude Hart on February 6, 1919, and they had two sons, Robert Burke, Jr. and Kenneth. Robert, Sr. was a furniture salesman by profession. Robert, Sr. died on July 20, 1931, and is buried in the Fernwood Cemetery in Henderson County, Kentucky. Gertrude lived 30 years more, passing away on April 13, 1962, and is buried beside Robert in Fernwood Cemetery.

James Clarke McGregor

Now we return to James Clarke McGregor, oldest son of Joel Henderson and Margaret Griffin McGregor. James Clarke was the father of Forrest Edwin McGregor. He was born in 1852 in Texas. He married Martha Elizabeth Graham, the daughter of a Brazos County farmer, William Alanson Graham, on December 5, 1877. The Grahams lived and farmed in the area around the Bright Light Baptist Church, not too far from the Gay-McGregor-Allen house and ranching property. The Graham family and their ancestors will be discussed in a later section of this chapter.

James Clarke McGregor

James Clarke and Martha Elizabeth McGregor quickly began their young family, and by the time of the 1880 census, their first two children were born. The oldest, Margaret Ruth McGregor, was born August 16, 1878, and Forrest Edwin McGregor was born February 15, 1880, both in Brazos County. The last child of the couple, Emma McGregor, was born December 11, 1883, also in Brazos County.

Shortly after the birth of their three children, the McGregors joined a large contingent of the Graham family to relocate to San Saba County. James Clarke and the rest of the group settled in the Algerita area, halfway between Richland Springs and San Saba. Unfortunately, James

Clarke fell victim to the McGregor heart issues, and died in 1886 at the age of 34. He is buried in the Algerita Cemetery, the final resting place for many of the Grahams and McGregors.

Martha Graham McGregor with Maggie, Forrest, and Emma

Martha Elizabeth Graham McGregor, still a very young woman, waited almost ten years before she married again, this time to Peter N. Johnson, a widower and native of Denmark. Peter and his first wife had four children who did not survive past infancy, and then four more sons before Mary Wells Johnson, his first wife, died in 1892. Peter N. Johnson and Martha Elizabeth Graham McGregor married in 1895, almost ten years after James Clarke McGregor had passed away.

In 1884, Peter erected the first rock building in Richland Springs. He had a general merchandise store, and was also appointed as postmaster. Peter and Martha had one child together, a son, Graham

Johnson, born in September, 1897. Their household in the 1900 Census of San Saba County consisted of Peter and Martha Johnson, Forrest McGregor and his sister, Emma McGregor, and four Johnson sons: Fred, Peter, Conrad, and Graham. Peter Johnson died September 30, 1911, and is buried in the Richland Springs Cemetery. Martha Graham McGregor Johnson passed away April 18, 1934, and is buried in the Algerita Cemetery.

Margaret Ruth (Maggie) McGregor, the oldest daughter of James Clarke and Martha McGregor, also met her mate for life when the McGregors and the Grahams arrived in the Algerita area. Andrew Jackson Lane had moved his family from McMinn County, Tennessee, to San Saba County in 1875, about 10 years before Margaret's family arrived in the area. On the way, the Lanes lived for a period of time in Georgia, Alabama, back to Tennessee, and finally, to Texas. In 1875, Andrew Jackson Lane purchased land east of Richland Springs and north of Algerita. Included in their family was Major James Lane, a son who was born in Ellis County, Texas, near Waxahachie, on March 6, 1874. Ellis County seems to be an initial stopping point at that time for families relocating to Texas.

Major Lane and Maggie McGregor married on November 29, 1896, in San Saba County. Coincidently, Major Lane was Uncle Major to my wife's other grandmother, Katie Marie Lane Adams, making both the new bride and the new groom direct ancestors of my wife. Major and Maggie had six children, all born in San Saba County.

The first child was a son, Hal Burns Lane, Sr., born December 8, 1897. Burns Lane, Sr. attended Daniel Baker College in Brownwood, Texas, where he met and married Bertie Cade in 1926, in Brownwood. Bertie Cade was born in Mercer's Gap in Comanche County, Texas on May 17, 1903. Burns Lane, Sr. spent most of his life as a teacher and administrator in the public school systems of Texas. He also served as San Saba County Judge from 1946 through 1948.

Hal Burns, Sr. and Bertie Lane had two children, Hal Burns, Jr. and Gwendolyn. In another coincidence, Hal Burns, Jr. was my math teacher and head of the Math Department at Howard Payne University, where I graduated with a degree in math.

The Ancestry of Forrest Edwin McGregor

Hal Burns, Sr. died at Big Bend National Park on December 2, 1968, from a heart attack while deer hunting. He is buried in the Richland Springs Cemetery, where Bertie, who passed away in 2000, is buried beside him.

Wilma Mattie Lane was born to Major and Maggie on July 3, 1899. Family lore has it that Wilma Lane and William M. (Bill) Swails had marriage plans multiple times over the years, but every time the date got close, Maggie would have an illness of some kind, and Wilma would call off the wedding to help take care of her mother. When Maggie passed away in 1945, the wedding took place.

Wilma was a teacher by profession, with a degree from Daniel Baker College, and taught in the San Saba Public School System until she retired in 1969. Wilma and Bill had no children, and both are buried in the Richland Springs Cemetery, Wilma in 1980 and Bill in 1987.

Forrest E. Lane, born to Major and Maggie on January 1, 1901, was tragically killed on August 17, 1918, in an elevator accident in Houston, Texas, while working for Bearing Cortez Hardware Company. He had worked just two days. He also was buried in the Richland Springs Cemetery.

The next child born to Major and Maggie Lane was another son, Leon Lane, born June 9, 1902, in San Saba County. Leon married Lucile Hodge, who was born May 15, 1915, in Marlin, Texas. They had one daughter, Margaret Ruth Lane, who was born July 12, 1941, in Austin, Texas. She married Calvin Ray Hector, and they had two sons, Bryan Lane Hector and Marcus Calvin Hector.

Leon was a public school teacher in the San Saba Public Schools, with a degree from Daniel Baker College. His last 23 years in the school system were as an administrator. Leon passed away January 31, 1987, and Lucille died on July 22, 2001, and they are both buried in the San Saba City Cemetery.

Ullman D. Lane, the fifth child of Major and Maggie Lane, was born February 5, 1904. His was another tragic story in the family of Major and Maggie Lane. He was a teacher in the Richland Springs High School, and died on August 23, 1928, in Lampasas, Texas, as a result of an injury suffered in a baseball game. He was only 24. He is buried in the Richland Springs Cemetery.

Cleo Lane was the youngest child of Major and Maggie, born March 19, 1905. Cleo was also a teacher, and held a Bachelors Degree from Daniel Baker College in Brownwood, and a Masters Degree from Southern Methodist University. She taught in the Dallas Public Schools for thirty years before retiring in 1975, and returning to San Saba County.

Professionally, there is a common thread which runs through most of the children of Major James Lane and Margaret McGregor Lane – service in the public school systems. The Lane children had a total of 165 years of teaching experience. What an impressive legacy, and what a tremendous asset this family was to their communities.

On the 1900 Census, Peter and Martha Elizabeth Graham McGregor Johnson were close neighbors to the Chapman family. On September 1, 1907, two of the neighborhood children, Vernon Chapman and Emma McGregor, the youngest child of James Clarke and Martha Graham McGregor, were married. They had one child, a daughter, Janis Adele Chapman. Adele was born September 5, 1920, and was adopted by the Chapmans in 1922 after her birth mother died while giving birth to her next child. Adele married Francisco Lozano Trevino in McAllen, Hidalgo County, Texas. She and Frank had four children, and are buried in the San Joaquin Valley National Cemetery in Merced, California.

Vernon Chapman was a grocer, and had grocery stores in various towns around North Central Texas. Emma McGregor Chapman died in Cleburne, Texas on August 27, 1950, and is buried in Richland Springs Cemetery. After Emma's death, Vernon married Annie Alice Garrett Burleson in 1957. Vernon died in 1962, and is buried next to Emma in the Richland Springs Cemetery.

Martha Elizabeth Graham McGregor outlived James Clarke McGregor by almost 50 years, and despite marrying again and raising another family, chose to be buried next to James Clarke in the Richland Springs Cemetery.

The next section of this chapter will discuss many of the ancestors of Martha Elizabeth Graham McGregor, including those who immigrated from throughout Europe, responding to the allure of vast amounts of free or very inexpensive land in Texas, as well as the freedoms they did not find in their homelands. Once they were here, they were willing to sacrifice for those privileges by fighting in the American Revolution, and helped establish our freedoms in this country. They made their permanent home here, because they had found what they were seeking.

Chapter Twelve

The Ancestry of Martha Elizabeth Graham

As stated earlier, the ancestors of Martha Elizabeth Graham McGregor, wife of James Clarke McGregor and mother of Forrest Edwin McGregor, came from many different countries. When many of her ancestors arrived in this country, the Revolutionary War was already on the horizon, and many of them fought on the side of their new country.

Martha Elizabeth Graham was the daughter of William Alanson Graham and Mary Ulmer, and was born November 30, 1860, in Jasper County, Mississippi. William Alanson Graham, as well as his father and grandfather, were among the first to move to new regions of the country as new land was made available to those brave enough to move their families to the edge of civilization.

William Alanson Graham, who often used the nickname "Lance", was born in Jasper County, Mississippi, on November 4, 1833, the same year that Jasper County was created out of Jones and Wayne Counties in Mississippi. He married Mary Ulmer, also a native of Jasper County, born in 1835. They married in Jasper County around 1853.

Mary Ulmer was a descendent of a large contingent of German and Swiss settlers who came to the Orangeburg, South Carolina, region, in the period 1735-1750. More will be discussed about the Ulmer family heritage in the Swiss and German connections section of this chapter.

William A. and Mary Ulmer Graham had nine children, the first six born in Jasper County, Mississippi. Their sixth child, born in Mississippi In August, 1866, was Hugh Jackson Graham. The seventh, John R. Graham, was born in Millican, Brazos County, Texas, in March, 1868. This makes the date for the migration of the family to Texas sometime during 1867. William A. Graham's parents, William and Susannah Ardalissa Terrell Graham, had fifteen children, six of whom moved, with their families, to Texas. However, his father and mother remained in Jasper County until 1882, when they moved to join their children in Brazos County. Four of the other siblings died in Mississippi before their parents moved, and four more had married and remained in Mississippi with their families.

The William A. Graham family, along with the families of many of his children, joined with the James Clarke McGregor family, and relocated once again, this time to San Saba County, where their son Forrest would meet and marry Mary Adelia Gibbons, daughter of Billy Gibbons. Once again, some of the Graham families would remain where they had established homes in Brazos County, including the parents of William A. Graham, William and Susanna Terrell Graham.

The children of William Alanson and Mary Ulmer Graham were:

Mary Susanna Graham, b. 6 Aug 1854 in MS, married Richard Dickens, d. 21 Jul 1810, buried Algerita Cemetery, San Saba County, 6 children

Jefferson Davis Graham, b. 1856 in MS, married Ellen Adella Wood, d. 27 Apr 1910, buried South Park Cemetery, Brazoria County, 6 children

Emma Jane Graham, b. 3 Nov 1858 in MS, married Thomas Browning, d. 10 Jun 1952, buried Algerita Cemetery, San Saba County, 4 children

Martha Elizabeth Graham, b. 30 Nov 1860 in MS, married James Clarke McGregor, married second husband Peter N. Johnson, d. 18 Apr 1934, buried Algerita Cemetery, San Saba County, 4 children

Laura Louise Graham, b. 12 Mar 1864 in MS, married Stephen Bailey, d. 26 Nov 1931, buried Meridian Cemetery, Bosque County, unk children

Hugh Jackson Graham, b. 13 Aug 1866 in MS, married Zilpha Wood, d. 23 Aug 1889, buried Algerita Cemetery, San Saba County, 1 child

John R. Graham, b. 2 Mar 1868 in TX, never married, d. 11 Nov 1929, Tom Green County, buried Algerita Cemetery, San Saba County

Minnie Graham, b. 30 May 1873 in TX, married John Stephenson, d. 9 Mar 1956, buried Mission Burial Park South, Bexar County, 1 child

Alberta Graham, b. 1876 in TX, married Neal Brown, d. 1949, buried Mission Burial Park South, Bexar County, 2 children

William Alanson Graham with three more generations

William Alanson "Lance" Graham was the son of William "Billy" and Susanna Ardalissa Terrell Graham, another family of pioneers who settled in Mississippi about the time it became a state in 1817. William "Billy" Graham was born December 12, 1809, in Green County, Tennessee. Susanna was born May 10, 1812, in Bay Springs, Mississippi Territory, in what later would become Jasper County. They were married before 1832 in what was Wayne County, Mississippi at the time.

William (Billy) Graham and Susanna Ardalissa Terrell Graham

As mentioned earlier, William and Susanna had 15 children, many of whom migrated to Texas in 1867, and some who remained in Mississippi. The Graham family consisted of:

Sarah Ann Graham, b. 13 Sep 1832 in MS, married Dempsey Dyess, d. 17 May 1908, buried Old Bethel Cemetery, Brazos County, TX, 6 children

William Alanson Graham, b. 4 Nov 1833 in MS, married Mary Ulmer, d. 4 Feb 1918, buried Algerita Cemetery, San Saba County, TX, 9 children

Edward Terrell Graham, b. 12 May 1835 in MS, married Frances McCurdy, d. 20 Nov 1917, buried Old Bethel Cemetery, Brazos County, TX, 4 children

John Thomas Graham, b. 27 May 1837 in MS, married Catherine Hargrove, d. 6 Mar 1930, buried Graham Cemetery, Jasper County, MS, 9 children

Simeon Greene Graham, b. 18 Dec 1839 in MS, married Sarah Wheeler, d. 23 Apr 1915, buried Union Seminary Cemetery, Jasper County, MS, 4 children

Seaborn F. Graham, b. 1841 in MS, never married, d. of measles in Civil War, 8 May 1863, buried Myrtle Hill Cemetery, Rome County, GA, no children

Wyley Graham, b. 1843 in MS, never married, d. before 1850, buried unknown, no children

James Samuel Graham, b. 18 Feb 1845 in MS, married Mary Hawthorne, d. 21 Nov 1905, buried Bright Light Cemetery, Brazos County, TX, 2 children

Andrew Jackson Graham, b. 4 Jan 1847 in MS, never married, d. 1858, No children

George Washington Graham, b. 4 Jan 1847 in MS (twin to Andrew Jackson Graham), married Jane Hosey, d. 11 Feb 1911, buried Bright Light Cemetery, Brazos County, TX, 7 children

Joseph Benjamin Graham, b. 26 Nov 1848 in MS, married Catherine Hudson, d. 6 Feb 1934, buried Algerita Cemetery, San Saba County, TX, 12 children

Mary Susan Graham, b. 12 Jan 1851 in MS, married James Pugh, d. 3 Jan 1930, buried Reads Chapel Cemetery, Jasper County, MS, 12 children

Albert Gallatin Graham, b. 19 Nov 1852 in MS, married Letha Allen, d. 18 Oct 1920, buried Union Seminary Cemetery, Jasper County, MS, 2 children

The Ancestry of Martha Elizabeth Graham

Jane Graham, b. 1854 in MS, never married, d. 1859, burial unknown, no children

Charles Hardy Bain Graham, b. 1857 in MS, married Sarah Perry, d. 1944, buried Bright Light Cemetery, Brazos County, TX, 10 children

The Graham Siblings Who Came to Texas

William and Susanna Ardalissa Terrell Graham migrated to Brazos County in 1882 after many of their children had established homes there. William died July 24, 1889, and Susanna died November 22, 1887, and both are buried in the Bright Light Cemetery in Brazos County, alongside several of their children.

Susanna Ardalissa Terrell was the daughter of John Terral, born 1784 in South Carolina, and Phoebe Dixon. Susanna evidently changed the spelling of her name to the more common spelling of Terrell instead of Terral. John Terral was the son of a Revolutionary War hero, Edward Young Terral, and Susanna Ardalissa Stephens Terral.

Edward Young Terral, often called "Ned", born July 10, 1765, in Little Pee Dee, SC, was the son of Joshua Terral and his wife Mary Ann Young.

Edward and Susanna were married December 21, 1782. Edward was a Patriot in the Revolutionary War. He enlisted from the Cheraws District in South Carolina. He is said to have fought in the Battle of the Cowpens when he was 15 years old.

The following is from *Records of Jasper Co. Mississippi* by Jean Strickland & Patricia N. Edwards, 1995: "The following story of a Revolutionary experience was told to John L. Lightsey by Edward Terral, who fought in the great American struggle for Independence. John L. Lightsey in turn related it to his son, Joseph B. Lightsey, who recorded it in his diary Wednesday, October 12, 1853. This diary is now in the possession of D. M. Lightsey of Louin, Mississippi.

"The story goes as follows: Edward Terral, who enlisted in South Carolina, at one time was with a company of men who were taken prisoner by the Tories. Night coming on, they halted. Their captors prepared their prison by cutting down pine trees and building a pen of the logs, this they called a 'Bull Pen', in which their prisoners were huddled after being tied. A guard was stationed in the door while the other members indulged in heavy eating and drinking.

"Sometime past the midnight hour when all were asleep, Mr. Terral succeeded in untying his hands, then one by one unloosed his comrades. He then told them they must make their escape, 'to stay there till the break of day was certain death, for the Tories had condemned them all to be hung the next morning'. All were more than ready to make the effort and follow directions with the exception of one fellow who was regarded as the lazy member of the unfortunate band, he having given up hope and accepted his fate.

"Mr. Terral, the leader, then announced he would knock down the guard who sat nodding at the door, run over and past him, and they were to follow suit. So saying, he laid the guard full length on the ground and the stampede followed. All passed out into the open except the lazy fellow afraid to take the chance. The constant beating of heels against the ground aroused the sleepers who seized their guns, firing after them without effect.

"On and on they ran until they reached the American camp. Here the Captain with his company pushed back to give the Tories a fight. When they reached the 'Bull Pen' the Tories were in the act of hanging their comrade they left behind, and just as the sun began to rise behind the eastern hills, a bloody fracas took place. The Americans killed and captured as prisoners each and every one of them. Those captured as prisoners, they hung.

"And so it was, they met the same fate they had planned for this brave little company of Americans whose ever present banner was 'Give me Liberty or give me death'. (Diary of Joseph B. Lightsey)"

By 1800, Edward Young Terral was in Marlboro County, South Carolina. By 1810, he was in Washington County, Alabama (Mississippi Territory). By 1812, he was on the Wayne County, Mississippi, tax rolls, and by 1819, he was on the Covington County, Mississippi tax rolls, where he was listed on the 1820 census. By 1823, he was in Copiah County, Mississippi, and by 1827 he was in Jones County, Mississippi, where he also appeared on the 1830 census. He died in 1833 in Jasper County, Mississippi, on the same property that was earlier in Wayne County.

William "Billy" Graham was the son of William Benjamin Graham, who was born about 1780 in Mecklenburg County, North Carolina. William Benjamin Graham married Nancy Anna Taylor in Wayne County, Mississippi, and in addition to William "Billy" Graham, they had at least five other children, 2 boys and 3 girls. The only other child who can be positively identified is Benjamin, born about 1819.

William Benjamin Graham was listed on the 1820 Census of Wayne County, as well as the tax rolls for Wayne County from 1816-1825. He died in about 1825, and Nancy began to appear as head of household on the 1830 census, along with William "Billy", Benjamin, and one young male child.

William "Billy" Graham was married to Susanna Ardalissa Terrell right after the 1830 census. In 1833, Jasper County was formed from Wayne and Jones County, so William and Susanna appeared on all the Jasper County censuses until 1882, when they moved to Texas.

Nancy Graham relocated to Clarke County, Mississippi, along with Benjamin, and both appeared on the 1840 and 1850 censuses there. After the 1850 census was taken for Clarke County, Benjamin married Martha, and in 1854, they had a son, William Graham. After Benjamin was married, Nancy moved in with her son William "Billy" Graham, and appeared on the 1860 census with his family. Nancy was not listed on any census subsequent to 1860, and it is assumed she died before the 1870 census. With the exception of the four Graham children who were still alive in 1882 when William "Billy" and Susanna moved to Texas, the William "Billy" Graham family era in Mississippi had ended.

Chapter Thirteen

Swiss and German Connections

When William Alanson Graham married Mary Ulmer in Mississippi, a whole new set of cultures were introduced into the McGregor/Graham family line. Mary Ulmer descended from German-Swiss immigrants, but they were not newcomers to America. Mary was a sixth generation American. The story of the migration of the Ulmers and related families is quite similar to the migration of the Irish during the Potato Famines which brought the Gibbons family to this country.

The Ulmer migration was part of the large German-Swiss Migration into South Carolina. Like the Potato Famines in Ireland, there were catalysts in Europe which fueled the immigration. For the German Protestants in Switzerland, the religious freedoms in America offered a refuge from religious persecution. This was the reason many Germans had already fled to Switzerland. Also, land rights for Protestants did not exist in Germany, but the land rights offered to others in South Carolina were extended to the German Protestants as well. For the Swiss, the primary attraction was economic.

According to *Orangeburgh German-Swiss Genealogical Society*, the first sixty years of history in the Province of South Carolina shows that colonists either settled on the coast or in the immediate vicinity. To induce settlers to the undeveloped "backcountry", a wilderness inhabited by only a few white traders and Indians, eleven townships were formed to be called The King's Bounty Land.

Each township contained 20,000 acres, encircled by a strip of land six miles wide to be held for future expansion. The decision, which was to leave a deep impression upon the character of the South Carolina people, was the policy which extended these land rights to Protestants of Europe. While other nationalities also settled in the townships, it was the Swiss and Germans that composed the greater number of these first settlers.

In the summer of 1731, Colonel Jean Pierre Purry drew up a little pamphlet in Charleston, South Carolina, entitled "A Description of the Province of South Carolina". This promotional literature exalted the superior merits of South Carolina to any other place in the world. Purry not only described the vast wealth produced by the colony, but he also explained the dangers of living in Carolina (climate, sickness, mosquitoes, and rattlesnakes). The pamphlet was disseminated throughout Switzerland, and set in motion what Swiss officials called "Rabies Carolinae", or Carolina Madness.

Orangeburgh Township was one of several townships established by the Colonial Government in order to encourage settlement in the South Carolina interior. A party of Swiss settlers was escorted to the township of Orangeburgh on the Edisto River in 1735. These were the first official settlers of Orangeburgh. Among those that arrived in 1735 were Jacob Ulmer and his four sons – the immigrant ancestors of Mary Ulmer Graham. Jacob was born in Germany but later moved to Switzerland and sailed to South Carolina on May 24, 1735. He landed at Charleston, South Carolina, on July 11, 1735. Jacob lived on land in Halfway Swamp, Orangeburg, SC until 1754.

Other Swiss and German families soon followed and settlers continued to come throughout the Colonial Era. At the end of the Colonial Era, Orangeburgh District included the townships of Orangeburgh, Amelia, Saxe-Gothe, and Winton. Although English, Scots, Irish, French, and others also settled in the area, at the end of the colonial period the inhabitants of Orangeburgh District were primarily of Swiss-German extraction.

The German-Swiss migration to the New World continued as more and more lands opened to the west. During the early and mid Nineteenth Century many Orangeburgh area families migrated to Alabama, Georgia, Arkansas, Texas, Mississippi, Louisiana and other points west.

Johann Friedrich (John Frederick) Ulmer, the second generation of Ulmers in this country, was born March 3, 1730, in Neuffen Baden-Württemberg, Germany. On September 26, 1752, he married Maria Barbara Shuler, born to Hans Joerg (George) and Anna Margretha Shuler.

Frederick was drafted in the fall of 1759 for service as a private in the militia company of Capt. Lewis Golsan in Col. John Chevillette's Battalion of the (Orangeburgh) SC militia for the Cherokee Expedition. On June 2, 1767, he petitioned for 100 acres of land in "St. Mathews Parish, formerly Orangeburgh Township, notwithstanding a former Survey for his Father." 'The 100 acres was for himself as a head-of-household, and was located on Bull Swamp. His wife and seven other dependents were included in his second petition for 400 acres of land on 29 September 1772, which was surveyed on "waters of Four Holes" in Berkly County with vacant land on all sides.

George Adam Ulmer, born March 20, 1754, the third generation of Ulmers, was the son of John Frederick and Barbara Ulmer. Adam married Ann, and served in the militia under Colonel John Griffin in Marion's Brigade. Adam supplied beef and drove cattle for the militia. No date or place of death has been found for George Adam Ulmer or for his wife, Ann.

His son Adam Ulmer, the fourth generation ancestor of Mary Ulmer Graham, was born in 1780 in Orangeburgh, South Carolina. He married Mary Margaret Horger in about 1801, in Orangeburgh. The Horger family was another of the early immigrants to South Carolina. Heinrich Horger, Sr. was the immigrant ancestor, arriving with his wife Catheran and child from Bern, Switzerland, in 1735. The child who traveled with them was their oldest son, Jacob Horger, Sr., born in 1725, in Switzerland. Jacob Horger, Sr. served as a Private in Captain John Rumph's Company, Thompson's Regiment, Orangeburg, with 140 days on duty payroll dated April 19, 1773. Jacob Horger, Sr. is of particular importance to the McGregor family. He was the ancestor that Fanora Mae McGregor Taylor used to gain her membership in the Daughters of the American Revolution.

Jacob Horger, Sr. married Louise Lovey Shaumloffel in Orangeburgh in 1743. Louise was the daughter of a German father, John Shaumloffel, and a Swiss mother, Anna Marie During. Jacob and Louise had eight children, including Jacob Horger, Jr., who married Margaret Inabinet in 1742 in Orangeburgh. Margaret was the daughter of another of the original German-Swiss colonists, John Inabinet, who sailed in 1735.

The Inabinets suffered through several tragedies during their attempts to immigrate to America. John Inabinet's father, Hans Inabinet, was heading the family immigration, but died enroute, and never got to realize his dream. Another relative, Peter Inabinet, was imprisoned in conjunction with non-payment of the immigration tax, and threatened with torture. He was imprisoned in a tower, and tried to escape with a rope his friends brought him. The rope broke, and Peter was discovered lying at the base of the tower. He subsequently died from his injuries.

Adam Ulmer, Sr., the husband of Mary Margaret Horger, was the first of Mary Ulmer's family to relocate from Orangeburgh. Adam Ulmer, Sr. left Orangeburg, South Carolina, going to the gold rush in Oklahoma in 1811. He described being in an earthquake where all the rivers ran backwards, confusing the people. He sailed the Tennessee River into the Tombigbee River to the flat land of Mississippi territory. He settled on Whiskey Creek in what is now part of Perry County, Mississippi. Adam lived in Perry County from 1812 until 1838, then moved to Jasper County, Mississippi, home of the Grahams. He served as Justice of the Peace in Perry County from 1818 to 1826. Adam, Sr. still owned land on Whiskey Creek after he moved to Jasper County. Adam Ulmer, Jr. had cows on his land until his own death in 1868. Adam, Jr. would ride a horse from Jasper County back to Perry County to check on the cows. He was crossing Whiskey Creek on horseback when the horse got tangled in some vines and drowned Adam, Jr. and his horse.

Another of Adam, Sr.'s sons, David Horger Ulmer, Sr., was the fifth generation of Ulmers in America. He married Mary Lovett in 1823, and their daughter Mary was born in 1835, in Jasper County, Mississippi, the home of William Alanson (Lance) Graham. Lance and Mary were married in Jasper County in about 1852. She accompanied Lance to Brazos County, Texas, in 1867, along with their first six children. Three more children were born in Brazos County, and then in 1883, the Grahams made their final move, this time to San Saba County, Texas.

It had been a long, winding road from Switzerland, to Orangeburgh, South Carolina, to Jasper County, Mississippi, then to Brazos County, Texas, and finally to San Saba County, Texas, where they made their final home. It took six generations of Ulmers and almost 150 years, but they had finally joined other Central Texas pioneers such as the Gibbons, McGregors, Davenports, Taylors, and Grahams, in their new home. They started their journeys as Englishmen, Irish, Scots, Germans, Swiss, and probably some other mixtures, but now they were all part of a new breed – Americans, and more specifically in most of the cases, Texans.

Chapter Fourteen

Conclusion

Although they followed many different paths, the ancestral lines depicted in this volume all eventually arrived in Texas or California, seeking the same things: land, economic opportunity, religious freedom, political freedom, and security for their families, along with, for some, the prospect for adventure.

The primary individual this book is based on, William Henry Gibbons, came to the New World seeking not only to escape deplorable economic conditions in his native Ireland due to the Potato Famines, but he also came with a willingness to work extremely hard to earn his fortune. He succeeded far beyond what most accomplished, yet at the same time, always remained concerned for those less fortunate around him.

Billy Gibbons and his family came from Ireland, but others came from all over the world: England, Scotland, Switzerland, Germany, and many other lands. Not a single family in these family lines came directly to Texas or California, but made many stops along the way, always moving toward more and better opportunities, until they found the place they had been seeking.

Often, some family members stayed behind on land acquired in one location, while others moved far away to find their own land, sometimes with the possibility of never seeing each other again. They were separated by the ocean between the old world and the new, or separated by vast miles of an unexplored continent, but they continued to move forward until they were satisfied with what they found.

Conclusion

Some came as farmers or ranchers and were tied to the land. Others, such as most of the Gibbons family, came from a merchant background, and were more driven by economic opportunity. The Gibbons family all ended up in California except Billy Gibbons, whose passion was more tied to ranching. Marie Gibbons Elliott and her husband Orson tried many different occupations, including farming, and even pursued their fortunes on other continents.

Some came not even speaking the language well, but all were willing to fight for the freedoms which we now enjoy. Many fought in the Revolutionary War and the War of 1812, and some even joined in the Texas War of Independence.

Eventually, through one means or another, they found their way to Texas and California, usually with large families, put down permanent roots, and became the nucleus for a new community. 'Gone to Texas' seems to have been the motto for many of these families.

Appendix A

Transcription of Letter from Maria Theresa Gibbons Elliott to William Henry Gibbons 1888

Buenos Aires   March 4, 1888

My Dear Brother William:

    We have not had a letter from you since the 29th of Nov or at least that was the date of your last letter and we received it just before coming here. We are both very anxious to hear from you and learn how you are and the family. I sent you a letter before starting for this place and Orson has written to you last week. We had two letters from Charlie and Lydia and they said they had a letter from you but did not say what was the date of it. This is a large city but Orson thinks that it will be very had to sell books here but he has an offer to sell out to a man whole sale of course. He would not make much but he is so anxious to return home. I too would be glad to go back but I think that we are here and I want to make as much as we can before returning as I am certain we will not have the same chance of making there. It is true that we did not make much in Chile but then we had a good deal to contend with there and I am glad that we were able to leave there at all for many persons much stronger than what we were died of Cholera. If Orson should sell out we will likely leave here in May or June. Don't tell them in Cala we will go to N.Y. from there we will go and see you and then to Los Angeles. So you tell Sister Mollie that I will stay longer the next time I come to see her and that I hope to find all of the children grown. Tell Ed that he must hurry up and be ready to go to Cala with us when I leave there but I am in hopes that you all will be able to move. I suppose that the babies have grown finely. I will be glad to see

Letter from Maria Theresa Gibbons Elliott to William Henry Gibbons 1888

them again as well as their Papa and Mamma. I had a letter from Delia since I arrived here. It was dated the 26th of November. She said she hoped to be able to leave there in April. I do hope and trust that she will. I will be glad when the poor woman joins her husband again. She has suffered a good deal alone since Thomas left her. They write us from Cala that John will bring his family out in May. If they do so then Delia will of course come with her. I will be truly glad to hear of John's family being with him. John found work for Thomas up in Shasta where he was selling books. He got him a very good job there or at least better than what he was doing in SF. John is a worker and he has made money since we left there. He has been kind to Thomas and I am thankful to him for that. I am so anxious to have poor Delia leave that place that I am grateful to any one who has in any way helped her. I feel in hopes that we will all be together ere long. You write Delia as often as you can and to us also for you well know that we are always glad to hear from you. I am in hopes that you have had some good rains there and that you have prospects for a good crop this year but that you bear in mind to sell out the first good opportunity you have. You can certainly make a living in Cala without having to work so hard. Besides I want you to live near us and you know that I don't want to live in Texas. So you will have to move to Los Angeles for there is where we hope to settle. The twins will be two years old the 14th of this month. I hope that they will keep well. I will be there to make them a birthday present next year. I have many things to tell you about our trip over the Cordilleria. I stood the trip well and one day we rode sixty five miles. Orson says that I can get along in these countrys better than he can as I can speak Spanish better than he does. You direct your letters in care of the U.S. Consul Buenos Aires S.A. Don't you wait to get letters from us. You always direct as I tell you to and we will get them. The weather is quite warm here now but next month it will be cool. Hoping soon to hear from you. With much love to Mollie and the dear children as well as your good self.

From your ever loving sister Marie

(Transcribed exactly as written – see folowing scans of letter)

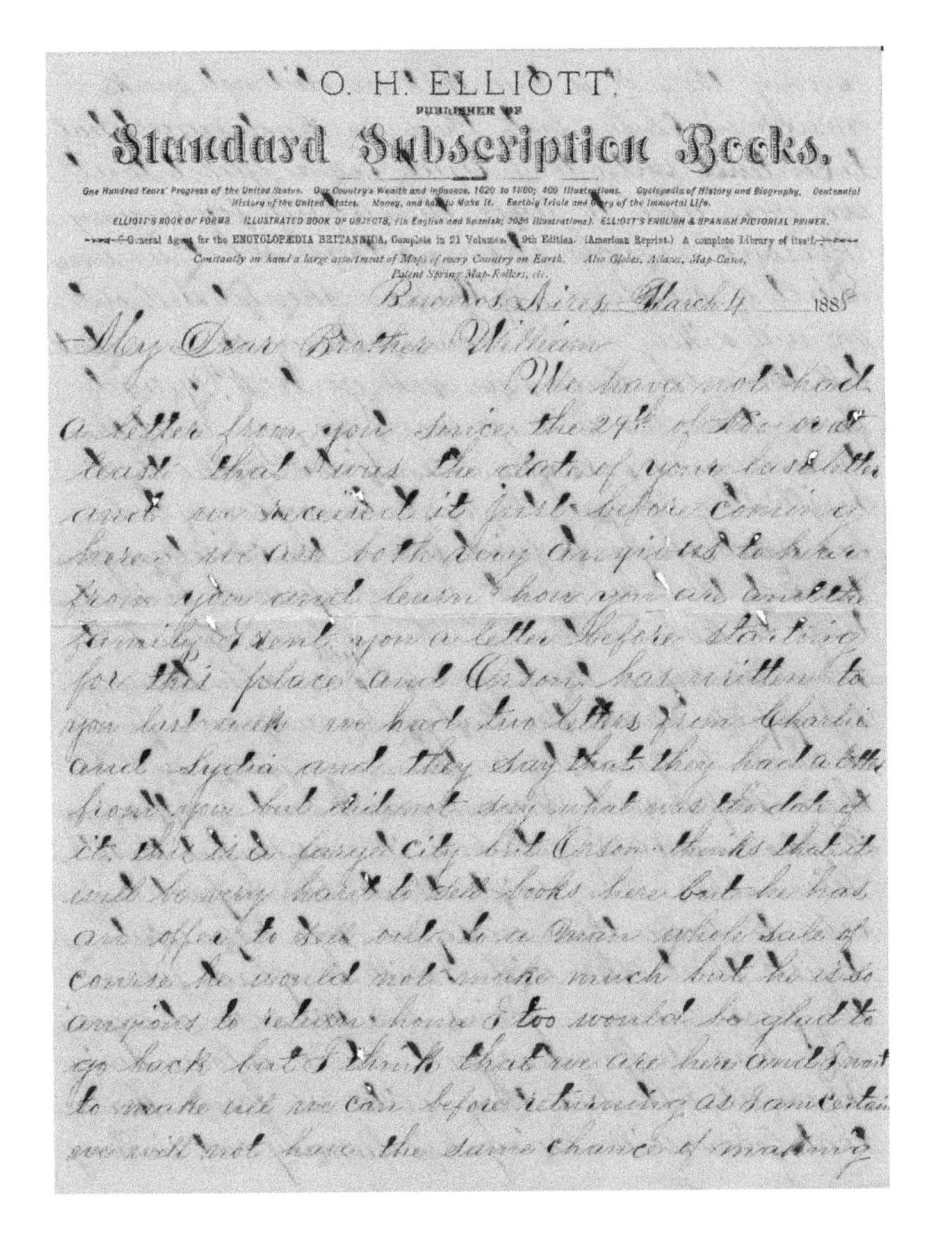

O. H. ELLIOTT
PUBLISHER OF
Standard Subscription Books.

One Hundred Years' Progress of the United States. Our Country's Wealth and Influence, 1620 to 1880; 400 Illustrations. Cyclopædia of History and Biography. Centennial History of the United States. Money, and how to Make It. Earthly Trials and Glory of the Immortal Life.
ELLIOTT'S BOOK OF FORMS. ILLUSTRATED BOOK OF OBJECTS, (in English and Spanish; 2036 Illustrations). ELLIOTT'S ENGLISH & SPANISH PICTORIAL PRIMER.
General Agent for the ENCYCLOPÆDIA BRITANNICA, Complete in 21 Volumes, 9th Edition. (American Reprint.) A complete Library of itself.
Constantly on hand a large assortment of Maps of every Country on Earth. Also Globes, Atlases, Map-Cases, Patent Spring Map-Rollers, etc.

Buenos Aires, March 4, 1885

My Dear Brother William

We have not had a letter from you since the 24th of December last that was the date of your last letter and we received it just before coming home. We are both very anxious to hear from you and learn how you and the family are. I sent you a letter before starting for this place and Orson has written to you last week. We had two letters from Charlie and Lydia and they say that they had a letter from you but did not say what was the date of it. . . . . fancy city but Orson thinks that it will be very hard to sell books here but he has an offer to sell out here. Orson whole sale of course he would not make much but he is so anxious to return home & too would be glad to go back but I think that we are here and has to make all we can before returning as I am certain we will not have the same chance of making

Letter from Maria Theresa Gibbons Elliott to William Henry Gibbons 1888

money there it is true that we did not make much in Chile, but then we had a good deal to contend with there and I am glad that we were able to have them at all for many persons much stronger than what we were died of it besides. If Orson should sell out we will likely leave here in May or June. dont tell them in Cala, we will go to N.Y. and from there we will go and do you tell them to Los angeles, so you tell Sister Mollie that I will stay longer the next time I come to see her and hope to find all of the children grown too Ed that he must hurry up and be ready to go to Cala with us when I was there last him in hopes that you all will be able to come. I suppose that the Babys have grown lively I shall be glad to see them again as well as their Papa and Mamma. I had a letter from Delia since I arrived but it was dated the 5th November. She said that she hoped to be able to leave there in April. I do hope and trust that she will. I will be glad when the poor woman joins her Husband again. She has suffered a good deal alone since Thomas left her. they write us from Cala that John will bring his family out in May.

O. H. ELLIOTT,
PUBLISHER OF
Standard Subscription Books.

One Hundred Years' Progress of the United States. Our Country's Wealth and Influence, 1620 to 1880; 400 Illustrations. Cyclopædia of History and Biography. Centennial History of the United States. Money, and how to Make it. Earthly Trials and Glory of the Immortal Life.
ELLIGIT'S BOOK OF FORMS. ILLUSTRATED BOOK OF OBJECTS, (in English and Spanish; 2030 Illustrations). ELLIGIT'S ENGLISH & SPANISH PICTORIAL PRIMER.
General Agent for the ENCYCLOPÆDIA BRITANNICA, Complete in 21 Volumes. 9th Edition. (American Reprint.) A complete Library of itself.
Constantly on hand a large assortment of Maps of every Country on Earth. Also Globes, Atlases, Map-Cases, Patent Spring Map-Rollers, etc.

188__

If so Aunt Delia will of course come with her. I was truly glad to hear of John's family being with him. When I arrived I wrote to Thomas up in Shasta where he was selling books. He got him a very good job there or at least better than he was doing in C & F. John is a worker and he has made nothing since we left there. He has been kind to Thomas and I am thankful to him for that. I am so very anxious to have poor Delia leave that place that I am grateful to any one who has in any way helped her. I feel in hopes that we will all be together ere long. You write Delia as often as you can and to us also for you well know that we are always glad to hear from you. I am in hopes that you have had some good rains there and that you have prospects of a good crop this year but you bear in mind to take the first good opportunity you have you

Letter from Maria Theresa Gibbons Elliott to William Henry Gibbons 1888

certainly can settle to living in Cala without
having to work so hard. Besides I want you
to live near us and you know that I don't
want to live in Texas so you will have to
move to Los Angeles, for there is where we hope
to settle the [child?] will be two years old
the 14th of this month. I hope that they will
keep well & will be there to make them a
birth day present next year. I have many
things to tell you about our trip over
the Andes [?]. I stood the trip well and
one day we rode sixty five miles. Orton
says that I can get along in these [country]
better than he can. He [speaks] Spanish better
than what he does. You [direct] your letters
in care of the U.S. Consul, Buenos
Aires, S. A. don't you wait to get letters
from us you always direct as I tell you
and we will get them. the weather is quite
warm here now but next month it will
be cool. Hoping to soon hear from you
with much love to Mollie and the dear
children as well as your good self
from your ever loving
Sister Marie

Appendix B

Drownings in Roundtree Cave, San Saba County, Texas
by J. Tom Meador

From *The Texas Caver*, December, 1978

Back in 1880 "Bob" Roundtree, his wife Sarah, their five sons and one daughter (1) lived at their ranch home, in northwest - central San Saba County. Nearby a windmill pumped water from a cavern lake, supplying the Roundtree family and their livestock with all the water they needed. The sinkhole entrance to this cave, which contains the lake, was located in the bottom of a small draw just a few feet from the Roundtree's ranch home.

After Bob Roundtree and his sons had finished their annual sheep shearing, they loaded the wool on wagons. Then Bob and his two oldest sons, Robert and Gillis, started on the long trip to market their wool at Austin, Texas, leaving Sarah and the younger children, in company with Miss Agness A. Terry (2), at home to tend the chores-so necessary to keep the ranch operations running.

Several days later, on Monday May 24th to be exact, a terrifying wind and electrical storm blew in. Tornadoes sometime accompany such storms and many families, in Texas, have "storm cellars" for such occasions. The Roundtree family didn't have a storm cellar, an impossible thing to dig in the thin soiled limestone karst where they lived.

In "fear of being blown away", Sarah Roundtree, her four children, along with Agness Terry, went down into the cave for protection. Unfortunately, for them, the wind and electrical storm soon turned into a heavy rain. A small river of water started flowing down the draw, cascading into the sinkhole, and rushing into the cave. Caught like

Drownings in Roundtree Cave, San Saba County, Texas by J. Tom Meador

"drowning rats in a trap", the women and children desperately tried to climb out. But the in-rushing waters swept them all back into the cave. Sarah Roundtree and Agness Terry were both thrown against the cave walls, and apparently were unconcious for a while. Luckily they did not drown.

Meanwhile the children were desperately clinging to anything that would keep them afloat. The two youngest children, Ross and Lawrence Roundtree (ages 3 and 5 years respectively) were washed still deeper into the cave where they drowned. After Sarah Roundtree and Agness Terry had regained conciousness and the torrent of water had subsided, the women and surviving children succeeded in climbing out of the cave.

"Uncle Billy" Gibbons (3) was the first man to arrive at the tragic scene. He had been out herding his sheep on the range nearby, and that evening drove them into the Roundtree Ranch as he was a "boarder" there. More help was soon summoned, and later after the water in the cave had subsided, the search for the boys began.

William F. Luckie (4) and Allen Hall volunteered to enter the cave. They began their "ghastly search" and slowly worked their way down deeper into the cave. In the process Luckie discovered the entrance to another room, which previously had never been entered. They spent nearly an hour in the cave before finding the bodies of both boys, where subsiding waters had left them.

Lawrence and Ross Roundtree were buried in the "Big Uncle Grave Yard" near Richland Springs, San Saba County, Texas.

At that time there were no telephones in the country and mail deliveries were slow and far apart. So Bob Roundtree did not know that his two youngest children had drowned until his return four days afterwards, to find his grieving family and two freshly made graves.

Agness Terry never fully recovered from the ordeal and exposure suffered at the cave. She developed a "fever" and died sixteen days later, on Tuesday June 9th, 1880. Agness Terry is buried in the same cemetery not far from the graves of the two Roundtree boys.

Footnote: (1) The Roundtree family moved to San Saba County in time to pay taxes for the year 1876. By 1880 "Bob" Roundtree had purchased his first land in San Saba County. He was a cattleman, but had apparently purchased sheep in 1880, and by 1881 he had 2000 head. In 1880 the Roundtree family consisted of: Robert M. "Bob " Roundtree, born ca. 1835 in South Carolina. Sarah J. Roundtree, born ca. 1842 in Tennessee. Robert T. Roundtree, born ca. 1856 in Texas. Gills M. Roundtree, born ca. 1860 in Texas. Larzo Roundtree, born ca.

1866 in Texas. Mattie Roundtree (the only girl), born ca. 1876 in Texas. Lawrence F. Roundtree, born May 2, 1874 in Texas. Ross M. Roundtree, born February 16, 1877 in San Saba County, Texas. (2) Miss Agness A. Terry was born ca. 18_ in Texas. Daughter of Cyrus and Virginia Terry, who ran sheep in San Saba County, (3) W. H. Gibbons, was known locally as "Uncle Billy". He was born ca. 1845 in Ireland. (4) William F. Luckie was born ca. 1857 in Texas. He was a farmer in San Saba County.

References: 1880 U.S. Census, Population Schedules for San Saba County Texas. 1880 U.S. Census, Mortality Schedules for San Saba County, Texas. Anonymous 1930. "Tragedy and History Recalled by Luckie", Frontier Times Vol. 7 No. 10, pp 434-435 July (reprinted from the San Saba News)

Capps, Joyce n.d. San Saba County Cemetery Inscriptions Privately Printed, with supplement.

Meador, J. Tom 1964 "Tragedy At Roundtree Cave" The Texas Caver Vol. 9, no. 1 January

Meador, J. Tom 1967 "Letter to the Editor" The Texas Caver vol. 12, no. 8, August

Reddell, James R. & James H. Estes 1962 "The Caves of San Saba County Part I" Texas Speleological Survey vol. 1, no 6 July.

Reddell, James 1973 "The Caves of San Saba County, Second Edition" Texas Speleological Survey Vol 1, No. 6, February.

Acknowledgements: I wish to acknowledge the help of "Pap" Murray, Edward Linthicum, Joe Ellie, and other "old timers" of San Saba County, from whom we first heard of the drownings. Assistance in the cave was provided by James Estes (with whom I first entered the cave in June 1961), Pate Cheatham, "Pete" Lindsley, John Vinson, and other Texas cavers of the 1960's.

Appendix C

A Short Biography of Orson H. Elliott

From FamilySearch.Org
BIOGRAPHY OF ORSON HYDE ELLIOTT

Orson Hyde Elliott was born 28 January 1842 in Springfield Township, Sangamon, Illinois to David and Miranda Reynolds Elliott. His father joined the Church of Jesus Christ of Latter-day Saints on 2 January 1831 at the age of 31.

His father was first married to Almira Holliday at the age of 22. They had one child, Lucina, born 3 August 1822. He went to work in New York as a blacksmith. While he was away his wife left him and went to live with another man.

He then married Margery Quick. They had four children, Edward E., Sarah Jane, Bradford White, and William. His wife died on 17 March 1831 just shortly after he became a member of the Church. He participated in Zion's Camp expedition to Missouri in 1834. He was appointed a member of the First Quorum of Seventy in 1835.

He married Miranda Reynolds on 8 March 1838 in Cuyahoga County, Ohio. He moved with the Saints from Kirtland to Missouri in 1838. They had five children, Caroline M, born 23 December 1838 in Missouri and died 16 July 1839. They were expelled from Missouri and settled in Springfield, Sangamon, Illinois where Orson Hyde was born 28 January 1842; John D. born 13 February 1844 and died 7 April 1844 in Nauvoo, Hancock County, Illinois; Jerome B. born 15 June 1845 and died 27 June 1845; and David born 24 November 1846. Miranda died from complications to childbirth on 30 November 1846.

He married Margaret Straway on 12 March 1848 in Mt. Pleasant, Henry, Iowa after they were expelled from Nauvoo, Hancock, Illinois. He had two children with Margaret. Eliza Lucretia was born 24 May 1849 in Mt. Pleasant, and Ephraim was born 1 January 1854.

They traveled to Utah with the Robert Wimmer Company leaving 1 July 1852 with 258 individuals and 71 wagons. The outfitting post was at Kanesville, Iowa (present day Council Bluffs). His father was 52 at the time. Margaret was 28. Also traveling with them were: William W. 22; Nancy, age 15; Orson Hyde, age 10; David Solomon, age 6; and Eliza Lucretia, age 3.

Orson was only ten but years later gave an account of their trek to Utah Territory. "After crossing the river all the Mormons were assembled together and then organized into companies of one hundred wagons each. As fast as they were organized they were started out on the road, across the plains. We had not been out more than a week when I ran away, intending to go back to my Aunt Laura. William came back after me, and when he overtook me I had taken off my shoes, tied them together, slung them across my shoulder, and was "humping it" for the Missouri river. How I was to get across when I got there, or how I was to reach Aunt Laura through a country of which I knew nothing, with no money in my pocket, was a problem I had not then taken into consideration. "Bill" had made enquiry from the emigrants whom he met on the road, and they had seen me and were able to describe me, and could tell him about where he ought to overtake me.

"At that time I did not think I was of sufficient importance that father would ever take the trouble to send for me. I looked down the road and saw William coming on horseback, galloping at full speed. I dodged into the brush and hid. He rode up and called out to me, saying if I would come back with him father would not whip me. I then crawled out of my hiding place, climbed up behind William, and he took me back to camp.

"I found father in great distress of mind. He had that morning received news from Salt Lake that my brother Bradford was dead. He asked me why I wanted to run away and leave him, saying he first lost Nancy by her getting married and staying behind, the Peter had run away and gone back to Mount Pleasant, Edward was in California, and now Bradford was dead. If I ran away, would he have any children left in his old age?

"The first night out we were surrounded by dense underbrush. It was almost impassable. A suitable place was found for camping. Our wagons were put in a circle formation with the cattle grazing inside the circle.

"At night, everyone was happy and sang songs and the men would teach some teachings of the gospel. At night the wagons and harnesses were repaired. The journey out west was long and tiresome. There were times when we would see as many as ten thousand buffalo in one drove. I remember one day we had to stop the wagon train to let them pass, and it took them two hours and a half to cross the road, so numerous were they. All this time we could do nothing but stand still and let them go, for all were afraid to attack them, lest they might stampede our cattle.

"At another time there were five hundred Sioux Indian families, consisting of more than a thousand persons all told, who passed, and again we were obliged to stop our train and let them cross the road. The cholera broke out among the emigrants that year, but we were spared the affliction.

"One night we were camped in a creek bottom, when a terrible rainstorm came up, and the wind blew down every tent in the camp. We were all obliged to pile into the wagon with Sarah and her family, and it was only a few moments before the whole creek bottom was flooded. The water came up almost to the wagon bed, and this taught father a lesson, not to camp again in any of the low creek bottoms.

"In September, 1852, we arrived at Fort Bridger, Green River, which was, as I remember, about one hundred miles from Salt Lake, Wade came out from Salt Lake City and met us at this point, and he brought with him some onions, potatoes, and other vegetables. He had an excellent pair of horses, so he took his family into his wagon and went on ahead. William and the McKinley family accompanied him, leaving father and his family to come on at a slower pace, as our ox team was feetsore and not able to go far in a day. A week later we reached our journey's end, and were all rejoiced that it was over." They arrived in the Salt Lake valley on 15 September 1852."

Orson was baptized into the Church of Jesus Christ of Latter-day Saints on 6 November 1853 at the age of eleven. In 1860 he was in Cumberland Township, Sierra County, California at the age of 18.

Appendix D

W. H. Gibbons Family Bible

NELSON & PHILLIPS' SUPERFINE EDITION.

NEW DEVOTIONAL AND PRACTICAL

PICTORIAL

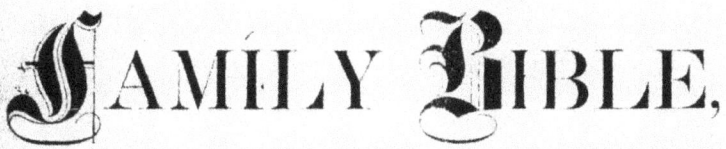

Family Bible,

CONTAINING THE

OLD AND NEW TESTAMENTS

APOCRYPHA, CONCORDANCE, AND PSALMS IN METRE,

Translated out of the Original Tongues, with all former Translations diligently Compared and Revised.

TOGETHER WITH A CAREFULLY ABRIDGED EDITION OF

Dr. WM. SMITH'S COMPLETE DICTIONARY OF THE BIBLE,

AND

A HISTORY OF ALL THE RELIGIOUS DENOMINATIONS OF THE WORLD, HISTORY OF THE TRANSLATION OF THE BIBLE, AN ILLUSTRATED HISTORY OF ALL THE BOOKS OF THE BIBLE, CHRONOLOGICAL AND OTHER USEFUL TABLES, TREATISES, MAPS, ETC., DESIGNED TO PROMOTE AND FACILITATE THE STUDY OF THE SACRED SCRIPTURES

COMPILED WITH GREAT CARE FROM THE MOST AUTHENTIC SOURCES.

Embellished with over 1000 Fine Scripture Illustrations.

NEW YORK:
NELSON & PHILLIPS,
No 805 BROADWAY.

MARRIAGES

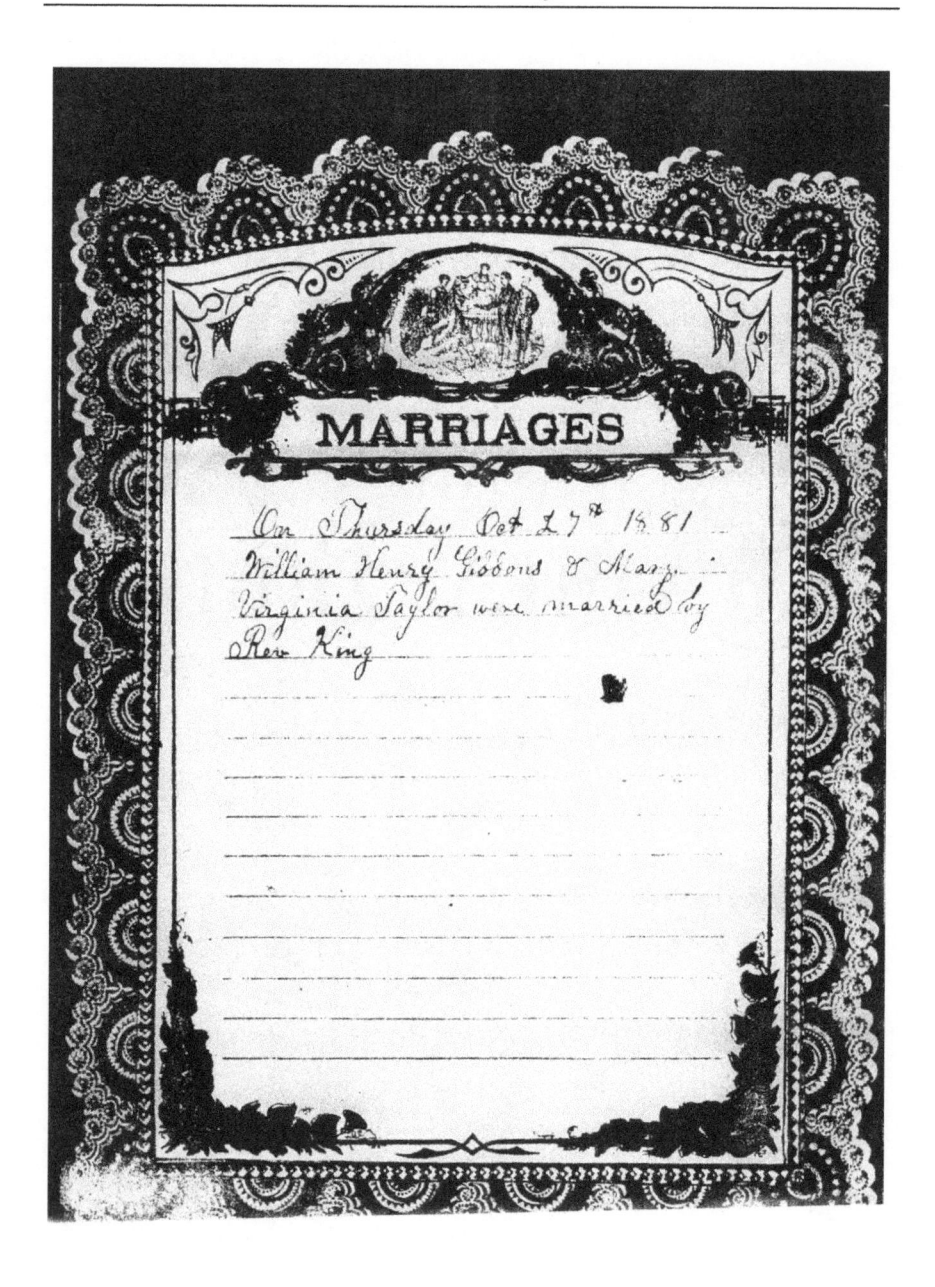

On Thursday Oct 27th 1881 William Henry Gibbons & Mary Virginia Taylor were married by Rev King

BIRTHS

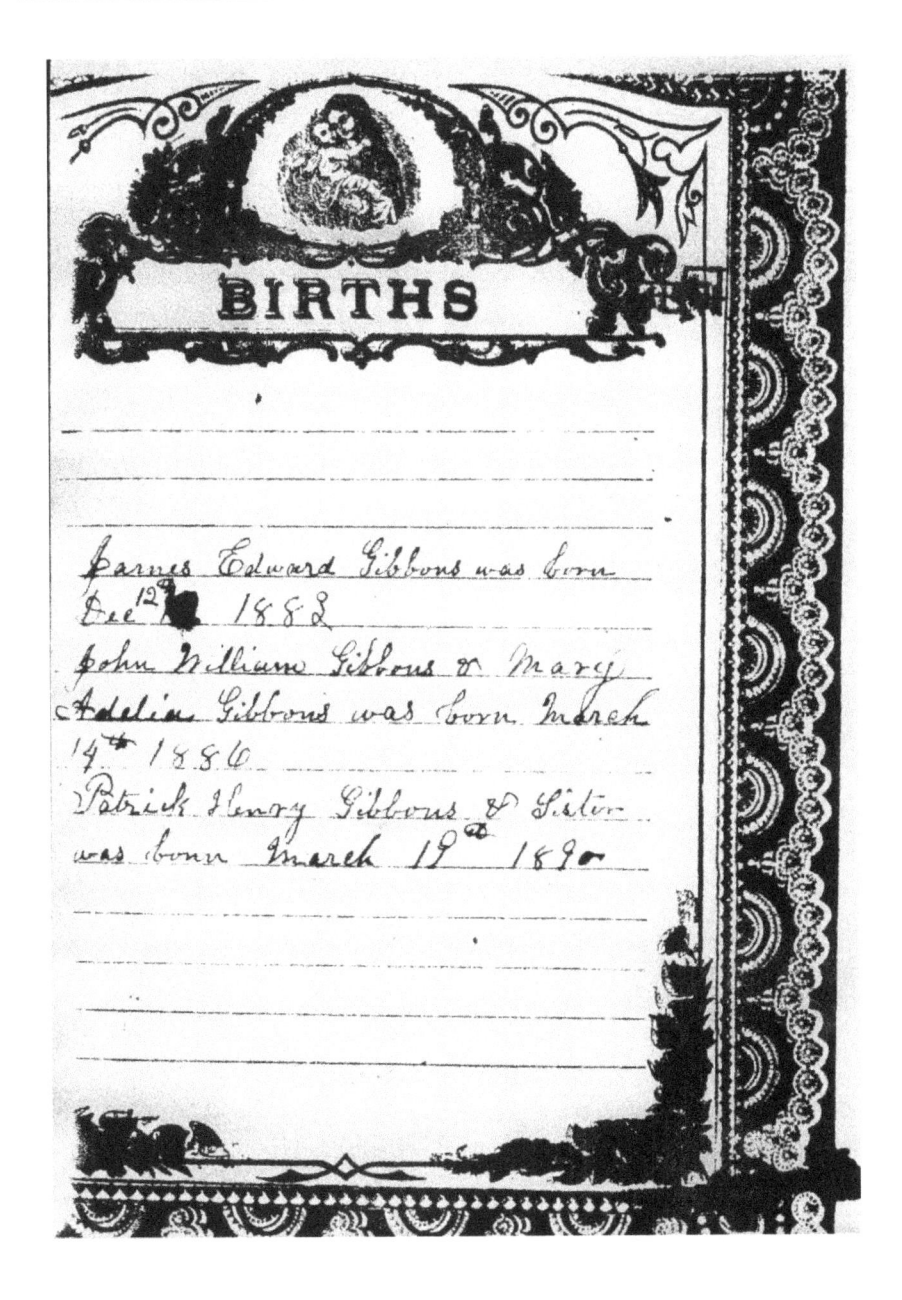

James Edward Gibbons was born Dec 12 1882

John William Gibbons & Mary Adelia Gibbons was born March 14th 1886

Patrick Henry Gibbons & Sister was born March 19th 1890

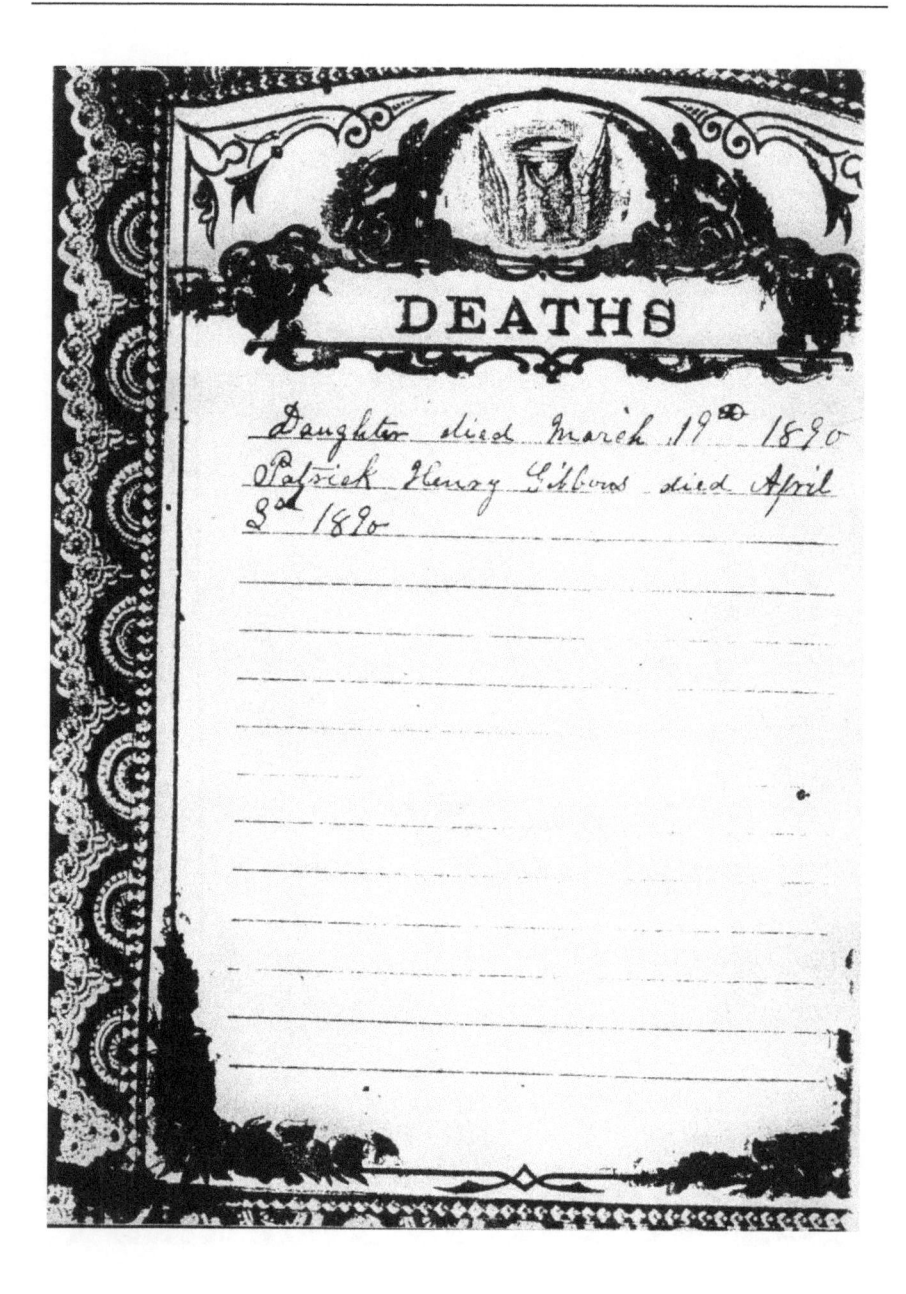

W. H. Gibbons Family Bible

DEATHS

Daughter died March 19th 1890
Patrick Henry Gibbons died April 2nd 1890

Appendix E

Deed Transfer W. H. Gibbons to O. H. Eliott

The State of Texas
County of San Saba
      Before me the undersigned County Clerk in and for the County of San Saba this day came and personally appeared O. H. Elliott assignee of M. T. Elliott a resident citizen of said County who being by one duly sworn declares that he is a bonafide settler upon 80 acres of vacant Public Land situated in said County and surveyed for W. H. Gibbons on the 16th day of June 1877 by J. H. Snellings Surveyor of said County. That he has occupied and improved the same as a Homestead for the period of three consecutive years beginning the 16th of June 1877 is married and that he makes this affidavit for the purpose of obtaining a title to the same for a Homestead under an act for the benefit of actual occupants of the Public Lands approved May 26 1873 and that he has not a homestead other than the above. This April 25 1881

      (signed) O. H. Elliott

Also personally appeared Jas. Forstad (note: the Elliott's Norwegian servant) and J. H. Allen two credible citizens of said county to me known who after being duly sworn, deposes and say that O. H. Elliott, the person first named in this affidavit has actually settled upon and cultivated as a homestead the land surveyed for the said W. H. Gibbons on 16th day of June 1877 by the surveyor aforesaid for the period of three years and that they nor any of them have any interest in said land.

      (signed) James Forstad
      (signed) J. H. Allen

Sworn to and subscribed before me, and I hereby certify that James Forstad and J. H. Allen are credible and trustworthy citizens of said county.

      In testimony thereby I hereto set my hand and the Seal of the County Court at San Saba this 25th day of April 1881

      (signed) county clerk

This indenture made this 25th day of April A.D. 1881 between M. T. Eliott on the first part and O. H. Eliott of County of San Saba Texas of the second part,

Witnesseth, that in consideration of one hundred dollars in hand paid by the said O. H. Eliott the receipt whereof is hereby acknowledged, the said party of the first part has quit claimed, remised and released and do hereby quit claim, remise and release unto the said party of the second part all their right title and interest in the following described premises in the County of San Saba ...(surveyor description of property) containing 80 acres each, the same being transferred to me by W. H. Gibbons and W. H. Bainbridge, both of San Saba County, Texas.

Signed by M. T. Eliott and signed and sealed by County Clerk

Appendix F

Hannon Family Register

78 John Taylor & Margaret his wife

John Taylor was born October 11th, 1775–	Departed this life Jan 25th. 1831. age 55 yrs 3 m. 14 d. in Montgomery co.
Margaret Taylor his wife was born March 14th, 1770	Departed this life Dec. 9th. 1830. age 60 yr 9 mo. 5 da. in the co. of Montgomery ala
John Bludworth Taylor was born Sept 15th 1803–	Departed this life in Mobile ala. aged
James Kenair Taylor was born Oct 15th. 1806–	
Margaret Maria Taylor was born Feb 29th. 1808	Departed this life 22nd. 1894. age 86 yrs. 9 mo. 23 a
Richard Henry Taylor was born Dec 24th– 1811.	Departed this life in Montgomery co. ala. aged –
Thomas Bludworth Jun. was born Sept 1st. 1768.	Departed this life Dec. 2nd. 1836. age 67 yrs. 3 mo. 1 Day in the city of Wetumpka. ala

Appendix G

Formal Requests from Billy Gibbons for Dates with Mollie Taylor

Bibliography

Brazos Genealogist, Volume 7, Brazos Genealogical Society, 1987-88

Burleson County, Texas, Marriages Book, Volume 1

The Charles Parish York County Virginia History and Registers

Correspondence on the Emigration of Indians, 1831-1833, Vol 1

Deed Book, Northampton County, North Carolina, 1759 – 1774

Deed Book, Northampton County, North Carolina, 1774 -1780

Griffith's Valuation, 1847 – 1964

International Genealogical Index Parish and Probate Records

Ireland Civil Registration Index, 1845 - 1958

Langley's San Francisco Directory

Polk's San Francisco Directory

The Quaich, Clan Gregor Research Magazine, Clan Gregor Centre, Edinburgh

Record of Estates in Northampton County, North Carolina

Richland Springs High School (W. H. Gibbons), Alumni Association and Graduates, Compiled by Richland Springs High School Alumni Association Historical Committee, 1991

Bibliography

San Saba County History 1856 – 1983, San Saba County Historical Commission, 1983

Stewart County Tennessee Deed Book 3, 1789-1818

Stewart County Tennessee Deed Book 4, 1810-1813

Stewart County Tennessee Probate Records, Roll #53

The Texas Baptist, 1860

Newspapers referenced:

    Brownwood Bulletin

    Bryan Eagle

    Richland Springs Eyewitness

    San Angelo Standard-Times

    San Francisco Call Bulletin

    San Francisco Chronicle

    San Saba News

Web Sites referenced:

    Ancestry.Com

    Brazos County History.Org

    digicoll.lib.berkeley.edu/

    FindAGrave.Com

    Forebears.IO

GenealogyBank.Com

Glorecords.BLM.Gov

GLOTexas.Gov
ObjGenealogy.Com

HistoryPlace.Com

Library of Congress, Loc.Gov/Resource/hhh.tx0603.sheet/?sp=1

Orangeburgh German-Swiss Genealogical Society (ogsgs.org)

Redfin.Com

Registers.nli.ie

Rootsireland.ie

Rootsweb.com/~txssaba/uncle.html

Selectsurnames.Com

SFPL.Org – City Directories of San Francisco Online

SurnameDB.Com

TexasHistory.UNT.Edu

Wakespace.lib.wfu.edu

Wikipedia.Com

Wikitree.Com

Adams, Mary Katherine, History Notes from Billie McGregor Adams, 2000

Arlitt, F. H. San Saba County, map, August, 1858; (https://texashistory.unt.edu/ark:/67531/metapth88953/), University of North Texas Libraries, The Portal to Texas History, https://texashistory.unt.edu; crediting Texas General Land Office

Ashburn, Sam, "Richland Springs Rancher Put $500 in Sheep and They Have Builded Large Fortune", San Angelo Standard-Times, San Angelo, Texas, June 2, 1929

Bloodworth, Travis William, The House of Bloodworth, Brentwood Christian Press, 1992

Bowser, David, "Hill Country Roots Run Deep for Rancher-Veterinarian Mays", Livestock Weekly, 1999

Burke, John, A Genealogical and Heraldic History of the Commoners of Great Britain and Ireland, Vol. II, 1835

Cawthorn, C. P., and Warnell, N. L., Pioneer Baptist Church Records of South-Central Kentucky and the Upper Cumberland of Tennessee, 1799-1899

Deutsch, J. B., Hill Country Roots Run Deep for Rancher-Veterinarian Mays, alevek@livestockweekly.Com, 2000

Hambrick, Alma Ward, The Call of the San Saba – A History of San Saba County, San Saba County Historical Society, Inc., 2011

MacNeill, Marcia Miller, W. H. "Uncle Billy" Gibbons (Facts and Fables about his life), 1998

Magnan, Nedrah Stringfellow, William Henry Gibbons, An Early Friend of Boys, San Saba Historical Commission, 1979

McLaney, Richard, Pioneer Settlers of Montgomery County, Alabama, *Pintlala Historical Association Newsletter, Volume XXVII, Number 4*, Dated Oct 2013

Mullins, Marian Day, Some Texas Land Grants, Volume 47

Neal, Mrs. Edgar T., Gibbons San Saba Ranch Grows Fine Blooded Stock, 1927

Quirl, G. G., Brief History of the Comanche Trail Council, Inc. Boy Scouts of America, September 6, 1954

Shannon, Dr. Catherine B., Irish Immigration to America, 1630-1921

Siddall, John William, editor - Men of Hawaii Volume 1, Published: 1917

Strickand, Jean, and Edwards, Patricia N., Records of Jasper County, Mississippi, 1995

Texas State Historical Association, The Handbook of Texas Online, http://www.tshaonline.org/handbook/online/index.html

Thom's Irish Almanac and Official Directory of The United Kingdom and Ireland, 1873

Van West, Dr. Carroll, and Johnson, Elizabeth, McGregor House, Rutherford County, Tennessee, and Tennessee Civil War National Heritage Area

Wigley, Donald B., Advancing the Frontier – The Life of Hezekiah Boone and His Descendents, 2009

Index

A

Adams, Billie Louise McGregor, 88, 97, 99, 100, 103, 113, 115, 117, 118, 120
Adams, Donna Louise, 117, 118
Adams, Francis, 8
Adams, Judy Muehlbrad, 120
Adams, Katie Marie Lane, 117, 185
Adams, Mary Katherine, 97, 99, 100, 103, 117, 118, 120
Adams, Norman Dean, III, 120
Adams, Norman Dean, Jr., 103, 118, 120
Adams, Norman Dean, Sr., 103, 113, 115, 116, 117, 118, 120
Adams, Shahala Deann, 120
Allen, E. E., 179
Allen, Hudson, 157
Allen, James, 149
Allen, Letha, 193
Allen, Nellie, 166
Amistead, Jane, 139
Amistead, Major William, 139
Anderson, Dr. James P., 118
Appling, Billy Joe, 95
Ashburn, Sam, 81, 92

B

Bailey, Stephen, 190
Bainbridge, William H., 43, 81, 82, 83, 84, 85, 86
Bartholomew, Ada Harlan, 171
Bartlett, William, Jr., 143
Beck, Alton, 93
Bennett, Minnie Lois, 179
Bentley, C. H., 121
Beverly, Robert, 139
Big Mama, 117
Biles, Phoebe, 149
Bingham, William H., 70
Blane, Elmira, 164
Bloodworth, Ann, 139
Bloodworth, David, 139
Bloodworth, Elizabeth, 139
Bloodworth, James, 139
Bloodworth, Jane Amistead, 139
Bloodworth, John, 139
Bloodworth, Mary, 139
Bloodworth, Sarah, 139
Bloodworth, Sarah Rooks, 139
Bloodworth, Susannah, 139
Bloodworth, Thomas, 139
Bloodworth, Thomas, Lord Mayor, 139
Bloodworth, Timothy, 139
Bludworth, Thomas Jr., 139
Bludworth, Thomas, Sr., 139
Bond, Norwood, 154
Boon, Mordecai, 175, 176
Boone, Daniel, 161
Boone, Hezekiah, 176
Bowser, David, 122
Boyd, Ellie, 166
Boyd, Melissa, 164
Boyett, W. C. (Dollie), 173
Brewer, John, 153
Brooks, Adelia Beatrice Gibbons, 3, 4, 11, 12, 32, 36, 37, 38, 45, 46, 49, 53, 54, 55, 56, 57, 58, 62, 63, 64, 66, 68, 69, 70, 71
Brooks, Austin, 62, 69
Brooks, Charles Ward, 54, 57, 66, 72, 75
Brooks, Dennis G., 69
Brooks, Eleanor Callan, 72, 75
Brooks, Ethel Mae Creamer, 69
Brooks, Florence, 63
Brooks, George Edward, Jr., 69

Index

Brooks, George Edward, Sr., 54, 57, 66, 69
Brooks, J. J., 54, 57
Brooks, John F., 63
Brooks, John J., 55, 57, 63, 66
Brooks, Kathryn, 69
Brooks, Luella Delia, 57, 73
Brooks, Martin, 53, 57, 58
Brooks, Michael A., 12
Brooks, Michael Edward, 12, 54, 55, 57, 62
Brooks, Milton, 54, 57, 66, 76
Brooks, Orson, 57, 66, 68
Brooks, Raymond J., 54, 57, 66, 71, 72
Brooks, Raymond J., Jr., 75
Brooks, Raymond J., Sr., 69, 75
Brooks, Robert, 62
Brooks, Sarah Adelia March, 62
Brooks, Thomas A., 4, 11, 12, 32, 38, 49, 53, 54, 55, 56, 57, 58, 62, 63, 64, 66, 68, 69, 70, 71
Brooks, Thomas J., 63
Brooks, William, 63
Brooks, William H., 54, 57, 70, 71
Brooks, Winifred, 36, 54, 55
Brooks, Winifred C., 57, 64
Brown, Arthur M., 26
Brown, Jean McGregor, 156
Brown, Neal, 191
Brown, Nettie Caledonia, 93
Brown, Newton C., 93
Brown, Sarah Ann, 127
Browning, Thomas, 190
Bullen, George, 148
Burck, Samuel Burck, 174
Burk, Caroline, 170
Burk, Garrett, 83
Burleson, John M., 90

C

Caffey, Thomas, 136
Camp Billy Gibbons, xi
Campion, Carney, 69
Campion, Kathryn Brooks, 69
Carroll, George Thomas, 106
Carroll, Jackie Wayne, 105, 106
Carroll, John Clayton, 106
Carroll, Monte Rey, 106
Carroll, Sheila Fay McGregor, 105, 106
Carroll, Sheila Faye McGregor, 106
Cass, Lewis, 134
Catoe, John, 154
Chapman, Annie Alice Garrett Burleson, 187
Chapman, Emma McGregor, 187
Chapman, Janis Adele, 187
Chapman, Vernon, 187
Chapple, Thomas, 11, 13, 35, 36, 38, 41, 80
Chapple, Winifred T. Gibbons, 10, 11, 13, 19, 35, 38, 41, 49, 80
Cherry, Adelaide, 161
Chevillette, Col. John, 201
Chew, Thomas, 135
Chilcutt, Anna, 136
Chilcutt, Elkannah, 136
Chriesman, Horatio, 179
Coffey, Judge, 36, 37
Collins, John Milton, 131
Collins, Margaret Caroline Hannon, 131
Conton, Florence E., 62
Crawford, David W., 177
Crawford, Herbert Lee, 177
Crawford, Lewis Dewitt, 176
Crawford, Minnie Bell McGregor, 176, 177
Crawford, Robert Dewitt, 176
Crawford, William McGregor, 177
Creamer, Ethel Mae, 69

D

Davenport, Anna, 129
Davenport, Annie, 127
Davenport, Aura Jane, 127

Davenport, Elizabeth Rusk Mann, 127
Davenport, Eudora, 127
Davenport, Fernando, 127
Davenport, Flavious R., 127
Davenport, John R., 127
Davenport, Kelbert, 127
Davenport, Luella Amazon, 127
Davenport, Luther C., 127, 129
Davenport, Lutitia, 127
Davenport, Newton M., 127
Davenport, Robert S., 127
Davenport, Septimas A., 127
Davenport, Sophia, 127
Davenport, Susan Davenport, 127
Davenport, Susan Mariah Taylor, 129
Davenport, Victoria, 127
Delaney, Sarah Ann, 125
Dickens, Richard, 190
Dietz, Logan, 148
Din, Edwin Harold, 26
Dixon, Phoebe, 194
Dodson, Elijah, 150
Dodson, Rev. Jesse, 150
Dodson, Sarah, 150
Dr. Nelson, 102
Duncan, Mahala, 167
During, Anna Marie, 201
Dyess, Dempsey, 192

E

Easton, Rev. Thomas Chalmers, 21
Eaton, Thomas, 169
Echols, Marjorie, 172
Edwards, Jesse, 137
Edwards, Mary, 137
Edwards, Patricia N., 195
Egan, Wilhelmina Kohrn, 17
Elliott, Marie Theresa Brooks, 45, 46, 53, 54, 55, 57, 59, 60, 61, 64, 66, 68

Elliott, Marie Theresa Gibbons, 3, 4, 11, 12, 36, 37, 38, 42, 43, 44, 45, 46, 49, 55, 59, 64, 68, 80, 82, 206
Elliott, Orson Hyde, 11, 37, 41, 42, 43, 44, 45, 46, 49, 59, 60, 68, 80, 82, 206
Equals, Ludie, 167
Eudora Frances Davenport, 127
Evans, Margaret, 139

F

Faircloth, Bill, 113
Faircloth, Brandon Taylor, 113
Faircloth, Forrest Baker, 113
Faircloth, Suzanne Taylor, 113
Fancher, Charles, 36
Farnsworth, Darlene Gibbons, 94
Farquhar, Albert O., 172
Farquhar, Anna Belle, 172
Farquhar, Essie, 172
Farquhar, Florence, 172
Farquhar, James, 172
Farquhar, James Edward, 172
Farquhar, Virginia (Jennie) McGregor, 172
Farquhar, Virginia McGregor, 172
Farquhar, William Eaves, 172
Fawcett, Alsey, 166
Fawcett, Alsey Franklin, 166
Fawcett, Green Harris, 166
Fawcett, William Bradford, 166
Fennell, William, 3, 35, 36, 37, 38
Fennell, Winifred T. Chapple, 3, 8, 36, 37, 38, 50, 56
Ferguson, J., 175
Fillmore, Millard, 134
Flowers, Ransford, 153, 154, 157
Flowers, Ransom, 145
Forstad, James, 44

G

Garrett, Elizabeth Ann, 160

Index

Gay, Eleanor, 179
Gay, Emily Margaret Lawrence, 179
Gay, Thomas, 179, 180
Gay, William, 179
Gibbons, Adelia Beatrice, 4, 8, 53, 54
Gibbons, Anna Rehage, 26
Gibbons, Anne Sue Miller, 93
Gibbons, Billy, 26, 71
Gibbons, Charles P., Jr., 14
Gibbons, Charles Paul, 3, 4, 8, 9, 10, 11, 12, 13, 14, 15, 16, 17, 19, 21, 23, 24, 26, 27, 28, 35, 36, 41, 42, 49
Gibbons, Charles Paul Jr., 24
Gibbons, Charles Paul, III, 24, 25
Gibbons, Charles Paul, Jr., 14, 16, 24, 25, 26
Gibbons, Charles Paul, Sr., 80
Gibbons, Delphia Inez, 93
Gibbons, Elizabeth Ann, 93
Gibbons, George William, 14, 16, 17, 18
Gibbons, Helen Herberg, 93
Gibbons, Hugh, 1
Gibbons, James, 1
Gibbons, James Edward, 89, 93, 94, 122
Gibbons, James Harold, 93, 94
Gibbons, Jane Loveland, 24
Gibbons, Jennie May, 95
Gibbons, Jennie May Walters, 95
Gibbons, John, 1
Gibbons, John J., 8, 10, 11, 35, 36, 41, 42, 49, 50, 55, 80
Gibbons, John W., 70, 122
Gibbons, John William, 90, 93, 94, 95, 96, 97, 104, 107, 108
Gibbons, Lydia, 14, 26
Gibbons, Lydia Brown, 27, 28
Gibbons, Lydia Brown Macy, 13, 16, 19, 23, 24, 27, 28, 35
Gibbons, Lydia Macy, 16, 17, 21, 23, 26

Gibbons, Marie Theresa, 8, 9, 10, 11, 35, 41
Gibbons, Marjorie Virginia, 93
Gibbons, Mary Adelia, 90, 95, 97, 99, 190
Gibbons, Mary Darlene, 93
Gibbons, Mary Elizabeth, 95
Gibbons, Mary Emily, 14, 21, 23
Gibbons, Mary Glennon, 3, 4, 8, 9, 12, 35, 41, 49, 79
Gibbons, Mary Virginia Taylor, 70, 88, 90, 91, 99, 100, 102, 107, 113, 121, 125, 127, 129
Gibbons, Mattie Elliott, 14, 23
Gibbons, Michael Edward, 3, 4, 8, 9, 10, 12, 35, 41, 49, 79
Gibbons, Nettie Caledonia Brown, 93, 94
Gibbons, Patrick Henry, 90
Gibbons, Virginia Katherine, 95
Gibbons, W. H., 43
Gibbons, Wilhelmina Kohrn, 17, 18
Gibbons, William, 8
Gibbons, William Edward, 93
Gibbons, William Henry, xi, 3, 8, 9, 10, 11, 12, 14, 16, 26, 36, 43, 44, 45, 49, 50, 55, 64, 70, 79, 80, 81, 83, 84, 85, 86, 87, 88, 90, 91, 92, 93, 94, 95, 99, 100, 102, 103, 107, 113, 119, 121, 122, 123, 126, 127, 129, 141, 190, 205, 206
Gibbons, Winifred Chapel, 14, 19
Gibbons, Winifred T., 8, 35
Gibiun, Ralph, 1
Giblin, Bridget, 3
Giblin, Bridget Galvin, 32
Giblin, Brigida, 4, 53
Giblin, Frederick Joseph, 22
Giblin, Gulielmum, 4
Giblin, Marie, 3, 4
Giblin, Mary Emily, 22
Giblin, Mary Glennon, 31, 32
Giblin, Michael, 3, 31, 32

Giblin, Michael Edward, 3
Giblin, Michaelis, 4
Giblin, Patricium, 4
Giblin, Patrick, 3, 13
Giblin, William, 3
Gibonson, Roger, 1
Gibun, Richard, 1
Gillum, Joel Harvey, 164
Glennon, Mariae, 4
Glennon, Maris, 4
Glennon, Mary, 8
Glennon, William, 8
Goebel, Frances Irma, 177
Goebel, George F., 177
Goebel, John William, 177
Goebel, Laura Lillian McGregor, 177
Goebel, Lillian Marie, 177
Golsan, Lewis, 201
Graham, Albert Gallatin, 193
Graham, Alberta, 191
Graham, Andrew Jackson, 193
Graham, Benjamin, 196
Graham, Charles Hardy Bain, 194
Graham, Emma Jane, 190
Graham, George Washington, 193
Graham, Hugh Jackson, 189, 191
Graham, James Samuel, 193
Graham, Jane, 194
Graham, Jefferson Davis, 190
Graham, John R., 189, 191
Graham, John Thomas, 193
Graham, Joseph Benjamin, 193
Graham, Laura Louise, 190
Graham, Martha, 196
Graham, Mary Susan, 193
Graham, Mary Susanna, 190
Graham, Mary Ulmer, 189, 192, 199, 200, 201
Graham, Minnie, 191
Graham, Nancy Anna Taylor, 196, 197
Graham, Sarah Ann, 192
Graham, Seaborn F., 193
Graham, Simeon Greene, 193

Graham, Susannah Ardlissa Terrell, 192, 194, 196, 197
Graham, William, 196
Graham, William (Billy), 192, 194, 196, 197
Graham, William Alanson, 183, 189, 190, 192, 199, 202
Graham, William B., 196
Graham, William Benjamin, 196, 197
Graham, Wyley, 193
Grahamm Edward Terrell, 193
Granbury, Moses, 168
Grant, Albert Sidney, 172
Gray, Captain Thomas, 161
Green, Belle, 21
Green, Herbert, 27
Green, J. Charles, 21, 27
Green, Lillie, 166
Green, Mary Emily Gibbons, 16, 22, 27
Griffin, Colonel John, 201
Griffin, Joseph B., 175
Griffin, Margaret J., 170
Griffin, Rebecca Jewell, 175
Griffith's Valuation, 1847 - 1964, 8
Guilfoyle, Maria, 8
Guinard, Mary Elizabeth Harlan, 171
Gustavsen, Betty Wynne, 178
Gustavsen, Florence McLeod, 178
Gustavsen, John Edward, 178
Gustavsen, Robert Harlan, 178
Gustavsen, William Edward, 178
Gustavsen, William Edward, Jr., 178

H

Hall, Louann, 88
Hannon, George P., 131
Hannon, Jean Elizabeth Taylor, 131, 132
Hannon, Joseph B., 131

Index

Hannon, Thomas Earle, 131
Hardin, Jaohn, 154
Hargrove, Catherine, 193
Harker, Kate, 27
Harlan, Ada M., 171
Harlan, Annie Mattinglee, 171
Harlan, Lillie, 171
Harlan, Mary Elizabeth, 171
Harlan, Robert, 171
Harlan, Robert D., Jr., 171
Harlan, Samuel D., 171
Harlan, Samuel D., Jr., 171
Harlan, Sarah McGregor, 171
Harris, Edward Howard, 120
Harrison, Nettie Ellen, 149
Harry, Mattie Elliott Gibbons, 23
Harry, Mrs. Charles W., 16
Harry, Willard Charles, 23
Harry, William J., 23
Hawthorne, Mary, 193
Hector, Bryan Lane, 186
Hector, Calvin Ray, 186
Hector, Marcus Calvin, 186
Herberg, Helen, 93
Hill, William Carroll Jackson, 179
Hogan, E. A. F., 161
Hogan, Edmund, 161
Hogan, John H., 160, 161, 162
Hogan, John McGregor, 161
Hogan, Nancy McGregor, 161, 162
Hogan, Patsy Wilburn, 161
Hogan, William C., 161
Holley, Arnold, 108
Holley, Brent Worth, 108
Holley, Keith Gregory, 108
Holley, Mary Jo McGregor, 108
Hoodenpyl, Philip, 148
Horger, Catheran, 201
Horger, Heinrich, Sr., 201
Horger, Jacob, Jr., 202
Horger, Jacob, Sr., 201
Horger, Mary Margaret, 201, 202
Hosey, Jane, 193
Huckabee, Bartlett, 149

Huckabee, Benjamin, 149
Huckabee, William, 149
Hudson, Catherine, 193
Hughes, Bernice Sophrania, 178
Hunter, Peter, 149
Hutchinson, Charles, 148

I

Inabinet, Hans, 202
Inabinet, John, 202
Inabinet, Margaret, 202
Inabinet, Peter, 202

J

Johnson, Conrad, 185
Johnson, Fred, 185
Johnson, Graham, 185
Johnson, Martha Elizabeth Graham McGregor, 184, 185, 187
Johnson, Mary Wells, 184
Johnson, Peter, 185
Johnson, Peter N., 184, 185, 187
Jones, John Henry, Jr., 175
Jones, John Henry, Sr., 175, 176
Jones, Martha Elizabeth Johnson, 175
Justice, John, 154, 156

K

Kennard, Ernest Lockett, 172
King George I of England, 135
King George III, 152
King Henry VIII, 1
King, Roxann, 95
Kron, Dr. Francis J., 149
Kuebler, Alma J, 45

L

Land, Bruce, 108
Land, Dorianne McGregor, 108

Land, Marthann, 108
Land, Quinnell, 108
Land, Ross, Jr., 108
Lane, Andrew Jackson, 185
Lane, Bertie Cade, 185, 186
Lane, Cleo, 187
Lane, Forrest E., 186
Lane, Hal Burns, Jr., 185
Lane, Hal Burns, Sr., 185, 186
Lane, Leon, 186
Lane, Lucile Hodge, 186
Lane, Major James, 185, 186, 187
Lane, Margaret Ruth, 186
Lane, Margaret Ruth McGregor, 185, 186, 187
Lane, Ullman D., 186
Lane, Wilma Mattie, 186
Lasswell Edward C., 73
Lasswell, Bertram J., 45, 64, 66
Lasswell, Edna, 64, 66
Lasswell, Edna L, 45
Lasswell, Edward C., 64, 65
Lasswell, Ida May, 45, 64, 66
Lasswell, Winifred C. Brooks, 45, 64, 65
Lasswell, Winifred C. Gibbons, 73
Latta, Renee Michele Yousey, 112
Leonetti, Walter A., 65, 66
Leonetti, Winifred C. Lasswell, 65, 66, 67, 68
Lewis, James Hampton, 127
Lewis, Lavania, 166
Lewis, Ora, 166
Lewis, Rev. J. M., 91
Lewis, Sarah Jane Taylor, 127
Lewis, Sarah Margaret Jane Taylor, 125, 128
Lewis, Victoria Louise Davenport, 127
Lewis, William Hampton, 125, 127, 128
Lightsey, D. M., 195
Lightsey, John L., 195
Lightsey, Joseph B., 195, 196

Little, Robert, 154
Loftin, Cecil L., 177
Loftin, Frank Elkna, Jr., 177
Loftin, Frank Elkna, Sr., 177
Lofton, R. J., 178
Lovett, Mary, 202
Lycett, Edna Lasswell, 66

M

Macy, Daniel Folger, 13
Macy, Lydia Brown, 13
Macy, Mary Brown, 13
Madison, Ambrose, 135
Madison, Frances Taylor, 135
Madison, President James, 135
Magnan, Nedrah Stringfellow, 81
Mann, Granvell, 127
Mann, John, 160, 164
Mann, Lucy Jane, 164
Mann, Lucy McGregor, 164
Mann, Martha Burton, 164
Mann, Nancy Fredonia, 164
Mann, Patsy, 168
Mann, Rebecca, 164
Mann, Robert Noah, 164
Mann, Sara A., 164
Mann, Sarah, 127
Mann, William, 163, 168
Mann, William T., 164
Mann, Willie, 167
March, J. Edwin, 62
Marks, Benjamin, 149
Marks, Tabitha, 148
Mason, Henry, 154
Matthews, Robert, 180
Mauzey, Michael, 148
May, 10, 13, 14, 28, 44, 45, 49, 50, 57, 207, 213, 215, 218
Mays, Buford, 95
Mays, Elizabeth Ann Gibbons, 95, 96
Mays, Glennon Buford, 95
Mays, Myron Daryl, 95, 122
McCurdy, Frances, 193

Index

McDigall, Isabell, 142
McGregor , Katharine, 142
McGregor Frank Bobbitt, Sr., 181
McGregor, Ahinoam, 148
McGregor, Ahixoam, 148
McGregor, Albert, 153
McGregor, Albert Leslie, 166
McGregor, Alexander, 158
McGregor, Alice, 172
McGregor, Aliza, 162
McGregor, Andrew, 141, 163
McGregor, Ann Rector Millican, 172, 173
McGregor, Anne Harris, 143, 160, 161, 162, 163, 164
McGregor, Annie, 173
McGregor, Anthony, 158, 159
McGregor, Arvilla, 160
Mcgregor, Arvilla Ann, 164
McGregor, Ava, 145, 146
McGregor, Avery, 149
McGregor, Bartlett, 141, 143, 144, 152, 160
McGregor, Bartlett, Jr., 143, 160, 161, 163, 168, 169, 170, 171, 172, 173, 174, 175
McGregor, Bartlett, Sr., 143, 144, 160, 161, 162, 163, 164, 165
McGregor, Billie Louise, 99, 102
McGregor, Carro Ellen Davis, 180, 181
McGregor, Cathy Renee, 109
McGregor, Cecile Bird, 180
McGregor, Charles Bennett, 180, 181
McGregor, Charles Franklin, 166
McGregor, Clarence Pinkney, 166
McGregor, Clayton Haliday, 166
McGregor, Clinton, 149
McGregor, Cora Loretta Rupe, 101, 104, 105, 106
McGregor, Cordia A., 166
McGregor, Cynthia, 155
McGregor, Cynthia Barnett, 149
McGregor, Daniel Chase, 167

McGregor, Dolly, 173
McGregor, Dorianne, 108
McGregor, Dr. Hiram Chase, 166
McGregor, Eliza L., 169, 170, 172
McGregor, Elizabeth, 150, 156, 157
McGregor, Elizabeth Ann Garrett, 162
McGregor, Elizabeth Mann, 160, 168, 169, 170, 171, 172, 174, 175
McGregor, Ella Dowling, 173
McGregor, Elner Elizabeth, 166
McGregor, Emily Margaret Lawrence Gay, 179, 180, 181, 182
McGregor, Emma, 183, 185
McGregor, Emmett, 172
McGregor, Ezekiel, 146, 147, 148, 149
McGregor, Fanora Mae, 99, 113
McGregor, Florence Ellen, 166
McGregor, Flowers, 152, 153, 154, 155, 156
McGregor, Forrest Edwin, 97, 99, 100, 101, 102, 109, 110, 113, 115, 120, 141, 163, 171, 175, 183, 185, 189, 190
McGregor, Frances, 155, 159, 162
McGregor, Francis, 159
McGregor, Frank Bobbitt, 181
McGregor, Frank Bobbitt, Jr., 181
McGregor, Frank Bobbitt, Sr., 181
McGregor, Gertrude Hart, 182
McGregor, Gramm, 163
McGregor, Gregory Edwin, 109
McGregor, Harris Valentine, 162
McGregor, Harris Valentine, Jr., 162, 163
McGregor, Harris Valentine, Sr., 160, 161, 162, 163
McGregor, Helen, 142, 153
McGregor, Henderson, 149
McGregor, James Bartlett, 142

McGregor, James Clarke, 104, 175, 183, 184, 185, 187, 189, 190
McGregor, Janet, 142
McGregor, Jason, 149
McGregor, Jean, 142, 155
McGregor, Jehu, 150
McGregor, Jemima, 149
McGregor, Joel, 161, 163
McGregor, Joel Algernion, 181, 182
McGregor, Joel Henderson, 168, 169, 170, 171, 175, 177, 179, 180, 181, 182, 183
McGregor, Joel Ira, 180
McGregor, Joel Ira, Jr., 180
Mcgregor, John, 154, 155, 156, 163
McGregor, John, 141, 142, 152, 153, 158, 160, 161, 162, 163
McGregor, John Clarke, 99, 100, 101, 103, 104, 105, 106
McGregor, John H., 169, 170
McGregor, Joseph Harper, 166
McGregor, Kenneth, 182
McGregor, Laura Lillian, 176
McGregor, Lavinna Anna, 149
McGregor, Leonora Isabella, 166
McGregor, Lewis, 152, 153
McGregor, Lucy, 160, 161
McGregor, Lucy Ann Savanna, 167
McGregor, Lucy Harris, 162
McGregor, Lucy Maxine Doran, 103, 107, 108, 109
McGregor, Madera A., 170
McGregor, Madora, 172
McGregor, Madora A., 174
McGregor, Mahala Duncan, 160, 167
McGregor, Malcolm A., 182
McGregor, Manson Clayton, 167
McGregor, Margaret, 142
McGregor, Margaret Griffin, 170, 175, 177, 179, 183
McGregor, Margaret Ruth, 183

McGregor, Margaret Scot, 142
McGregor, Margaret Thomson, 152, 153, 154
McGregor, Marion Franklin, 167
McGregor, Martha Anna Smith, 181, 182
McGregor, Martha Elizabeth Graham, 183, 184, 185, 187, 189, 190
McGregor, Martha Louise Bobbitt, 180
McGregor, Mary, 155
McGregor, Mary Adelia Gibbons, 86, 88, 99, 100, 101, 102, 103, 104, 113, 115, 117, 118, 141, 175
McGregor, Mary Ann, 146, 150
McGregor, Mary Flowers, 154
McGregor, Mary Forrestine, 99, 110
McGregor, Mary Jane, 150
McGregor, Mary Jo, 108
McGregor, Mary Leona, 167
McGregor, Mary Lucinda, 160, 161, 163
McGregor, Mattie, 175
McGregor, Mexico, 149
McGregor, Mildred L., 182
McGregor, Minerva, 149
McGregor, Minnie, 176
McGregor, Montague M., 162
McGregor, Nancy, 149, 158, 159, 160, 161
McGregor, Nannie Susan, 167
McGregor, Ned, 173
McGregor, Noah, 160, 161, 164, 165, 166, 167
McGregor, Noah Edward, 167
McGregor, Noah Lee, 166
McGregor, Oroha, 149
McGregor, Patricia Elizabeth, 166
McGregor, Peter, 142
McGregor, Polly Payne, 153
McGregor, Priscilla Elizabeth, 166
McGregor, Ransford, 153

Index

McGregor, Rev. William, 141, 143, 145, 146, 147, 148, 149, 150, 152, 155, 160
McGregor, Richmond, 150
McGregor, Robert Burke, 182
McGregor, Robert Burke, Jr., 182
McGregor, Ruth Ellen Shrader, 166
McGregor, Ruth Emily, 181
McGregor, Sallie Sarah Allen, 166
McGregor, Sarah, 149, 150, 155
McGregor, Sarah Allen, 160
McGregor, Sarah Ann Young, 149
McGregor, Sarah Flowers, 145, 146, 148, 155
McGregor, Sarah Jane Ware, 148, 149
McGregor, Sarah Martha, 169, 170, 171
McGregor, Sarah Mattie, 177
McGregor, Sheila Fay, 105
McGregor, Susan, 149
McGregor, Susannah Ware, 148
McGregor, Sylvia Ann Millican, 109
McGregor, Taylor Gibbons, 99, 100, 101, 103, 107, 108, 109, 110
McGregor, Temperance, 149
McGregor, Tennifly, 162
McGregor, Theodocia Iris (Dosia) Jones, 175, 176
McGregor, Tilden Plummer, 166
McGregor, Vesta, 149
McGregor, Walter Bartlett, 173
McGregor, Washington, 166
McGregor, Wiley, 149
McGregor, Wiley A., 149
McGregor, William, 142, 150, 154
McGregor, William Bartlett, 166, 169, 170, 171, 175, 176
McGregor, William Emmett, 166
McGregor, William Jefferson, 148
McGregor, William, Jr., 143, 145, 146, 149, 150, 158, 159
McGregor, William, Sr., 153, 154, 155, 156, 157, 158, 159
McGregor, Willie, 176
McGregor, Willis, 146, 147, 148
McGregor, Willis Nard, 149
McGregor, Joel, 160
McGregor. John H., 172, 173, 174
McLaughlin, John, 8
McLaughlin, Molly, 8
McLeod, A. L., 175
McLeod, Alex Earl, 178, 179
McLeod, Alexander L., 177, 178
McLeod, Bessie Bruce, 179
McLeod, Carlyne Compton Walker, 178
McLeod, Dolly, 178
McLeod, Earnest LeRoy, 177
McLeod, Eva Byrd, 177
McLeod, Girley M., 178
McLeod, James Allen, 178
McLeod, Jenobia Byrd, 178
McLeod, Mattie Pearl, 178
McLeod, Milton, 178
McLeod, Samuel Charles, 178
McLeod, Samuel Harlan, 178
McLeod, Sarah Mattie McGregor, 177, 178
McLeod, Walter William, 177
McLeod, William David, 178
McLeod, William Jake, 178
McNeill, Marcia Miller, 79, 80, 84, 88, 95, 121
McNeill. Jerry, 95
Megregor, Elizabeth, 154
Meredith, Mary C., 176
Meredith, Richard, 176
Meyers, Melgena, 149
Miller, Anne Sue, 93
Miller, Jake G., 70
Miller, Marcia Ann, 95
Miller, Maxwell Hugh, 95
Miller, Pancho, 115, 116
Miller, Sandra Sue, 95
Miller, Virginia Gibbons, 95, 108
Miller, William Gibbons, 95

Millican, Ann H. Rector, 172
Millican, John, 175
Millican, Wesley J., 172
Mitchell, Jessee, 154
Mitchell, John W., 149
Morris, Arvilla Ann McGregor, 164
Morris, Enoch, 164
Morris, Jasper N., 164
Morris, Mary, 164
Morris, Narrard, 164
Morris, Nathaniel Newton, 164
Morris, Sarah, 164
Morris, Sophronia Ann, 164
Morris, William, 160
Morris, William Thomas, 164
Mudersbach, Luella Brooks Pepper, 69
Mudersbach, Luella Delia Pepper, 73, 74
Mudersbach, William, 73, 74
Muehlbrad, Judy, 120
Myers, Mary, 150

N

Nancy, 132, 133, 155, 158, 159, 160, 161, 218
Napiers, Col. Richard C., 161
Neal, Mrs. Edgar T., 81, 84
Newsom, Karen Rushing, 112
Newsom, William, 112
Noland, Thomas Pearl, 177
Norman, Anna, 136
Norman, Charles Wesley, 136
Norman, Elizabeth, 137
Norman, Emily Maria, 137
Norman, Fannie Deer, 136
Norman, Henderson H., 137
Norman, Hiram, 136
Norman, James, 137
Norman, Job, 136, 137, 138
Norman, John, 136, 137
Norman, Margaret J., 137
Norman, Mary, 137
Norman, Mary Edwards, 137
Norman, Mary Elizabeth Williams, 138
Norman, Permelia Ann Myrick, 138
Norman, Rebecca, 136
Norman, Rebecca Caffey, 136
Norman, Rebecca Chilcutt, 136, 137, 138
Norman, Rebecca Elizabeth Chilcutt, 136
Norman, Riley, 137
Norman, Sarah E., 137
Norman, Thomas, 137
Norman, Thomas Webb, 137, 138
Norman, William Riley, 137, 138

O

Oliver, John T. P., 132
Oliver, Maria Margaret Taylor, 132
Oliver, William K., 132

P

Parker, Cynthia Jeanne, 95
Parker, Elizabeth, 148
Patrick, Patsy, 95
Payne, Mary, 155
Pennington, Margaret, 149
Pepper, Louella Delia Brooks, 73
Pepper, Luella D. Brooks, 45, 54
Pepper, Luella Delia Brooks, 59, 65, 66
Pepper, Spencer, 73
Pepper, Spencer F., 45
Perry, Sarah, 194
Perryman, Elizabeth Ann Gibbons, 94
Piper, Lon, 121
Portwood, William Gibbons, 93
Portwood, William Gibbons, Jr., 93
Powell, R. J., 115
Pugh, James, 193
Purry, Colonel Jean Pierre, 200

Index

Q

Quinlivan, Father John, 92

R

Reed, Ann, 164
Reese, Mary, 149
Rehage, Anna Mary, 26
Reynolds, Thomas, 135
Reynolds, William, 164
Roden, Harry Victor, 61
Rooks, Sarah, 139
Ross, Lucy, 162
Rossiter, Florence, 167
Roundtree, Lawrence, 83
Roundtree, Lonzo, 83
Roundtree, Mittie, 83
Roundtree, Robert M., 83
Roundtree, Robert T., 83
Roundtree, Ross, 83
Roundtree, Ross M., 83
Roundtree, Sarah J., 83
Rowntree, Ann Eliza Taylor, 127, 130
Rowntree, Robert M., 84
Rowntree, Robert Thomas, 127, 130
Royall, M.L., 173
Royder, Jefferson Pettus, III, 181
Royder, Jefferson Pettus, Jr., 181
Royder, Ruth Emily McGregor, 181
Royderm Gwendolyn, 181
Rumph, John, 201
Rushing, Bradley, 110, 111
Rushing, Bruce Kevin, 111
Rushing, Karen, 110
Rushing, Mary Forrestine McGregor, 103, 110, 111, 113, 120
Rushing, Rebecca Blue, 111, 112
Rushing, Scott Bradley, 110
Rushing, Scott Bryan, 111
Rushing, Stanley Nelson, 103
Rushing, Stanley Nelson, Jr., 110, 111
Rushing, Stanley Nelson, Sr., 110, 111
Rushing, Susan Ziehe, 112
Russell, Hardy, 148

S

Safley, Anderson, 149
Safley, Myrick, 147, 148
Salinas, Fred Lee, 119, 120
Salinas, Maisie Fidela, 120
Salinas, Manda Greg Wigley, 119
Salinas, Ryker Lane, 120
Sanchez, Johnny, 120
Sanchez, Johnny Dean, 120
Sanchez, Shahala Deann Adams, 120
Sandifer, Cynthia McGregor, 155
Sandifer, Frances McGregor, 155
Sandifer, John, 156
Sandifer, Robert, 155
Sandiferm John, 155
Schaefer, Barbara Corrine, 28
Schaefer, Elizabeth Robertson, 28
Schaefer, F. A., 27
Schaefer, Frederick August, 28
Schaefer, Gustav Edmund, 27, 28, 29
Schaefer, Lydia Brown Gibbons, 28, 29
Schaefer, Lydia Gibbons, 19
Schaefer, Lydia Macy, 28
Schaefer, Mrs. Gus, 16
Schimpferman, Jane Gibbons, 25
Schimpferman, William, 24
Sealem E., 175
Seeger, Ernest, 173
Sempringham, St. Gilbert of, 1
Shanley, Eva Byrd McLeod, 177
Shannon, Catherine B., 5
Shaumloffel, John, 201
Shaumloffel, Louise Lovey, 201
Shelby, John, 137

Sherman, General W. T., 137
Short, Theodore, 70
Shuler, Anna Margretha, 201
Shuler, Hans Joerg, 201
Shuler, Maria Barbara, 201
Simmons, Ann, 170
Sims, Teresa, 149
Sims, Winton Edward, 178
Smith, Ida Eldridge, 166
Smith, Louie, 166
Solomon, Ava McGregor, 146, 147, 148, 150, 160
Solomon, Bennett, 150
Solomon, Bennett II, 148
Solomon, Diana Gordon, 147
Solomon, Frances "Fanny", 148
Solomon, Goodwin, 147
Solomon, Hixie, 148
Solomon, Jane, 148
Solomon, Martha B., 148
Solomon, Mary "Polly", 148
Solomon, Rev. Bennett, 147, 148
Solomon, Sarah A., 148
Solomon, William, 147
Solomon, William Jr., 147
Solomon, William S., Sr., 148
Solomon, Willis, 147, 148
Sorelle, David, 177
Steele, Ollie Ruth, 173
Stephenson, John, 191
Stiles, Mary Jane, 145
Stiles, Robert, III, 150
Stone, John, 163
Stowe, Leslie Forrestine Yousey, 112
Strickland, Jean, 195
Sullivan, Bertha, 97
Sullivan, Ray, 97
Susan Mariah Taylor, 127
Swails, William M., 186
Swails, Wilma Mattie Lane, 186
Swann, William Lane, 149

T

Taylor, Aaron, 132
Taylor, Andrew, 132
Taylor, Ann Elizabeth Norman, 125, 126, 128, 130, 131, 136, 137, 138
Taylor, Annie Eliza, 126
Taylor, Aura Jane Davenport, 127, 129
Taylor, C. D., 175
Taylor, Charles Edward, 103, 113, 117, 118
Taylor, Charles Thomas, 113, 114
Taylor, Col. John, 131, 132, 133, 139
Taylor, Dr. James Job, 104, 125, 126, 128
Taylor, Dr. Job, 100
Taylor, Elbert Neal, 126, 127, 129
Taylor, Elizabeth Lee, 134
Taylor, Eudora Frances Davenport, 129
Taylor, Fanora Mae McGregor, 103, 113, 118, 181, 201
Taylor, George Thomas, 133
Taylor, James, 133, 135
Taylor, James K., 86
Taylor, James Kaneer, 125, 126, 128, 129, 130, 131, 132, 138, 139
Taylor, James the Elder, 134, 135
Taylor, James the Younger, 134, 135
Taylor, James W., 126
Taylor, Jean Elizabeth, 139
Taylor, Jesse Riley, 133
Taylor, John, 132
Taylor, John Bludworth, 131, 132
Taylor, John William, 129
Taylor, Joshua, 133
Taylor, Margaret, 132
Taylor, Margaret Caroline Bludworth, 131, 132, 139
Taylor, Maria Margaret, 132

Index

Taylor, Mary Virginia, 86, 87, 126
Taylor, Missouri Elizabeth Massey, 128
Taylor, Missouri Massey, 125
Taylor, Nancy, 132, 133
Taylor, Ola Massey, 100
Taylor, President Zachary, 133, 135
Taylor, Richard, 132, 133
Taylor, Richard Bludworth, 100
Taylor, Richard Henry, 126, 127, 129, 132, 138
Taylor, Richard Lee, 133, 134
Taylor, Roxie, 125
Taylor, Sarah Dabney Strother, 133
Taylor, Sarah Smith, 131
Taylor, Susan Mariah, 126
Taylor, Suzanne, 113
Taylor, Thomas Andrew, 133
Taylor, Thomas H., 113
Taylor, Thomas Hardaman, 126, 129
Taylor, William, 132, 133
Taylor, William T., 133, 134
Taylor, Zachariah, 133
Taylor, Zachary, 133, 134
Tayor, Sarah Garrett Foster, 133
Terral, Edward Young, 194, 195, 196
Terral, John, 194
Terral, Joshua, 194
Terral, Susanna, 195
Terral, Susanna Ardalissa Stephens, 194
Thompson, Judge A. W., 21
Thompson, Lillie Harlan, 172
Thompson, Mrs. A. W., 21
Thompson, W. C., 172
Thompson, Wallace L., 21
Tippit, Sallie A., 167
Toma, Hazel M., 69
Trevino, Francisco Lozano, 187
Tucker, Marvin Wait, 164
Turner, George, 148

Turpin, Andrew Walker, 19, 28
Turpin, Mrs. A. W., 16
Turpin, Ruth E., 19, 28
Turpin, Winifred Chapel Gibbons, 19, 20, 28
Tyron, William M., 168
Tyson, Avrilla Ann McGregor, 164
Tyson, Harriet F., 164
Tyson, Uriah, 164

U

Ulmer, Adam, Jr., 202
Ulmer, Adam, Sr., 201, 202
Ulmer, Ann, 201
Ulmer, Barbara Shuler, 201
Ulmer, David Horger, Sr., 202
Ulmer, George Adam, 201
Ulmer, Jacob, 200
Ulmer, John Frederick, 201
Ulmer, Mary, 189, 199, 202

V

Van Buren, Martin, 134
Vaughan, William Thomas, 164
Vaughn, Melinda, 166
Veil, Charles Herbert, 19
Veil, Ruth E. Turpin, 20

W

Walker, Lucy, 166
Wallace, A., 165
Walters, Jennie May, 95
Ware, James M., 149
Ware, Peter, 148
Ware, Roland, 148
Ware, Susannah, 148
Ware, Temperance, 148
Washington, General George, 161
Weldon, Casey, 108
Weldon, Mary Jo McGregor, 108
Wheeler, Sarah, 193
White, Baker, 153

White, Willie McGregor, 176
Wigley, Devin Adams, 119
Wigley, Donald Burt, 119
Wigley, Donna Louise Adams, 97, 103, 119
Wigley, Jeffrey Burt, 119
William Bradford, 166
William, Fennell, 36
Williams, Nancy McGregor, 159
Williams, Sarah McGregor, 155
Wilson, General James H., 137
Wilson, James, 165
Wilson, John, 177
Wood, Ellen Adella, 190
Wood, Zilpha, 191
Woodall. Dr. J. B., 95
Wornom, Samuel, 154

Y

Yarborough, Asa, 162
Yarborough, N. Elems, 167
Young, Martha C., 149
Young, Mary Ann, 194
Young, Sarah Ann, 149
Yousey, Bill, 112
Yousey, Karen Rushing, 112

CPSIA information can be obtained
at www.ICGtesting.com
Printed in the USA
LVHW091241260222
712095LV00001B/26

9 781608 628315